BASIC SKILLS EDUCATION IN COMMUNITY COLLEGES

Nearly two-thirds of students require some form of remediation before taking college-level classes, and community colleges have become increasingly important in providing this education. Unfortunately, relatively few students complete the developmental courses required to make a transition to college-level work. Based on a three-year study of over twenty community colleges, *Basic Skills Education in Community Colleges* analyzes developmental education practices, exploring what goes wrong and what goes right, and provides a series of recommendations for improved practice.

Including both classroom observations and interviews with administrators, faculty, and students, this valuable book balances critique with examples of innovation. Part One explores the instructional settings of basic skills—the use of drill and practice and remedial pedagogy in math, reading, writing, and ESL, as well as innovations in colleges that show developmental education need not follow remedial pedagogy. Part Two examines institutional factors shaping basic skills and provides recommendations for improving the quality of basic skills instruction. The research-grounded observations and recommendations in *Basic Skills Education in Community Colleges* make this an invaluable resource for scholars, administrators, and faculty aiming to help students progress through developmental education to college-level work and beyond.

W. Norton Grubb is the Emeritus Professor and David Pierpont Gardner Chair in Higher Education at the Graduate School of Education, University of California, Berkeley, USA.

Robert Gabriner is Professor of Educational Leadership and Director of the Educational Leadership Doctoral Program for Schools and Community Colleges at San Francisco State University, USA.

BASIC SKILLS OF EDUCATION IN COMMUNITY COLLEGES

Inside and Outside of Classrooms

W. Norton Grubb

with

Robert Gabriner

NEW YORK AND LONDON

First published 2013
by Routledge
711 Third Avenue, New York, NY 10017

Simultaneously published in the UK
by Routledge
2 Park Square, Milton Park, Abingdon, Oxon OX14 4RN

Routledge is an imprint of the Taylor & Francis Group, an informa business

Library of Congress Cataloging in Publication Data
Grubb, W. Norton
 Basic skills education in community colleges : inside and outside of classrooms / W Norton Grubb.
 p. cm.
 Includes bibliographical references and index.
 1. Community colleges. 2. Community colleges—Curricula. 3. Basic education.
 I. Title.
 LB2328.G78 2013
 378.1'543—dc23
 2012027439

ISBN: 978-0-415-63474-8 (hbk)
ISBN: 978-0-415-63475-5 (pbk)
ISBN: 978-0-203-09429-7 (ebk)

Typeset in Bembo and Stone Sans
by EvS Communication Networx, Inc.

Printed and bound in the United States of America by Publishers Graphics, LLC on sustainably sourced paper.

We dedicate this volume to the many community college instructors, counselors, and student service personnel teaching basic skills classes, only a tiny fraction of whom we have observed. They teach under difficult conditions, made even harder at the moment by fiscal crises in most states. We hope they find themselves and their perspectives accurately recorded in this book.

CONTENTS

LIST OF FIGURES

ACKNOWLEDGMENTS

The origins of this volume lie in a somewhat different book that I published almost 15 years ago: *Honored But Invisible: An Inside Look at Teaching in Community Colleges* (Routledge, 1999). That book looked at instruction in all subjects of the community college by observing in classrooms and interviewing instructors and administrators, to get a view from inside and outside the classroom. Remedial or developmental education was only one of the subjects in that work. Since then, basic skills instruction has increased substantially and, for reasons examined in chapter 1, has come to be of increasing concern. Pamela Burdman, then a program officer at the Hewlett Foundation, urged me to take a closer look. My first debt is therefore to the Hewlett Foundation and its support over 3 years of planning, interviewing, and observing classrooms in a variety of community colleges. The David Gardner Chair in Higher Education at the University of California, Berkeley, which I hold, supported additional costs of the research.

My greatest debt is to the many community college instructors and administrators we observed and interviewed in the course of this research. As I have detailed in the methodological appendix, we ended up interviewing 323 individuals and observing 169 classes in approximately 20 colleges. The individuals, with few exceptions, welcomed our inquiries and gave freely of the insights and experience they had gained over many years of working in community colleges. Without their full participation, this book would not be possible.

I thank Robert Gabriner of California State University, San Francisco, the second author of this volume. Bob participated at an early stage in conceptualizing the research and in identifying specific colleges to study. He was also a member of several research teams that visited colleges. He and I visited Chaffey College together, and he wrote the first draft of chapter 6 on student services at Chaffey. Finally, he read all of the initial working papers that came from this project and provided invaluable comments, including some that tamped down my exaggerated prose.

I thank the researchers who conducted the site visits to the many community colleges we examined for this book. They included Elizabeth Boner, Katherine Frankel, Lynette Parker, and David Patterson, all of the School of Education at UC Berkeley; Laura Hope, Eva Schiorring, Bruce Smith, Richard Taylor, Ian Walton, and Smokey Wilson, all members of the Research and Planning Group of the California Community Colleges. Typically, two researchers visited each campus, one from UC Berkeley and one from the RP Group, to provide the perspectives of both academics and practitioners. The researchers carried out 2- to 3-day site visits to an initial round of 13 colleges; they revisited some of the colleges; and they examined innovations in other colleges to produce the interviews and observations on which this book depends. They also read drafts of working papers and chapters, contributing their insights and additional material from the colleges they had visited. In every way, they have been indispensable to this volume.

The student interviews in chapter 2 were carried out by Tom DeWit and Sean McFarland of Chabot College, whom I thank for their ideas and participation. They have a larger project in which students interview other students about specific topics in their education. Katherine Frankel and I provided initial questions for these student-interviewers to use; then she and I watched 22 video transcripts to extract themes and quotations. Chapter 2 does not have the vividness of the original videotapes; however, editing of the student voices was necessary for readability because while students were extremely informative they were also very repetitious.

At the School of Education at UC Berkeley, the work of Jan Haase and Frankie Temple was invaluable for managing the complex accounts of this research and, so far as possible, for insulating me from the central campus bureaucrats.

Finally, I thank members of my family who were crucial to writing the manuscript: my son, Alex Grubb, who edited the penultimate version of the book; my daughter, Hilary Grubb, who has become the guardian of the family's health; and my wife and amanuensis, Erica Grubb, who entered several rounds of changes into the computer when I became unable to do so. They illustrate the advantages of having family members who are both loving and capable.

W. Norton Grubb

David Gardner Chair in Higher Education
University of California, Berkeley

1

UNDERSTANDING THE QUANDARY OF BASIC SKILLS

Framing the Issues in Community Colleges

Yet another "crisis" has been building in U.S. education, though the language of crisis is often overused as a way of getting people to pay attention.[1] At many levels of the system, students enter unprepared for the appropriate level of academic work, and then need to participate in remediation in some form, which is called variously, basic skills instruction, developmental education, academic skills, intervention, skills for success, or foundational skills to avoid the unavoidable stigma of "remediation."* In K–12 education, this happens at several transitions: in the ninth grade; at the transition to middle school; and perhaps much earlier in third or fourth grade, as teachers progress from teaching basic literacy and numeracy skills to using them to develop content knowledge. The transition from high school to community college suffers from another crisis or quandary of remediation, as I will document, but the problem seems almost as acute in the 4-year regional colleges of the country.[2] Short-term job training, welfare-to-work programs, and adult education are other places in the vast system of education and training where basic skills instruction takes place.

All these manifestations of the remediation problem are serious, but the transition from high school to community college is especially difficult. In an era when a college credential seems necessary for middle-class jobs and achieving the American Dream, increasing numbers of students are being pushed, or counseled, toward college as the only route to individual advancement. The

---

* In this book, I will use these terms as synonyms since many nuances have been lost; for example, the notion embedded in "developmental education" of a developmental trajectory for all students, or the view that "all education is developmental." For a strong exception, see the description of Chaffey College in chapter 6.

pursuit of equity in this country for low-income students; for African Americans, Latinos, and other racial or ethnic minorities; and for immigrant students has led to promoting higher education as the appropriate policy, rather than, for example, trying to equalize the distribution of earnings or eliminate racial discrimination in employment. And the overheated rhetoric about the centrality of education to economic growth and competitiveness, which I have critiqued as the Education Gospel (Grubb & Lazerson, 2004), has been extended to community colleges, too. As Barack Obama said at the Community College Summit:[3]

> Given these relationships [with business, industry, and government], community colleges are uniquely positioned to raise the skill and knowledge base of our workforce. The President recognizes the critical role colleges play in developing our nation's human capital.... The President's plan will also improve college access and completion by supporting programs and activities designed to boost college persistence and increase graduation rates.

But none of these goals for individual advancement or developing the nation's human capital can be realized without mastery of basic skills.

The quandary of community colleges can be divided into two issues. A large and increasing fraction of students who enroll in community colleges, and who take initial assessments to see if they are prepared for college-level courses, are directed into basic skills courses; one figure often bandied about at the national level is about 60%. Based on a national sample of students tracked between 1988 and 2000, Attewell, Lavin, Domina, and Levey (2006) found that 58% of students attending community colleges took at least one remedial course. Another data set, based on 83 community colleges surveyed by the Achieving the Dream project, found that 59% of students enrolled in at least one developmental course over a 3-year period (Bailey, 2009). Various data problems—students who manage not to go through the assessment process, as well as students directed into remediation who do not take recommended classes—mean that this figure is subject to considerable uncertainty. Overall, however, several sources indicate that the figure is well over 50%.

In California, where the research for this book took place,** the figures are somewhat higher. Peter Bahr (2011) has found that, in the cohort entering in Fall 2002, 49.7% of entering students *enrolled* in one or more remedial courses (Perry, Rosin, & Woodward, 2010, p. 26). More recently, many people in the colleges we visited claimed that about 80% of entering students are *assessed* into developmental education; at certain individual colleges, this number is as high as 95%—implying that virtually no entering students are ready for college-level

---

** See the appendix for the methodology used for the data in this book.

work. I sometimes refer to this as the magnitude or extent of the remedial problem. These high proportions are not, of course, the fault of community colleges (though there are issues in the assessment process that may artificially inflate or deflate these numbers, as examined in chapter 7). Many instructors blame high schools—indeed, California is near the bottom of all states in the quality of its educational system.[4] Other factors specific to California include low tuition levels in colleges (meaning that fewer students select themselves out because of financial reasons) and the existence of many community colleges with every possible mission and, therefore, highly heterogeneous students (the subject of chapter 2). But with a few exceptions, colleges have concentrated not on preventing such high numbers of remedial students—for example, by working closely with high schools—but on increasing and improving their own developmental education.

The second issue in the quandary of developmental education involves the proportion of basic skills students who complete a remedial sequence, move into college-level coursework, and complete a credential of some sort or transfer to a 4-year college—the "success" of remediation. The Achieving the Dream data indicate that, of those referred to a developmental reading course, only 44% completed the full sequence. The figures are even worse for math, where only 31% of those assessed into developmental classes entered college-level math. Many more students have missed being assessed at all, and their success rates are unknown. Of the least prepared students, only 22% completed sequences in reading and 16% in math; that is, those students who enter three or more levels below college-level math.

For California, again, the figures are worse. One source found that only a quarter of students enrolling in a basic reading class ever enroll in transfer-level English, and only 10% of students enrolling in basic math end up in transferable math (Center for Student Success, 2005). Bahr (2010) has calculated that of all students who initially enroll in a basic math course, only 24.6% successfully enroll in a college-level math course within 6 years. The rates for racial groups vary widely, from 29% for Whites and 33.7% for Asians, to 20.3% for Latinos, and 11.8% for African Americans. Rates of success are related to other obvious factors indicating that both preparation in high school and students' own behavior affect success rates; for example, the extent of deficiency in math, students' academic goals, success in the first math class, persistence in enrolling (instead of "stopping out"), and delaying the first math course. In addition, most students assessed into remediation advance only one level (in rare instances, two levels). Therefore, if students are assessed three or four levels below college level, there is very little chance they will complete a developmental sequence.

When success rates are calculated for individual colleges, they vary substantially. In data collected by the California Chancellor's Office for the 2005-2006 cohort, the rates of progressing from developmental education into college courses in English varied from 57% for one middle-class suburban college to 17% in several urban colleges, and 16% in an urban college with a high proportion of career-technical students. Rates of progress in math, usually lower than those in English, varied from 32% to 43%. Again, because of differences in data quality and how students are categorized, there is some uncertainty about the precise magnitude of these numbers. However, there is little question that these success rates are low; indeed, many administrators and instructors worry about how low they are. As one chair of counseling said:

> What we see is a revolving door with that level of student coming in. And so, it makes recruitment extremely difficult and frustrating because, obviously, you have a lower retention rate [in basic skills courses]: you recruit a bunch of people, they come in, they fail, they leave. You recruit another bunch of people, they come in, they fail, they leave—so it's just a constant revolving door.

Until success rates can be improved, the promise of the community college as the route to success for nontraditional students, or as the locus of equity for low-income and racial minority students, or as a pathway to the American Dream cannot be realized.

The consequences of such high rates of developmental education and low success rates primarily affect students, of course, who come to college for education to become successful economically, only to find they have to retake many of the courses they have passed earlier in K–12 schooling. (As will be seen in chapter 2, this is a source of considerable anger.) But these consequences have effects on community colleges too, because they have turned into places where increasing amounts of remediation take place:

> Basic skills accounts for 90%, I'd say, of what we do. If you take a look at just the courses that are offered, we have very limited offerings. Over the years, we have gotten narrower and narrower in terms of what we're actually offering, and these are always basic skills classes, paring down, paring down to the core gut-level basic skills classes. Pathetic—not what anyone wants.

Several colleges in our sample have suffered crises of identity in the process. One used to be a transfer-oriented institution for African American students. With a shift in its population to increasing numbers of Latinos and immigrants, it found itself providing more developmental courses, including English as a second language (ESL) for immigrants. As one faculty member described the shift, "You've got in excess of 90% of students who are, quote, 'basic skills,' below college level. Without a basic skills component, the college does not exist." This left the college in a dilemma: while many faculty wanted to address basic skills issues, others (particularly older faculty wedded to its transfer mission) didn't want to be just a "remedial campus." At another institution, the vice president of academic affairs pointed out the tension between providing basic skills instruction and college-level courses, and said that "while we don't wish to become a basic skills institution," they had to recognize the needs among incoming students and strike a balance among its offerings. Yet another college has been debating this issue for over a decade: 10 years ago, they convened a basic skills task force, but "we didn't really understand that those [remedial] students were such a big part of our campus, and there was more a sense of 'Well, we're more of a transfer institute.'" But the upsurge in the need for basic skills in the past decade has forced this college, like so many others, to reevaluate its priorities.

The issue of increasing basic skills coursework is, in turn, part of the discussion of mission. If community colleges become "remedial campuses," then they may not be able to fulfill their academic or transfer roles, their role in preparing students for employment, or their economic development role in providing short-term training for employers. Colleges may then be put in the devilish position of either resolving basic skills issues before students can take advantage of transfer or occupational missions, or (in effect) turning away students because they don't address the need for remediation. As one president said of basic skills, they become a prerequisite for the college's occupational responsibilities:

> As far as the economic well-being of this area, it's all tied to having an educated, trained workforce. If we wish to be a player, our part would be to support the economic expansion of opportunities here. So, that's where basic skills sits for me. It isn't to prepare them all to go off to transfer; that's not real, especially in this community. What they want to do is prepare themselves to have a better life.

So, the magnitude of remedial education has, in some cases, changed the missions of colleges, though this change may have been too fast for the colleges and instructors to keep up with it.

Some aspects of the "crisis of identity," or comments about basic skills accounting for the "90% of what we do," are exaggerated (as claims in educational "crises" often are). Even while a large majority of *entering* students may assess into basic skills courses, this does not mean that *overall enrollments* in basic skills courses are overwhelming other offerings. In the fall of 2009, for example, only 7.9% of enrollments in California colleges were in basic skills courses (including 7.1% of enrollments in English courses); the only real exception came in math, where 29% of all math students were enrolled in developmental math.[5] So, even if there is a serious problem with entering cohorts needing more developmental education, the other academic and occupational missions of community colleges still account for the vast majority of enrollments. The comprehensive community college is alive and well—it's just that developmental education has become a larger part of its mission.

This book represents my effort to figure out what might be responsible for such low levels of success in basic skills sequences. There are many potential causes, and everyone has his or her favorite explanation. But with the current state of knowledge and data, no one, absolutely no one, has any idea about which reasons are more important than others, and no one has the quantitative data that might enable a statistical analysis of which causes are more important. Until such data and results emerge, we are left looking at a broad range of issues to illustrate the enormous variety of ways in which basic skills instruction could be improved.

My efforts in this volume are based on 3 years of research in community colleges. By the end, a team of fellow-researchers and I had visited about 20 colleges, observed 169 basic skills classes, and interviewed 323 instructors and administrators—as the methodological appendix describes in detail. These data provide the sources of all the quotations and classroom observations used in this book; they underlie all the conclusions we make about the current state of developmental education. For reasons that will become clear, this methodology reflects the conviction that observations inside classrooms, as well as an understanding of the institutional context, are necessary to analyze teaching and learning activities in any educational setting.

But before I can launch into such an analysis, it is essential to frame the dilemmas of basic skills, both to provide some immediate understanding of the dismal numbers presented above, and to clarify fruitful areas and methods of investigation. Accordingly, in this chapter, I first examine the admirable tendency in U.S. education to develop second-chance efforts for students who are lagging behind, but where second chances necessarily operate under difficult conditions. The analysis of second-chance efforts makes it easier to understand, if not accept, the low success rates of developmental education.

Like much of education and training, basic skills instruction is, by definition, an instructional encounter. The simple model of an instructional setting presented in the second section of this chapter, "The Triangle of Instruction," and illustrated in Figure 1.1 can help tease apart the different elements: It is the triangle of the student, the instructor, and the content, all residing within a complex set of institutional influences.

In this research, the dominant instructional setting is obviously the basic skills classroom (see chapters 3 and 4). If the research underlying this book had included apprenticeships, for example, the instructional settings might have also included workshops and workplaces. Other instructional settings include student services such as tutoring, brief workshops, and "student success" courses (see chapters 5 and 6). These settings led to the research design employed in this work, especially its emphasis on classroom observations as the principal way to know what happens inside instructional settings. In addition, the so-called triangle of instruction helps identify some of the potential causes of low success rates in remedial education. The final section of this chapter provides an overview of the book's central argument, along with a roadmap to subsequent chapters.

Second-Chance Programs: Their Promises and Challenges

Because the magnitude of the developmental dilemma is largely beyond the control of community colleges, this book will not examine it much further. (A limited exception occurs in Chapters 7 and 10, where I look briefly at what colleges can do to make high school students "college ready.") Instead, this book focuses on the success of basic skills programs by asking why so many students are "stuck behind the wall of remediation," as one instructor described the issue.

Given the high levels of inequality in the American education system—achievement gaps are stubbornly high, as is the growth in inequality among students as they progress from kindergarten to postsecondary education[6]—the United States has fortunately been more generous than other developed countries in providing second-chance programs. These include remedial coursework at all levels, including many "interventions" in K-12 education, dropout recovery programs for high school students, and an enormous range of public and private efforts to improve the transition from high school to college and to offer forms of "college readiness" that neither parents nor schools have provided. Community colleges are the institutions of first choice for some students, particularly those who are uncertain about college, those who are unwilling or unable to leave their own communities, or those who have limited financial resources. However, community colleges are often viewed as second-chance institutions for many other students, providing an entry point into postsecondary education for those whose high school work was mediocre, or those who decided in their 20s (or 30s or 40s) that earlier decisions not to attend college were mistaken. Other postsecondary second-chance programs include short-term job training, welfare-to-work programs, and government-supported adult education.

The creation of so many second-chance efforts is testimony to an underlying belief in equity in American education. Such programs are often linked to the belief in the public schools as "a great equalizer of the conditions of men, the balance wheel of the social machinery," as Horace Mann put it, or to the American Dream of individual advancement through hard work—including hard work in schooling (Hochschild & Scovronek, 2003). However, second-chance efforts always operate under difficult conditions. The students in question are, by definition, those who have failed in some other part of the system—perhaps due to the poor quality of their earlier education, their own lack of work or persistence, or other problems that schools are not equipped to resolve (e.g., needing to take care of siblings, learning disabilities, or mental health problems). Chapter 2 will review student issues, including instructors' perceptions of why they show up in developmental courses. The peer effects in second-chance options may not be beneficial, since the other students have also failed in some way and may have restricted ambitions or limited ability to help their classmates with schoolwork.[7] The nature of the instructional problem is self-evidently difficult, like trying to move a student reading at the fifth grade level to "college-level" reading, or to motivate a student whose previous school attendance has been spotty at best. One English instructor noted, "If you're literally taking students from sentence-level errors and working from sentences all the way up to college-level writing in a span of a few semesters, that's a tall order, obviously."

Almost inevitably, second-chance efforts are funded at lower levels than first-chance efforts (though a few very intensive and expensive programs exist as tests of more comprehensive approaches),[8] and resource constraints will show up throughout this study (especially in chapter 8, on funding and resources). Teaching in second-chance programs is usually left to the instructors who are the weakest or most marginal to the institution—adjunct instructors in community colleges (examined in chapter 9), emergency-credentialed and inexperienced teachers in high schools, or instructors hired "off the streets" without any instructional preparation in adult education and job training programs. And because of the ways in which inequality in education works, most of the students in second-chance efforts come from low-income, African American, Latino, or other racial minority or immigrant families, and they cannot count on their families for financial or academic support. The common phenomenon in community colleges of students who are the first in their families to attend college is a testament to the equitable intentions of these institutions, but it simultaneously creates various problems with college readiness, and with financial and academic support (explored in chapter 2).

Second-chance programs therefore concentrate a number of conditions that are detrimental to their success, and it's unclear what their success rates should be. Surely, given these various problems, 100% success is unattainable and unrealistic, and many college instructors we interviewed have gotten accustomed to dropout rates throughout the semester of 50% or more, as the "revolving door" metaphor illustrates. Perhaps the 31% to 41% success figures compiled by Achieving the Dream, or the 16% success rate in math for California students who enter at the lowest level, are as high as can be expected. There are no absolute benchmarks for success in any second-chance programs, and the best that can usually be done is to compare the success rates in supposedly high-performing colleges with those in low-performing colleges, or in pilot programs with those in regular programs. The question of what success rates could be or should be is especially difficult in community colleges, with the enormous heterogeneity of their students (see chapter 2), the great variety of K-12 education from which they come, and the enormous differences in their goals and aspirations. Thus, it is both conceptually difficult and statistically impossible, given the limited data in most colleges, to decide when success rates are high enough—even though there is a consensus that existing rates are too low.

In the absence of conceptual agreement and better data, the only practical solution is to examine the practices in basic skills to see whether they are consistent with practices that have been generally found to be the most effective, and then to examine whether institutional support of basic skills is consistent with high-quality instruction.[9] This forces us to examine basic skills efforts from two perspectives: from the perspective of the classroom and from the vantage point of institutional policies that might support or undermine what happens in classrooms.

The Triangle of Instruction

Developmental education, like much of what happens in formal schooling and postsecondary education, is first and foremost an instructional enterprise involving, at the very least, one instructor, one student, and some kind of content. This can be simply described as the *triangle of instruction* (Figure 1.1), where

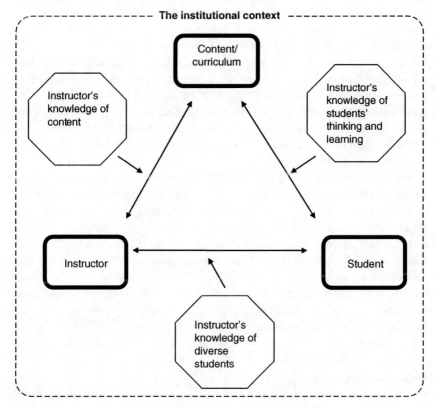

FIGURE 1.1 The Triangle of Instruction

the learning that takes place is a function of all three components. This simple model of the classroom can be interpreted as a kind of equilibrium model, as can indeed other instructional settings, including math and writing labs, tutorials, computer-based instruction, experiential learning, the varied workshops of occupational education, and the employment settings of work-based learning. So long as the teacher and student have similar conceptions of the purposes of a course, including the same ideas about what learning is and how best to learn, then consistency between the two prevails. However, if the instructor and student or the instructor and content (often embedded in a textbook) disagree, then some problem is likely to arise. Therefore, it is necessary to be aware of potential inconsistencies within the classroom among the three elements of the instructional triangle.

Alternatively, the schema in Figure 1.2 directs us to the interactions among each pair of elements. One of the interactions is between the instructor and content. Content knowledge, or mastery of the subject matter, is universally recognized as important for strong teaching, and community colleges usually ensure this by requiring all instructors to have masters' degrees (or, for occupational instructors, experience in their field). But the instructor's conception of the content is also crucial: one math teacher may understand math as a set of procedures to learn by rote—how to convert decimals to fractions, how to solve a one-variable equation—while another may understand it as a way of thinking about relationships (including spatial relationships). Likewise, an historian may think of history as names and dates or, conversely, as a set of deeper issues (economic institutions, governmental forms like democracy, struggles for power, etc.) that transcend any specific event. This is similar to what Shulman (1987) has referred to as pedagogical content knowledge—the understanding not only of alternative approaches to teaching and learning, but also how they may appear in different content areas.

Similarly, it is important to examine the interaction between the instructor and students since that will surely affect their teaching; for example, what instructors know about their students and their backgrounds, and what they think about their students' capacities (both examined in chapter 2). Instructors' warmth and support of students are widely recognized as elements of strong teaching, so the personal relationships between teachers and students are also part of the triangle of instruction and the potential success of the classroom. Indeed, the sympathy of community college instructors for their students, and their efforts to provide them with as much encouragement as possible, are distinctive features of the classrooms we observed. (Chapter 3, which focuses on the dominant approaches to remedial instruction, begins with observations about such relationships.) And, of course, content—the material that students learn, like basic math, basic reading and writing, English for immigrant students—is what matters to the outcomes of formal schooling. But the content of the classroom can also be understood as a set of attitudes toward learning, especially whether the content is engaging, motivating, and perceived by students as relevant (or irrelevant) to their purposes. And so, as I will illustrate in chapters 3 and 4 about conventional instruction versus innovative instruction, one consequence of some teaching is that students lose motivation and drop out of basic skills sequences. This lower success rate of conventional remedial coursework does not occur in more innovative classrooms where student engagement remains high.

Therefore, the elements in the triangle of instruction influence both what students learn and whether they make adequate progress in their coursework— two different dimensions of remedial success rates. But the important point is that *it is impossible to understand the triangle of instruction, and therefore the nature of basic skills teaching in community colleges, without entering the classroom in some way.* Some people have depended on instructors to report what they do (e.g., Seidman, 1985), though this is unreliable because instructors may exaggerate the extent to which their teaching is student-centered or "active" or constructivist. Others have depended on administrators' conceptions of who is a good teacher (Roueche & Baker, 1987); but most administrators don't spend any time observing classes and as a consequence they are ignorant about what the instructional triangle looks like even in their own colleges.[10] The only trustworthy way to learn what happens inside instructional settings is to observe them. Such systematic observations are the mainstays of the research discussed in chapters 3 to 6, which comprise section I of the book, and took place in 13 different colleges, plus several other colleges with examples of potentially exemplary or promising practices.

In addition, the triangle embeds the instructional setting within its institutional and policy contexts. These include a wide range of policies, from those specific to certain colleges to practices that virtually all community colleges have adopted. These practices include the course as the basic unit of instruction; state and federal policies that determine the amounts and uses of public funding; and policies developed by other players such as academic senates, faculty unions, accrediting associations, and occupational licensing boards. All these influences external to the classroom may affect instructors, students, and content in different ways, working either to improve or lower the quality of instruction. In the most extreme cases, certain factors can collapse the whole basic skills enterprise or reduce it to a peripheral and impoverished mission of a college, and in the process almost surely contributing to low success rates. These include a lack of funding from the state level; a lack of support from college administrators who don't want their institutions to be "empires of remediation"; a faculty that stresses standards and rigor but is unwilling to teach basic skills courses (or basic skills within their own classes);[11] and students who are trying to evade basic skills courses that they (sometimes correctly) see as irrelevant and boring.

In order to understand developmental education or any other form of instruction in virtually any educational institution, it is also necessary to learn about institutional influences on instruction. Therefore, in each of the colleges we visited, we interviewed a variety of administrators to understand these institutional decisions. Specifically, we interviewed the dean of instruction; the dean of basic skills, if one existed; the heads of the math and English (or writing) departments; the head of the reading department (if separate from English); the head of the ESL department; those in charge of student support services, including reading and math labs and workshops; the head of Extended Opportunity Programs and Services (EOPS), a support program in California for "students handicapped by language, social, economic and educational disadvantages"; and, in some colleges, the head of the Disabled Students Program and Services (DSPS), the program for students with various disabilities.[12] The appendix to this book provides further details about our research methods, the kinds of people we interviewed, the content of interviews, the process of observation, the selection of colleges, and other methodological issues.

In addition, we questioned instructors not only about their own practices, but also about institutional support for basic skills. In this way, we hoped to get many different perspectives on institutional influences. These results are presented in section II of the book. Chapter 7 focuses on the trajectory of basic skills courses, the dilemmas of initial assessment, the alignment of sequences of courses, and articulation with college-level coursework. Chapter 8 examines funding and resource issues, and Chapter 9 identifies other institutional influences on basic skills.

One limitation of this analysis is that we confined our research to colleges in California; partly for logistical simplicity, partly to eliminate the additional complexity of a variety of states with different policies, and partly because our source of research funds, the Hewlett Foundation, was particularly interested in California. In several ways, California may be atypical. Its spending for students in community colleges is lower than that of most other states, and its K–12 system is of lower quality than most others, as measured by test scores on the National Assessment of Educational Progress (NAEP). The proportion of entering students needing remediation is higher than in other states (as I have already documented), and the governance of and policy structure for education in California are quite fragmented and incoherent for both community colleges and K–12 education. However, California enrolls about one quarter of community college students in the country and is therefore important in its own right. It has an exceptionally varied community college system, thereby allowing us to examine the full variation of colleges, and, judging from the nature of the national discussion, California colleges experience most of the same issues that colleges in other states do.[13] We have, then, every reason to believe that California colleges are representative of the nation as a whole.

Why the Quality of Instruction Matters

Before I continue, it is crucial to understand what I mean by the quality of instruction because this issue arises inevitably once we enter the classroom. In one sense, it seems ludicrous to articulate the importance of instruction, but it often seems like the last topic anyone wants to discuss. The vast amount of writing about basic skills rarely mentions teaching. Even in K-12 education, where a new conventional wisdom has declared the quality of teaching to be the most important element of effective schools, the discussion about what "good teaching" means has been incredibly confused. The perspective I take is that good teaching can be identified by the behavior of instructors in the classroom, not mainly by their credentials (which may reflect content knowledge only, as is usually the case in community colleges) or what they know about instruction (since more extensive *knowledge* may not lead to improved teaching *practices*). Moreover, good teaching cannot be properly identified by ex post measures of what students have learned, including value-added measures, both because of horrendous technical problems with value-added measures and because they cannot tell us what about an instructor has improved student learning. To understand the quality of basic skills instruction or any other kind of teaching it is absolutely necessary to enter the classroom to see what instructors are doing, and no discussion about the institutional and policy contexts of teaching can compensate for the lack of observation.

Classroom practices have been described in many ways, though many observers have divided practices into two polar opposites. On the one hand are pedagogical approaches called constructivist, student-centered, progressive, conceptual, active, teaching for meaning, or innovative, while the opposite approaches are called behaviorist, teacher-centered, traditional, conventional, information transfer, or passive. The former are concerned with students being active creators or constructors of their own understandings, while the latter are more concerned with transferring information and procedures from teachers (or textbooks) to students. Many different vocabularies have been used to describe these two approaches. The instruction for computer programming uses the terminology of *systematic* versus *minimalist* teaching; mathematics often uses "complex instruction" to refer to conceptual approaches; Grubb and Associates (1999, ch. 3) has used the terms *systems* vs. *skills* approaches to describe teaching in occupational subjects; and a confusing discussion about behaviorist "teaching" versus constructivist "learning" has taken place in community colleges.[14] These different vocabularies may refer to different aspects of instruction: *behaviorism* refers to the rewards and punishments that may (or may not) motivate students; *constructivism* is a theory of learning; *teacher-* and *student-centered* often refer to the source of expertise and often the source of talk in a classroom. Therefore, descriptions of classrooms using these vocabularies have to be understood flexibly, since different observers may use different language to refer to these two approaches.

Of course, any time there are two polar opposites like behaviorist vs. constructivist approaches, there is also everything in between; that is, instructional practices that draw on both schools of thought. In John Dewey's introduction to *Experience and Education* (1938), he wrote: "Mankind likes to think in terms of extreme opposites. It is given to formulating its beliefs in terms of Either-Ors, between which it recognizes no intermediate possibilities" (p. 17). In discussing traditional and progressive pedagogies, he lamented that "the problems are not even recognized, to say nothing of being solved, when it is assumed that it suffices to reject the ideas and practices of the old education and then go to the opposite extreme" (p. 22). These intermediate approaches to instruction have been called "balanced," as in balanced literacy programs, or hybrid instruction. Many recommendations about teaching, including the National Academy of Sciences reviews mentioned below and those aimed at postsecondary instructors, in effect recommend balanced instruction (Grubb & Associates, 1999, ch. 1).

There are at least seven reasons to think that more constructivist or balanced approaches are superior to those described as behaviorist. Some of these are based on relatively well-specified statistical models, while others represent the consensus of instructors about what works. Rather than looking for a single kind of evidence providing overwhelming "proof," many different arguments support the use of more constructivist or balanced instruction.

First, some statistical evidence demonstrates that more balanced instruction, or "teaching for meaning," increases learning as measured by different test scores.[15] My own research on high schools (Grubb, 2009), based on NELS88 data, indicates that learning in math, science, reading, and history is enhanced by the way teachers use time, depressed by conventional teaching, and enhanced by more balanced teaching, and increased when teachers have more control over the curriculum. Placement in vocational, general, and remedial tracks depresses all test scores as well as progress through high school—teaching in those tracks is more likely to be behaviorist and teacher expectations are likely to be lower. Research by Knapp et al. (1995) has shown that in schools with high proportions of low-income students, a greater number of practices involving "teaching for meaning" improves test scores; for example, conceptual approaches rather than the emphasis being on procedure and information transfer. The research by Newmann, Bryk, and Nagoaka (2001) on Chicago elementary schools indicates that more balanced instruction increases test scores on both basic skills tests and more comprehensive tests, so constructivist approaches do not lead to lower scores on the ubiquitous basic skills tests. The most improved elementary schools in Chicago were distinguished by instructionally oriented leadership, a coherent instructional guidance system, and student-centered learning (Bryk, 2010; Bryk, Sebring, Allensworth, Leppuscu, & Easton, 2010). Finally, John Hattie's review (2009) of the enormous literature of meta-analyses largely confirms the effectiveness of constructivist methods.

Second, the National Academy of Sciences has undertaken numerous reviews of the enormous empirical literature on instruction. These include research on reading difficulties among young children (Snow, Burns, & Griffin, 1998); a companion volume aimed at parents, promoting success in reading (Burns, Griffin, & Snow, 1999); a report on the teaching of math (Kilpatrick Swafford, & Findell, 2001); a summary of *How People Learn* (Bransford, Brown, & Cocking, 1999); another on *How Students Learn*, compiling vast amounts of research on learning in math, science, and history (Donovan & Bransford, 2005); a report on engagement and motivation in high schools, a volume with substantial implications for learning in community colleges (NRC, 2004); and, most recently, a report on *Improving Adult Literacy Instruction* (Lesgold &Welch-Ross, 2012, especially ch. 4). These examinations clarify the importance of instruction, even with regard to issues like motivation and engagement that are often thought to be characteristics of *students*. More specifically, they highlight the centrality of balanced instruction; for example, by combining specific "skills" (phonemic awareness, mastery of mathematical procedures) with efforts to understand and communicate through text and with conceptual understanding of mathematical approaches and procedures. These reports generally depend on empirical research in small settings, none of which can be considered "proof," but the consistency across studies adds to the evidence for balanced instruction.

In particular, the review of engagement and motivation (National Research Council [NRC], 2004) outlines several recommendations for engaging instruction. Students are more likely to be motivated in programs with close adult–student relationships where they have some autonomy in selecting tasks and methods and can construct meaning, engage in sense-making on their own, and play an active role in learning. They will be more engaged in well-structured educational environments with clear purposes, a challenging curriculum, high expectations, and a strong emphasis on achievement. Students are more likely to be motivated if they have multiple paths to competence and can enhance their understanding of school and its relation to future goals. But most teaching in basic skills, especially the remedial pedagogy described in chapter 3, does not look like this. To move to more engaging instruction, more balanced approaches are necessary.

Third, a review of professional development clarifies the importance of sustained work on pedagogical content knowledge (Little, 2006). This is the application of general pedagogical approaches (e.g., the use of more complex questioning, problem-based learning, and student-centered procedures) to specific subjects like math, business, and automotive repair (Shulman, 1987). It requires an integration of both content knowledge and general pedagogical knowledge, rather than viewing strong instruction as dominated by either one or the other.

Fourth, by definition, basic skills instruction pays attention only to those mathematical and linguistic capacities that are considered basic, and not to conceptual abilities that include those cited by Conley (2007) as part of college readiness, or "higher order" or "21st century skills" like problem-solving abilities or communication skills. When developmental classes confine themselves to basic skills, they do a poor job of preparing students for college-level courses,[16] or for transfer to 4-year colleges. Indeed, shifting the terminology of remediation from "developmental" education to "basic skills" instruction seems a step backward, since the term *developmental education* implies improvement on many dimensions of cognitive ability, not just basic skills. In addition, as instructors in one college with an exemplary system of student support consistently maintained, "All education is developmental"; segregating basic skills from more advanced competencies labels students and may subject them to stigma, or the kind of stereotype threat analyzed by Claude Steele (2010).

Fifth, in the specific area of basic skills instruction, most students (including most immigrant students) have been taught by behaviorist methods for 12 or 13 years of formal schooling.[17] Given these conditions, it seems inappropriate—daft might be a better expression—to try still one more round of traditional teaching. To be sure, students in community colleges may be more motivated to learn than they were in earlier grades, as they confront the challenges of adulthood. Otherwise, however, it seems absurd to try the same methods when these approaches have failed so many times before. As one department chair defended his belief in group work (which he described as "hands-on")[18] in place of lecture, "Inside the box didn't work in high school, so let's do something else." Another instructor, a math instructor, noted that

> If they didn't get it for the last however many years of their life, most of them are not going to get it in 17 weeks. Being a former high school teacher, I know different things to do like collaborative learning—I want them to talk and do collaborative work in groups.

Sixth, while community colleges have many well-known examples of innovation (analyzed in chapter 4), they can be undermined by conventional and unimaginative teaching. For example, learning communities—where students take two, three, or even four courses simultaneously, as one way of contextualizing instruction—lack coherence when two (or more) instructors vary in their instructional approaches. As one instructor in a pairing of basic reading with Introduction to Computers related, "It's hard working with another instructor locked into a lecture format—horrible because lectures don't reach 'new students.'"[19] Similarly, the effort to teach basic skills (including ESL) in the context of an occupational subject can be as drill-oriented as any "academic" version of basic skills. If instructors in such paired courses neglect to consult with one another, the result is two parallel courses without integration. In many ways, the *structure* of instruction—the attempts to create learning communities or paired courses, the various mechanisms of acceleration—may improve the conditions for better instruction, but without specific attention to instruction itself, a new structure may not enhance learning.

Finally, there is some evidence that more constructivist approaches to teaching reduce the incidence of stereotype threat. As conceptualized by Claude Steele (2010), stereotype threat causes students to perform worse when a negative stereotype is triggered (e.g., African Americans in school, women in math, or White males in basketball). These triggers may be subtle, but the lower performance they cause may be quite serious. Some evidence from a variety of classrooms suggests that behaviorist teaching is more likely to trigger negative stereotypes than in more "active" or constructivist teaching that engages students in the creation of learning (D. Steele et al., n.d.). This result in effect replicates the finding by Knapp and his colleagues (1995) that more constructivist teaching improves learning among the most vulnerable and lowest performing students.

In the community colleges we observed, there is indeed a great variety of instruction—"there's a lot of individuality to making that decision"—replicating the divisions between behaviorist or teacher-centered instruction versus constructivist or student-centered teaching. Some instructors are frankly behaviorist, concerned with information transfer: "Mostly, I lecture in my class and ask for their questions," said one. Another commented, "To be honest, I pretty much lecture, just because it's supposed to be a class at a certain time and the students are supposed to be there"—as long as standard practice is to hold classes, he felt he was "supposed to" lecture. Another instructor expressed her belief in worksheets and drill, the essence of remedial pedagogy, because it lent itself to mastery learning—the notion, prevalent in the 1980s and 1990s, that students must master certain skills before advancing to the next stage.

But many of their colleagues rejected the practices of conventional teaching: "That's what I knew what to do [traditional lecturing] when I got here, and that doesn't work very well.... These are not students who would just sit well and listen to a lecture." Instead, they tended to talk in terms of "active" or "hands-on" learning, as well as "interactive" and "problem-based" teaching. One noted that "Piaget has been talking about hands-on learning since when? Years and years and years—and some people are looking at it now as like, 'This is new'?" These instructors try to vary their classrooms to incorporate balanced approaches, not eliminating lecturing but combining it with other methods. As one ESL instructor remarked, "We try to use, for every hour, no more than 20 minutes of lecture ... [there is] a lot of ... student group work, student presentations." Others acknowledge using "an eclectic mix [of teaching approaches] ... from other people I've known, my second grade teacher, my grad schools."

Several talked about the need for contextualizing instruction, or clarifying how any particular competence is useful in different settings, either academic or occupational.[20] One math instructor acknowledged that "math instructors are not good at providing real-world examples," while another, when asked how he could motivate students, replied that he could

> give better illustrations—some students always tell me, "I don't want to learn this stuff, it doesn't seem relevant to my life, I don't want to learn math, what is this all about?" I could get better at getting, like, real-world examples and bringing them into the class ... that would motivate them.

Furthermore, when colleges try to change instruction, they refer to many of the practices of constructivist and student-centered approaches. When one college got a Title III grant from the federal government (formally known as Aid for Institutional Development), it explicitly used it to change teaching: "The focus is on faculty and staff development and helping them understand the learner-centered method of teaching, as opposed to 'I taught it, so why didn't they learn it?'" So, when instructors talk about instruction, many of them replicate familiar dimensions of instructor-centered, behaviorist instruction concerned with fact transmission and procedural knowledge *versus* student-centered and constructivist instruction incorporating various forms of "active" and conceptual learning, often contextualized.

However, there are many more dimensions of instructional quality than the traditional/progressive, behaviorist/constructivist divide—too many to have been empirically validated or evaluated, so the evidence for them is often taken from the logic of practice. Some dimensions of instructional quality are supported by virtually everyone: content mastery; warm and supportive relationships with students; explicitness about the purposes of instruction; clarity in presentation; care in providing the prerequisites for understanding before developing new material; developing checks for student understanding; and using student errors to diagnose how students are thinking about a topic.[21] Other dimensions of quality are specific to particular approaches: some instructors might use project- or problem-based learning (in sciences and occupational areas in particular), and others might not. Some instructors try to vary the classroom, changing topics or exercises every 15 to 20 minutes in the interest of motivating students; others do not. Some instructors would emphasize the duration of instruction as crucial to outcomes and high standards, while others would caution that what counts is not time itself but the amount of *engaged academic learning time* (Cotton, 1990).

Within each of these approaches to instruction, then, there are better and worse forms that instruction can take. For behaviorist teaching, the techniques of direct instruction suggest a careful progression of introducing a new topic, presenting it to students, having students practice with guidance (or "scaffolding"), and finally having students work independently. Behaviorist teaching that neglects this progression is likely to leave some students without mastery of the new topic; for example, instructors who present a new topic or skill, and then move on to the next one without scaffolding or independent performance.

For constructivist instruction, the efforts to develop student-centered methods can work well or poorly. Student groups can be truly cooperative or dominated by a few students, or characterized by nonparticipation when students have not been socialized about the reasons and methods of participation. Projects can be engaging and "relevant" or "academic" and even demeaning when they are too childish. Attempts to contextualize an academic competence can draw on contexts that are meaningful to students or only those that the instructor fabricates.

In effect, there are some dimensions of quality that everyone agrees are important; others may be subject-specific, or more controversial. Certain dimensions of quality may be particular to constructivist teaching, and somewhat different elements of quality may be important in behaviorist teaching. In addition, balanced instruction requires skill in developing an appropriate mix of behaviorist and constructivist approaches, and skilled instructors can usually specify why they move from one to the other.

To clarify the alternatives, the "landscape" of instructional possibilities looks like those in Figure 1.2. The x-axis displays, from left to right, behaviorist teaching passing through balanced instruction toward increasingly constructivist teaching. The y-axis describes low-quality to high-quality instruction,

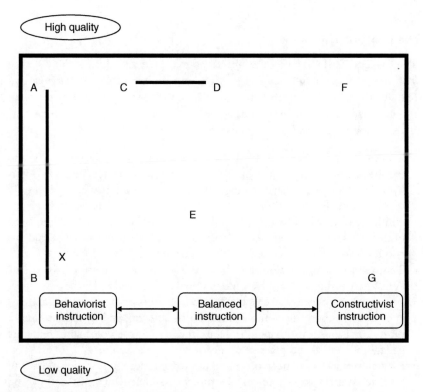

FIGURE 1.2 The Landscape of Instructional Approaches

though quality in reality is multidimensional (and difficult to visualize) rather than one-dimensional. While balanced instruction seems, based on the arguments above, more effective than either behaviorist instruction or extreme constructivist instruction, high-quality teacher-centered instruction (point A) might be more effective than low-quality student-centered instruction (point G). Figure 1.2 displays possible combinations of instructional approaches, not their effectiveness; no one has figured out how to measure all the dimensions of instruction included in this figure, and no one can say which of these instructional combinations is most effective. All one can say with any confidence is that movement to the right from extreme behaviorist teaching (segment A-B) is probably an improvement, and movement toward the top (improvement in quality) is surely beneficial, if we can agree on the crucial dimensions of quality. Ideal teaching, like that in the National Academy of Sciences reviews, might be described along the segment C-D, with high-quality balanced instruction. If instruction is both behaviorist and low-quality (point X), which describes a great deal of the "remedial pedagogy" we have observed, there's obviously room for improvement toward the top right. For the moment, what is important is to understand the different dimensions of the basic skills classroom in order to clarify which features might be worth reforming.

The Logic of This Book

In creating a methodology for examining developmental education, we started with several hypotheses about what might explain low success in remediation. The practices that we investigated contributed to our hypotheses about what might impede progress through basic skill sequences, and they will be examined systematically in subsequent chapters:

- The variety of students in developmental classes, their differing needs, and their levels of preparation may affect success rates, as chapter 2 analyzes. This hypothesis sometimes leads to suggestions that community colleges should develop admissions requirements or tests, as selective colleges do, in order to eliminate some or all basic skills students, but this is contrary to the mission of the college as an "open-access" institution. The heterogeneity of students also leads to an enormous variety of support services.
- The quality of instruction, and how motivating and relevant it is to students, may influence both how much they learn and whether they complete a remedial sequence (see chapter 3). I will also examine (in chapter 4) the enormous extent of teaching innovation in colleges, and investigate under what conditions it is sufficient to break the hold of the dominant "remedial pedagogy"—drill and practice on decontextualized subskills.
- Student services have been increased to provide more support to students in both academic tasks—in forms like tutoring, supplemental instruction, and writing and math labs or workshops—and in the noncognitive aspects of

college success, in such forms as student success courses, guidance and counseling, and tutoring and supplemental instruction (see chapter 5). However,
if these services are inadequate or poorly integrated with developmental
classrooms, then they may not be effective, and students will not have the
supplementary support they need. Conversely, effective student services provide yet another setting, complementary to classrooms, for developmental
instruction (see chapter 6).

• Basic skills courses are typically aligned in a sequence, initialized by an
assessment test that it is hoped leads to successful college-level coursework.
This trajectory of events, like every other sequence of courses in formal
schooling, may be smooth and integrated. Conversely, it may suffer from a
lack of articulation among courses (vertical alignment) and of consistency
among courses taught at the same level (horizontal alignment). If misalignment occurs in several ways, then this by itself will reduce success rates
since some students will be unprepared for subsequent courses. In contrast,
well-aligned assessment and courses ought to simplify the process of getting
through the sequence. Some advocates have called for shortening the time
required for basic skills courses, by compressing two courses into one and
accelerating the sequence (e.g., Hern & Snell, 2010). This may indeed help
some students, particularly those who have to complete only one developmental course before moving into college-level work.[22] But the articulation issues for other students, involving the consistency of similar courses
("horizontal articulation") and of courses in a sequence ("vertical articulation"), are considerably more complex than acceleration alone could remedy.
Therefore, more systemic policies may be necessary to smooth the trajectory
of remediation.

• The institutional characteristics of community colleges affect basic skills
instruction (see the Triangle of Instruction again, in Figure 1.1). As mentioned before, these include the issues of assessment and alignment, or the
dynamic aspects of developmental education (see chapter 7); funding and
resources (in chapter 8); the role of adjunct or part-time faculty; the nature
of professional development; and the nature of the community college as a
laissez-faire institution, leery of imposing constraints on faculty or students
(all in chapter 9). So, there are many more issues to analyze and, potentially,
to "fix" than just the ones that show up in instructional settings.

• Finally, all these analytic chapters have implications for change and reform.
Chapter 10 therefore briefly recaps the highlights of each previous chapter,
with recommendations based on our findings.

In contrast to our broad efforts to identify the potential causes of low success, others have fastened on one or two specific innovations. For example,
Hern and Snell (2010) have focused on accelerated courses, where instructors
concentrate more material in a shorter period of time. Others, like Hughes and
Scott-Clayton (2010) or Safran and Visher (2010), have emphasized problems

in assessing readiness for college-level courses. MDRC has focused on a series of random-assignment studies on learning communities, where cohorts of students take two or more courses together.

But the problem is that no one has any idea which of these potential influences on success rates is more important than any other. The data to measure with any precision the quality of instruction, and then to see what effect this has on learning and progress, do not currently exist. Similarly, while some colleges have improved student services in particular ways, it isn't possible to say whether such efforts are more or less effective than improving alignment or articulation, or enhancing instruction. Until data about colleges and their students improve significantly, the best that can be done is to examine common practices and see if they live up to what we know (or suspect) about effective practices. This may not tell us which reforms are the most important, but they at least provide an agenda for improvement in developmental education, the subject of chapter 10.

In the end, the current remedial quandary cannot be resolved by community colleges alone; the magnitude of the problem is largely out of their control. Even if success rates could be vastly improved, the sheer number of students needing some form of developmental education constitutes a serious problem, one that has turned some colleges into places where other missions may be squeezed out. Resolving the remediation "crisis," both in community colleges and in all other education and training institutions with underprepared students, will require a Deweyan "both-and" solution, *both* improving the quality of developmental education *and* trying to improve the quality of each level of K–12 schooling so that the need for remediation is not so great. I will put off such a "both-and" strategy until the final chapter, accumulating information and perspectives along the way about what might contribute to such an approach.

2

DEVELOPMENTAL STUDENTS

Their Heterogeneity, Readiness, and Perspectives

Students are crucial participants in the classroom, one of the elements in the triangle of instruction discussed in the previous chapter that consists of the instructor, the student, and the content. The first section of this chapter, therefore, examines the roles of students in the developmental classroom based on our observations of classrooms; the second section addresses the comments of instructors about students; and the third section looks at the responses of students themselves.

What is most striking about the students in community colleges is how varied they are. Some could have attended 4-year colleges, but chose not to for reasons ranging from family responsibilities to finances; others have barely managed to achieve their high school diplomas. The largest number of students are of conventional college-going age (i.e., from 18 to 24), but a substantial number in virtually every college are older students who are returning to school for a variety of reasons. Some students have clear plans, but many are "experimenters," using the college as a low-cost and convenient way to try college and see whether they can find a sustaining interest. Some are full-time students but most are part-time, with employment and family responsibilities competing for time with school responsibilities—the work-family-schooling dilemma. But what really counts for the purposes of this book are the learning needs of different students and these prove to be just as varied. The first section describes five types of students who coexist in the basic skills classroom, each of whom has a different learning issue but all of whom are in the same classroom, which enormously complicates the job of the instructor.

This chapter relies heavily on instructors' perceptions of students, which is appropriate since such perceptions may affect their expectations of students and their approaches to instruction. Instructors have enormous sympathy for their students, and understand all too well the pressures in their lives, the competing demands of family and employment, and the "busied-up" conditions of their schedules. But at the same time, they also perceive many developmental students to lack the preparation necessary for college—the common phrase is that "they're not ready to be college students." Indeed, based on classroom observations, there is some truth to that: many students do not behave like the stereotype of committed college students. They arrive late to class, spend time on cell phones and computers, and fail to complete homework. However, there is a problem of causality: do they behave this way because they somehow have not learned to behave in any other way, or are they responding to the fact that their developmental classes are so conventional, so dominated by the drill and repetition of remedial pedagogy? In our observations, such distracted behavior is much less common in classes with more student participation and interaction. Therefore, the dominance of remedial pedagogy may be responsible for a great deal of unmotivated activity.

But whether this is true or not, the crucial question is how instructors, and colleges themselves, respond to the perception that students "are not ready to be college students." Many individual instructors, as well as colleges that provide student support services (especially courses like "College Success"), are doing what they can to teach developmental students "how to be college students," rather than assuming that their behavior is inherently unengaged. So this, too, is a dimension of developmental education—teaching students not only the basic and other academic skills they will need for college-level courses, but also instilling the behaviors that will make them successful in subsequent education.

Finally, students can speak for themselves, and in the third section results are summarized from interviews of a small number of students: 22 to be precise. Fortunately, given this limited sample, the perspectives of students prove to be highly similar to one another, as well as to our findings from classroom observations and interviews, as we will see in subsequent chapters.

The nature of students is somewhat different from the other topics in this book. Community colleges have some influence over the kind of instruction that takes place in classrooms and student services (chapters 3–6). In addition, potentially they can control at least some of the institutional conditions that shape developmental education (chapters 7–10). But as long as they remain open access institutions without entrance standards, they have to accept the students who come to their doors. As one instructor declared to her president,

> Teaching college is like being in Vegas. If you get a hand of cards, and you don't like them, you can't say, "Gee, can you take them back and give me some better ones?" I can't look at my students and say, "Wow, you're unprepared, so I'm going to send you over there and I want better students." ... I like my students. I think my job is the best job ever.

Some instructors may carp about the "quality" of their students, as we will see later in this chapter, but they recognize that they cannot influence the composition of their student body without completely reshaping the community college. So, the range of students as well as the magnitude of remedial problems are givens, to which colleges may react in different ways but cannot readily avoid. In many ways, then, the analysis of developmental education teases apart the variety of ways that community colleges react to student conditions that are not of their own making.

Heterogeneity in the Classroom

One important source of information about students is, of course, the classroom, of which we observed close to 150. In observing classes, many different types of students present themselves. From our observations, there are at least five quite different kinds of students, with different learning needs, in developmental classes:

"Brush-up" or "Refresher" Students

Some students have mastered basic skills in the past—the various formulas for math, the academic patterns of reading and writing—but have forgotten them. Instructors estimate that "no more than 10%" of students are brush-up students, suggesting that their numbers are relatively small. Sometimes they end up in developmental classes because they did not study for the initial assessment test, and did not understand how important the test is to placement; sometimes they are older students who have not been in any academic setting for a number of years. They may have various other advantages since instructors often believe that older students are more motivated, with better prepared plans for their postsecondary education.

Brush-up students do not need to go back to the beginning of math or reading and writing sequences; they need a quick review of topics they have already learned. According to instructors, this is particularly likely in math classes since many students may not have taken math for the last 2 years of high school, and their math skills are therefore rusty. In class, these are the students who understand everything the instructor does, who have answers to all questions; they are in the process of remembering what they have already learned, rather than learning material for the first time. Instead of being placed in conventional developmental courses, they might be better served by a computer-based review of basic academic material or some other individualized program that allows them to move at their own rapid pace. But developmental classes are not usually structured to allow a great deal of internal variation in the pace and content of material, so they are stuck with following the same pace as students who have truly not learned basic academic skills.

Students Whose Initial Assessments have been Incorrect

The process of placements into developmental courses includes an initial placement exam—often ACCUPLACER or the COMPASS test in the colleges we visited. But students are often unaware how important these placement exams are, and they often do not take them seriously (see the third section of this chapter and chapter 7 on "Assessment and Alignment"). As a result, they are sometimes placed in remedial courses that they do not need; but without a way of testing out of the class, they are stuck in a sequence of developmental classes. Like brush-up students, these are students who generally know everything that is being taught in class so that the briefest review is enough to bring these topics back to them. What they really need is either some mechanism to test out of a remedial sequence once it is clear that they have been misplaced, or a mechanism to get them to take the placement exam more seriously. For example, several colleges in our sample have instituted preparation programs for the placement exam, taking place 2 to 3 weeks before the beginning of the semester; these programs serve the needs of both brush-up students and students who might otherwise be misplaced because of failing to take the exam seriously.

A very different kind of misplaced student includes those whose primary language is not English, but who have been placed into developmental reading or writing instead of ESL. Rather than the drill and practice common in developmental reading and writing classes, they need the broad range of language-related exercises more typical of ESL classes. Evidently, however, placement procedures are not always precise enough to distinguish ESL students, and we will therefore return to the assessment and placement issue in chapter 7.

Students Who have Learned very little about Basic Academic Skills in Their Prior Schooling

The majority of students are surely those who genuinely need further instruction in basic academic skills. This is not because they have not seen these subjects before;[1] fractions and decimals, or subject–verb agreement and parts of speech, are part of every elementary school curriculum, with periodic review in middle school. Instead, these students seem to have mastered this material just well enough to follow the procedures necessary to pass tests, but not well enough to retain academic concepts over a longer period of time. This is evident in their basic lack of understanding, in many cases, of numbers and place values, or when to use multiplication with a set of numbers and when to use some other operation. These students may also be unclear about parts of speech and their function in reading and writing. They may have learned about topic sentences at some point, but not well enough to use this idea in their strategies for either reading or writing. These are the students for whom developmental courses are designed with sequences of material going all the way back to the basics of number and sentence construction if necessary.

Why so many students have learned so little about basic academic skills, never mind the higher order competencies necessary for college, is a genuinely puzzling question. It is one we will take up in the final chapter in considering how one might create an educational *system* that does not require so much remediation as ours does. However, from community college instructors themselves, the dominant answer is that the K-12 system has failed: "We're all remedial colleges because the K-12 system is failing them," one instructor mentioned. There's a great deal of high school bashing, blaming high schools for not being demanding enough: "The bar's just set too low," commented an instructor in a middle-class college with well-regarded feeder high schools. "It's always amazing when you talk to high school students and their parents, how little they know," commented another instructor, referring both to academic knowledge as well as "college knowledge" about the process of applying to and getting through college.

To be sure, high school bashing is part of a larger practice in which each level of the education system blames the level just below it for the weaknesses of students. The pattern of passing on some students who are not ready, in this case, not college ready, is a systemic problem, not one confined to high schools. But there is at least some evidence that K-12 bashing is justified in California: ever since the state passed a proposition limiting property taxation, the quality of schooling has deteriorated substantially due to inadequate funding and other resources. In the most recent NAEP assessments, California eighth graders ranked in the bottom seven states in reading and among the bottom nine states in math, so they are genuinely underprepared relative to their peers in most other states. This is surely one of the reasons that the proportion of entering students needing remediation in California (around 80%) is higher than the national figure of about 60%.

Of course, there are other sources of blame for low academic performance aside from the quality of the K-12 system. Some instructors engaged in a cultural critique of life in the United States, with computer games and cell phones and other electronic gadgets distracting students from the hard work required for academic success. Recently, there has been a wave of newspaper stories about psychology experiments related to delayed gratification, where children who are unable to delay gratification turn into poorer students. This is, among other things, another cultural critique of the United States, oriented to the desire for instant gratification rather than "the long-term gratification of reading a book," as one instructor put it. Like high school bashing, such criticisms by instructors help explain why many students have such a weak command of basic skills, though they also defend community college instructors against blame for the continued poor performance of developmental students.

So, even though there may be some brush-up students and misplaced students in developmental classrooms, there is little doubt that most of the students present do need some remedial coursework. When instructors teach to the middle of the class, these are the students who are the targets of their instruction.

Students with Learning Disabilities (LDs)

In observing classes, it appears (even to untrained observers) that a number of students suffer from learning disabilities. These are students who work through problems at an excruciatingly slow pace, who seem to have trouble retaining simple information or directions, and who remain genuinely confused about what a number or a verb is, even after several explanations. To be sure, the observers in this project are not trained to detect signs of learning disabilities, just as instructors are not, but the behavior of some students alerted us to this possibility.

A few instructors talked about the problems of having students with learning disabilities in their classes, corroborating our perception that such students are present. One instructor in a middle-class college went through a list of potential diagnoses: "Some students are learning disabled, not diagnosed; those with really low IQ are 10% of my class, or ADHD, or borderline retarded." Another commented on the effect on student morale:

> Then you get students with learning disabilities, too, and that's even worse. They already know they suck, and then to have a class just come around and beat on them.... There is nothing they can do about it because they just can't learn as quickly as other people can.

Another instructor in a Learning Center was uncharacteristically blunt (and politically incorrect) about the problems for instructors:

> Most of the students here [in basic courses at the bottom] are like—they have mental problems, honestly. These are DSS [Department of Special Services] students.... And I used to teach these classes, and I know that it's really hard to deal with this kind of student. One [kind of student] is like a normal regular student—understands the concepts and everything and knows how to behave; but other students, they don't understand. And besides this, they don't know how to behave in class ... just as an instructor, you cannot deal with these people.

This passage, contrasting "normal regular students" with students having "mental problems," was essentially a complaint that conventional instructors are not trained to deal with the various cognitive and behavioral problems of students with learning disabilities ("just as an instructor, you cannot deal with these people").

One of the underlying problems is that instructors are not prepared to diagnose or to treat learning disabilities. In K–12 education, programs in special education are responsible for carrying out this function, and they enlist teachers as well as parents in identifying and then treating many different kinds of learning disabilities. But for adults in community colleges, Departments of Special Services are quite small and have no authority to seek out LD students. If students do not self-refer, then there is no way that these already limited resources can be used to address these problems.

Of course, neither we nor anyone else knows the magnitude of learning disabilities in developmental classrooms. Our point here is not that learning disabilities account for a large number of the students in basic skills classrooms, but rather that, unlike K-12 education, there is no workable mechanism operating in the colleges we examined to respond to this problem. Until such an approach can be developed and institutionalized—either by expanding DSS services, or by publicizing such services in student success courses—developmental instructors must cope with LD students as best they can, within the mix of the many types of students they face.

Students with Mental Health Problems

Again, observations in classes suggest that quite a few students have a variety of mental health problems: compulsions, depression leading to extreme passivity, different kinds of anxiety, and sometimes more extreme problems. One instructor talked at length about the extent of posttraumatic stress syndrome in the community because of the prevalence of gang- and gun-related violence. Sometimes, student behavior in class makes these conditions obvious, but of course, at other times—especially with depression and anxiety that often are not manifested in "problem" behavior—neither we as observers nor instructors are in any position to know about these conditions. Indeed, instructors usually do not know and often *cannot* learn about such conditions; as one instructor said:

> The reality for me, when I taught arithmetic, is that they had so many issues beyond arithmetic skills.... We're not allowed to know. If we have students that are on medications or have emotional issues—unless the student comes up and self-identifies.... If they are willing to talk about it, often you can get them to supportive services. Every so often, though, you will get somebody in complete denial, and there's not much you can do except try and keep on.

As in the case of students with learning disabilities, the diagnostic capacities of community colleges with respect to mental health conditions are limited, and there is no mechanism (like special education in K-12, or sometimes school-based health centers) to assure that any diagnosis is matched by treatment, something that students would need their own health insurance to pay for.

Although all five kinds of students may be in a developmental classroom, the instructor won't know much about the needs of individual students and will typically only utilize conventional teaching aimed at the middle group, those students who have not mastered basic skills in K-12 education. But brush-up and misclassified students need something completely different; either a mechanism to test out of a developmental sequence, or an individualized remedial program, perhaps computer-based. And students with disabilities and mental health problems need services that the instructor and (usually) the college cannot provide. The result is an unknown number of students whose needs cannot be met within the conventional framework of developmental education.

Faculty Conceptions of Students: "They're Not Ready to Be College Students"

A crucial component of any instruction is the way instructors view and treat their students. A commonly held notion about teaching is that instructors need to know their students well, particularly in student-centered teaching where instructors draw on the background and experiences of students. Sometimes the advice to be knowledgeable about and respectful of students becomes exaggerated as the only dimension of teaching that matters, as one can sometimes see in the notions of "student support" as a conception of teaching, the notion of "caring" as the basis of pedagogy, or a "therapist" approach to teaching (Grubb et al., 1999, pp. 36–38). But, short of such extreme statements, the notion of respecting students is widely considered to be a crucial dimension of instruction; that is, empathizing with the conditions of their lives and supporting them psychologically as well as cognitively.

As emphasized in chapter 3, instruction in basic skills classes is almost invariably supportive, with teachers praising students for participation and answers while avoiding the demeaning treatment one sometimes sees in high schools. In addition, most instructors are quite knowledgeable about the enormous variety of students and the kinds of lives they lead. One full-time math instructor, an individual who has taught at several levels of the education system, declared:

> Oh my God, they're all over the place. On the extremes, they vary from your bottom four students in a basic math class who have absolutely no concept of what anything means. Sometimes it's learning disabilities, sometimes there are students here who honestly have marginal IQs ... and then on the other side of it are top students—they could be functioning at Berkeley and be just as successful as they are here. They generally were not successful in math before, but they really want to learn and they'd like to get through it this time. But they're very responsive, as opposed to junior high kids, let's say.... Single mothers with three kids, working 40 hours a week, and trying to come to school. I had a guy who would come directly from his night shift to the 8:00 class ... so you know, work, kids, illness, mental problems. And the occasional one who just, you know, "Hi, I'm here, fine, great, did well, see you." They're the

ones who just go through it no problem at all, too—they're just reviewing. There's everybody, you know?

In the span of a few minutes, the instructor has identified the tremendous
variation in student performance, the issues of family and work responsibilities,
and what we call "brush-up" students ("the ones who just go through it no
problem at all, too—they're just reviewing"). This instructor has also introduced, along the way, the problems of learning disabilities and more pervasive
developmental delays ("marginal IQs") that were identified in the previous
section.

Another dean of student development used the card-playing metaphor again
when she acknowledged the difficulty of

> getting the faculty to acknowledge that we have students coming to us
> who are unprepared to go on to do collegiate work.... It's almost like
> denial at times: "We're a college and this shouldn't be." Well, the reality
> is society has dealt us a different hand and we have a responsibility now;
> we're in a situation where we can do some things. And I think more and
> more, the faculty are embracing that idea—that we can do some things.

Furthermore, she credited a series of basic skills symposia supported by the
state's Basic Skills Initiative, bringing together faculty from all disciplines to
describe their students, "and that makes them more aware that they, too, are
basic skills faculty. Not all of them are willing to buy into that, but more
and more are." When colleges create induction programs for new faculty or
adjuncts, they often include a course or module about community college students to be sure that everyone understands the enormous variation. There are,
of course, exceptions, like a math department we visited, described as being
"dismissive" of students. In another college, an English instructor and cochair
of basic skills noted that

> There are some [faculty] who have students that don't have college skills,
> and [they say] "What are they [unskilled students] doing here? And even
> "Why are we teaching them?" So we try to—when I say "we," the coun-
> selors and those of us [instructors] who care deeply—together try to pro-
> tect them a little bit, and in the beginning while they are building their
> skills, get them into classes with instructors who do care and who aren't
> going to just dismiss them for their skill level.

In several colleges, a similar coterie of faculty, anywhere from five to a
dozen, were highly committed to basic skills and "care deeply and try to protect students," while other faculty in the same department were more ambiva-
lent. But, by and large, the faculty we interviewed understood and respected
the enormous variety of students they face.

At the same time, instructors make many statements about students that are quite pejorative, and it's worrisome to think that these negative perceptions of students might influence their teaching. Their comments about students and their deficiencies run the gamut from comments about inadequate academic skills to observations about their work habits to statements about their lack of potential. One instructor, a full-timer who had been teaching for 15 years with a background in GED instruction,[2] seemed particularly frustrated with his students. In an interview standing outside the classroom, he called the work of his students "shit," and felt that their time was better spent on in-class practice rather than on developing new approaches. During his career, he has had to "adapt to reality" and "lower his standards" because of the low reading levels of his students. For example, he wanted to incorporate more advanced authors like Sandra Cisneros, but selected an easier work instead (Miguel Street by V.S. Naipaul). He also asserted that his students lack cultural literacy, or general knowledge of high culture, and that this eroded academic literacy; he suggested that the college sponsor trips to museums (including the nearby Getty Museum) as a remedy. However, despite his disparaging comments about student skills, his classroom behavior showed evident concern for students, and they seemed quite responsive to his approach.

Many other instructors complained about preparation in high schools, noting that it was possible to avoid writing-intensive courses in the junior and senior year, and that the emphasis on fiction in conventional literature classes did not prepare students well for the nonfiction stressed in college. Also, they noted that most students who passed the high school exit exam—which most observers think is geared to the eighth or ninth grade level ("the bar's just set too low")—thought they were well-prepared for college. As one instructor in a middle-class college noted, "There's a disconnect in that 98 or 99% of the students graduate with the high school exit exam. They wing it. They come here, and we have 85% of them, they can't get through our placement test." Another instructor noted the disjunction: "The high school teachers were concerned that they thought their students were doing well, but then they come take our placement test and place below college level." This was one of the few colleges in our sample to work consistently with high school teachers.

Basic skills instructors understandably complain about students' academic competencies—low levels of these skills are what have gotten them into developmental classes. But just as important as academic skills, many instructors noted the life circumstances that prevent their students from being "ready to be college students." Some of the dimensions of being "not ready" come from the conditions of their lives: the work-family-schooling dilemma:

> We find at the 97 and 99 level [the lowest level courses] that students often lead more chaotic lives than students in 101 and 102 ... I have a student who's very motivated, but his mother's in jail and he's having to look after his brother who has mental health problems—and work and go to college.

Another, using the same language of chaos, commented that

> I also believe that we have a group of students that have the desire, but they're in crisis or chaos mode. And with that comes, "I want to but I don't know how." And we need to have programs that really work to reopen their possibilities ... I would love for student services and the Academic Success Center to come together and create that model.

This refers to the need for student support services, the subject of chapter 5, and the integration of support services with academic instruction. But most student services provide academic support, not support for the personal crises and chaos that come from the confluence of family, work, and schooling, or from childcare needs, or employment and money pressures, or transportation needs, or from mental health issues. Even the college with the best student support—Chaffey College,* profiled in chapter 6—cannot readily cope with such personal issues. Similarly, one college surveyed its students to find out what they needed to be successful; the most common response was an academic mentor, but the second most common answer was gas cards so they could get to class, though the college had no way to respond to this income-related need. More generally, three separate studies based on interviews with students have found that the distractions of work and family life are the most powerful reasons that students leave community colleges,[3] so it's not surprising that this overload, the "busied-up conditions of students' lives," often prevents them from paying full attention to their basic skills classes.

But a less obvious and more difficult aspect of students is their apparent lack of understanding of what "college" requires, including planfulness, commitment to schooling, independence, initiative, and academic stamina or "grit" (Duckworth, Peterson, Matthews, & Kelly, 2007). One vice-president for student services mused about what we call basic skills:

> How do you define "basic skills"? I see lots of our students who need basic responsibility, interpersonal skills—almost everything. So, it's not just reading and writing or math. According to many of the nationwide surveys, the employers pay attention to the interpersonal skills, relationship skills, and communication skills. So, I feel a high proportion of our students are really in need of enhancing that part.

Planning is another dimension of these kinds of "basic skills": One chair of a Learning Assistance Center stated, "We have a set of students that may not ever see a counselor, and they just start taking courses." Many others complained that a lot of students "don't know what they're here for," and that without

---

* With the exception of Chaffey College, all names of instructors and colleges in this book are pseudonyms. Because of the difficulty of maintaining Chaffey College's anonymity, we received permission from the college to use its real name.

clear plans they cannot formulate a coherent program of study, or understand the role of basic skills courses in their educational trajectories. In part, this is a complaint that the "experimenters"—students who come to college to find out what they might want to do in their adult lives (since career-oriented guidance and counseling in high school are so poor)—are not particularly ready to learn since they are there to find out if they should be in college.[4] "I have some people who want to take the class for information, and don't intend to do any of the work," as one instructor described them. Almost all colleges provide guidance and counseling to address the issues of planning, but, as we will see in the section on student voices, and in chapter 5 on "Student Support Services," there are too few counseling resources in most community colleges. Such services are being cut back under fiscal pressure, and faculty often complain that counselors are disconnected from programs of study and are therefore ignorant about requirements. At the same time, the same Learning Assistance chair said that

> We also have the group [of students] that follows the prescribed program, and they may or may not do well. That depends on their initiative and their follow-through. I think we need to do a better job making sure that our students understand their role and responsibility in their own education.

Another English instructor, who had been fretting about the low pass rates in one of the basic English courses, said, "It just occurred to me that the people who pass the course are the ones who, from the beginning of the semester, spend 30 minutes in my office each week." This instructor was illustrating the kind of initiative—going to office hours, seeking out help from tutoring and student assistance centers—necessary to be a "college student." One instructor linked this kind of initiative to class-related habits learned in the home:[5]

> I've come to believe that people's cultural or family background is a huge determinant of success. And I separate them—I'll use this language informally—hourly or blue-collar versus professional or white collar. And the mentality of the hourly employee is you do what's required, what you're told to do or asked to do, and of course for a certain length of time. And if the task is not finished, it's not your concern. The next shift finishes, or whatever. Professional people are goal-oriented. And you do as much or as little as required to reach that goal.

Similarly, many directors of tutorial or student success centers agreed that the students who showed up were not necessarily the ones who needed the most assistance, but rather the more motivated and aggressive students. As one learning specialist at an Academic Skill Center noted, after describing an Early Alert system that "intrusively" contacts students in academic trouble, "We still know that the motivated students are the ones who come to Supplemental Instruction. The basic skills students, what we call the developmental students, they are not historically the people that seek tutoring." As a result, many such centers are constantly trying new ways to attract a wider variety of students, like using Facebook to "make it cool" and developing other forms of "social networking and finding students where they are."

Another dimension of college readiness, or unreadiness, emerging from our interviews with instructors and administrators is student fear, the anxiety they feel in coming to college. This is the subject of a book-length work by Becky Cox called *The College Fear Factor* (2009), stressing that fearful students often use counterproductive strategies like avoiding office hours, tutoring efforts, group work with other students, and other contact that might reveal their weaknesses. As one director of basic skills in our study noted,

> I know there are a lot of students who kind of want to remain anonymous and stay under the radar. And a lot of it has to do with anxiety—they are just anxious and they don't know how they're going to place on those exams.

In response, many instructors take some time, especially at the beginning of a course, to engage in confidence-building. As one English professor noted,

> I find that once they have it [the first essay assignment] in front of them, they get sort of stressed out about it: "What do you want? What is it exactly that you are going to want?" Then, in a class like English 10 [the most basic English class, three levels below transfer], I feel like I spend at least the first quarter of the semester building their confidence. When you talk about measuring their learning, it is not really measuring it in terms of grading it in the beginning—if they do the work, they get the points in the beginning. And I give them lots of feedback, lots of wins. I'm not evaluating so much.

When the observer noted that students seemed depressed (i.e., "squashed down by school for quite a while"),[6] the instructor replied, "That is a pretty accurate perception. That's why I say I spend the whole first part of the semester building them up a little bit. There is almost nothing better I can do to help them." Many colleges also have courses and workshops intended to build confidence. One had a human development course, a life management course, and a math anxiety course. Many colleges have developed student success courses designed to teach "how to be a college student," to bolster confidence, to provide access to the variety of student services on campus, and often to help students in planning a program (see Zeidenberg, Jenkins, & Calcagno, 2007 on the effectiveness of these courses).

Perhaps the most difficult issue in being a "college student" involves the level of work required. On the one hand, most instructors understand the "chaotic," "busied-up" conditions of students' lives. They sometimes accommodate these demands by making sure that all assignments can be done in class (avoiding the need to assign homework), or by giving short assignments—one- or two-page reading assignments, a one-page paper—which means that the intensity and pacing of classes is incredibly slow. At the same time, many instructors insist that learning requires a certain amount of time, a minimum level of effort, and a basic amount of persistence or stamina or "grit" at academic tasks, and that their students fail to understand this. One vice-president of instruction illustrated the shift:

> One of the other things is our students' concept of time. Saying to a student that it's going to take you three semesters to catch up, we might as well say to them that it's going to be their lifetime. Also, the expectation of study has changed. Our faculty still believe the Carnegie unit—for every hour in class, 3 hours outside. But I'm not sure it's a mantra that is still being taught as [students] come up. The student's life today is much more crowded than mine was ... I go back to the days when I taught art. Our classic example is dexterity for students. Students can't cut by the time of junior high school because we took the scissors away, because they were dangerous. So, they don't have dexterity. And I look at it the same way for study, that we have made things simpler along the way, or not helped them expand their attention span for study.

This is yet another complaint about the preparation of students in their earlier schooling, where some of the requirements for academic success—persistence, work, "grit," "expectation of study," attention span—have not been instilled in them earlier. So, "college readiness" turns out to have many dimensions, many of them falling in the category of understanding what college requires rather than specific academic skills.

At the extreme, as exemplified in the previous section, instructors alluded to mental health problems, learning disabilities, and more pervasive developmental delays (what used to be called mental retardation) as reasons for students' poor performance. One instructor nicely illustrated the conjunction of negative perceptions with assertions of support:

> I have very fragile students. There are a lot of reasons they are at the level they are, and sometimes it's their own fault. But none of that matters, and part of my job is to make them see, "You can do this. You can be successful. And whatever your problems are in the past, we can overcome those."

Another asserted that many of his students—from a low-income community with high levels of gang violence—showed signs of posttraumatic stress disorder. Yet another was blunter in referring to developmental delays: "These students are damaged in some way. If you're 20 years old, and you're still taking arithmetic, there's something wrong here." In short, faculty perceive and label an enormous variety of ways in which their developmental students "are not ready to be college students."

What can we make of the generally supportive teaching in developmental education, while instructors still make negative comments about students and their readiness to be college students? On the one hand, there's a long (and regrettable) tradition in American education of student-blaming, of ascribing slow progress through schooling—or slow progress through the endless sequence of developmental courses—to the characteristics of students themselves. As one instructor noted,

> The first thing people want to do—this administration is doing this—is use that cop-out as a way not to address it [slow progress] because any kind of change, you got to look at yourself and say, "OK, maybe I need to do some things differently and take part of the responsibility for it." But it is easy to say, "Oh no, it is just the students. They don't know anything. They're not going to be anything." So, it is easier to do that.

Therefore, it is distressing to see so many instructors describe students in the same terms—"not ready to be college students." On the other hand, based on our classroom observations, their descriptions are often true. Many students don't come to class on time, many students don't come to class prepared, and many don't do their homework. Many students are distracted during class by phone calls, texting, the Web, and off-topic discussions about family issues. The demands of family life and employment are all too real, and many students who need help from office hours and student services don't avail themselves of that assistance.

The question, it seems to us, is whether instructors use their perceptions of "students not ready for college" to slow down their courses, to water down the content, to declare that "I can't teach the way I want to because they're not ready for college," versus doing something to make students ready for college. These actions include the efforts that individual teachers make to socialize students to college-level norms, to introduce them to discussions and projects as methods of learning that are superior to information transfer, and to curb their distractions and get them to focus on class content. This also happens when departments develop coherent approaches to instruction, like the discussion-based approach to math in one department, or the English department that shifted away from the sentence-paragraph-essay approach to one based on the reading of entire texts, or the use of Reading Apprenticeship to enable students themselves to generate higher level questions (see chapter 4 on "Innovation in Basic Skills Instruction").

At the institutional level, student success courses and orientations to college also present some of the habits and attitudes of "being a college student." At the college with the most comprehensive roster of student support services—Chaffey College, described in chapter 6—part of the belief system is that all educational efforts must consider not only the cognitive dimensions of learning, but also the noncognitive and affective dimensions, including attitudes about learning. Accordingly, different kinds of workshops and tutoring get students to engage more actively with course material, to play more independent roles in their own learning, to shift to metacognitive perspectives, and to rely on their own efforts and on peers rather than instructors (or tutors) to get the correct answer.

To be sure, it might be better for everyone if these dimensions of being a college student, or being "college-ready," were instilled in high school. But as long as instructors and colleges are willing to take the steps necessary to resocialize students, then their recognition that so many students are not "college ready" turns from a pejorative perception into a diagnosis of what work needs to be done.

The Voices of Students

Finally, I turn to the voices of students themselves, and their reactions to basic skills instruction. Altogether, we videotaped 30 students in classes where students were already videotaping other students.[7] The intent was to put students at ease, since we knew from other sources that students prefer talking to other students rather than to researchers. We analyzed about 22 of these interviews thoroughly. What students said about basic skills generally paralleled what we learned through observations and interviews, so we can be reasonably sure that the perceptions of students are congruent with our own.

In the first place, many students admit that they didn't take high school seriously. Some of them acknowledged that their high school did not prepare them well for college. Similarly, students did not take the assessment for basic skills seriously: "I did not realize that's one of the ways you choose your courses," said one. "There is less preparation than for a driver's license," said another. Still, these students were shocked to find themselves placed in basic skills courses. Their anger in finding themselves in developmental education comes from their characterization of such classes as "a waste of time. It feels like high school again ... I've already taken these courses, like, why am I taking them again?" Many students view basic skills courses as easy and boring; after admitting that developmental education is easier than high school, one student complained, "We can't be lower than high school—that's kinda sad."

Given the extent to which students fail to take high school seriously, administering assessment tests earlier during high school might at least give them some motivation to take the process seriously. For example, the Early Assessment Program devised by the California State University system administers an assessment in the junior year; this could be extended to sophomore and senior years, if appropriate, as a way to get high school students—most of whom say they want to go to college—to take high school as preparation for college more seriously. Such a strategy might also include summer brush-up programs to help those who have forgotten some of what they learned in K-12 education. Given students' widespread anger at having to take basic skills courses in college, community colleges ought to try everything in their power to reduce the numbers of individuals referred to developmental courses.

One of the patterns I have already noted in this chapter is that, in many classes, students do not pay much attention. They text, walk in and out of class, have side conversations, and don't contribute much to class discussions. Faculty often say that such behavior indicates "not being ready to be college students." But the students themselves have different explanations that fasten the blame squarely on instructors. One said that if students are not paying attention, "It's because the class is boring, straight out of the book, information on the board." When the class is interesting, there is less texting and other inattention. The same student said, "Professors should find out why students are walking in and out of class," rather than assuming that they don't know any better.

Another problem is the "fear factor" identified by Cox (2009). One student phrased this succinctly: "The reason why we don't know too much is because we're afraid to ask, because when you're ignorant, you don't want to look like a dumbass. You kind of want the answer to come to you." Other students admitted that, because of their fear of asking questions ("I didn't want to sound stupid"), they did less well than they could have. The fear factor thus leads to self-defeating practices.

Another series of complaints reflect the opinion that the basic classes in which students are placed are irrelevant to their intended majors. This is particularly true of complaints about math. As one student said, "If my major has nothing to do with math, it doesn't have anything to do with what I'll be doing [this semester]." Another said, "Why should we have to take all this English all over again? I wish I could go directly to my major." Many complaints about basic courses were essentially that "I'll never have to do this again." One student noted that "I don't need to be sitting here wasting my time on essays that have nothing to do with nursing. I didn't come here to start all over again; I came here to continue." This is an argument about the irrelevance of much remedial education, and it reflects the highly goal-focused approach of community college students—they don't want to waste any time on coursework they see as "irrelevant" to their ultimate goals (Cox, 2009). This suggests that rather than having to take general assessments, students should be taking these tests only in subjects relevant to their intended majors.

When students complain that their courses are boring, they have clear views of what good teaching requires: careful explanations, as many times as necessary; not going too fast; and introducing humor into the classroom (one student said instructors should be "a combination of Will Farrell and Dana Carvey"). The persona of the instructor is important, too. "Be more patient. If you're more calm and nice and don't get so aggressive toward the class," then classes are better. (I assume that this "aggressiveness" is a result of instructor exasperation, an all too human reaction, though one that undermines trust in the classroom.) Good teaching also includes some group work, as a way of introducing a social dimension to the classroom; and it relies on stories about how lessons in the classroom are used in the real world. In other words, students want some context for the basic skills they are asked to learn.

Students also recognize what constitutes bad teaching, including simple presentation of information (like reviewing PowerPoint slides) and going over material from the textbook that students can read on their own. Another element of bad teaching is working at the blackboard, where the instructor's back is always to the class. One student recommended that instructors look at their teaching from the students' perspective: "Are you going too fast? Are you not explaining well enough? Are you just writing on the blackboard and just telling us to write it down? Just be a teacher." Here, "a teacher" means someone who explains carefully, who engages in discussion rather than "chalk and talk," who understands when students are falling behind. Another student commented, "Teachers who can't see different viewpoints will always have failing students." In general, students want student-centered and constructivist approaches rather than the teacher-centered and behaviorist approaches to instruction that are so prevalent (see chapter 3), though they would never use that language.

Good teaching is also a kind of implicit bargain between students and teachers. As one student said, "The teacher's job is to teach so that the student can get on with his job, which is to learn." The same kind of implicit contract exists for hard work: "If you [the teachers] set the standards low, then we [the students] are gonna aim low. If you set standards high, then you're gonna give us the opportunity to step up." Unfortunately, according to a large number of students, the most common experience is a "low standards equilibrium," where standards are low, students are bored ("we're always staring at the clock"), and they fail to pay much attention to what goes on in the classroom.

Another dilemma emerges from students' conceptions of "good teaching." While one student praised an instructor because "he talked down to a level we can understand," other students complained about how easy basic skills classes were. The trick, evidently, is to make classes difficult enough so that they are not boring or repetitive of high school learning, while at the same time providing opportunities—in class or in student support services like tutoring—for students to ask questions and get any clarification of the material that they need. This calls for some differentiation of instruction, since "talking down to a level we can understand" will bore some students at the same time that it meets the needs of others. This point will be revisited in chapter 5 on "Student Support Services," where I distinguish short, skill-oriented support from the longer, more conceptual approach of the conventional classroom.

Good teaching also requires caring and trust on the part of the instructor. Caring, in the most basic sense, refers to being patient with students and showing a willingness to provide explanations, rather than just sending them to another source of information. Trust also requires instructors to get to know students—both their names and their life circumstances. Instructors can signal their lack of caring in many small ways, including dismissing questions, sending students to support services without first trying to help them, and, of course, belittling them in any way. Moreover, students are exquisitely attuned to signs of indifference. As one student commented, "What really gets on my nerves is when you ask for help and they [teachers] give you handouts. Teachers could take just a minute to talk to me about what I'm doing wrong." When instructors betray a lack of caring, students begin disengaging from the classroom by texting, leaving the room, and having side conversations. In extreme cases, the class will "collapse," with students challenging the authority of instructors.[8]

Students generally have a positive view of student services, which provide places where students can go for individual attention and careful explanation of what they find confusing. They also allow students to interact with other students, who are "nicer, more patient" than most faculty. On the other hand, many students reveal the "fear factor" that Cox (2009) identified: as one student said, "Some students are too shy or afraid to participate [in support services]; more shy than afraid." In short, student services are both attractive and threatening, which confirms a point from chapter 5: self-assured students are likely to take advantage of student services, but those in greatest need of support are the least likely to show up because of their fear or shyness.

But other dimensions of trust and caring create unavoidable dilemmas. As most teachers recognize, students have extremely busy lives. This sometimes translates into implicit battles over homework. As one student expressed it, "I'm so tired of homework. They [instructors] don't get that we have our own lives. We have other classes, and we work, too, so it's like there's no time to sleep—we're walking zombies." Unfortunately, eliminating homework, even in recognition of the work-family-schooling dilemma, also lowers standards, so instructors are caught in a bind. The same problem came up in a vivid bus metaphor from a different student who admitted to being overwhelmed and "shut down":

> The class I'm in now, I feel like I got on the bus and somebody put their foot on the gas and they have not really let up ... I fell off the bus and it just kept on rolling. It rolled over me, then went two stop signs, and then came back and picked me up.

This particular course apparently ended well when the instructor perceived which students were falling behind. But the sense of a class as an accelerating bus, contrasted with the notion that basic skills are slow and boring, reveals another dilemma of developmental education.

Finally, many students admitted a general lack of direction. This problem started in high school, where guidance and counseling failed to prepare them for the tasks of college. As one student said, "My high school didn't teach me how to be independent, like planning what courses and programs to take." Unfortunately, it continues in college, where the lack of counselors, and the difficulty in seeing the ones who are there, combine to make advice inaccessible. In the words of one student, "Trying to see a counselor is, like, impossible. You can't even get the help you need." Another complained that "counselors are rude and rushed." Many students also mentioned that counselors lack the information they need about course requirements and majors ("Sometimes counselors don't know what they're talking about"). One student noted that "before you come in here [to the counselor's office], you're supposed to know what to do." The big exception to these complaints was the counseling offered in a learning community for racial minority students, where individuals uniformly praised counselors for being knowledgeable about the program and its prerequisites. This argues for learning communities or other smaller units like departments having their own counselors, rather than the common practice of general-purpose counselors who may know relatively little about specific programs of study.

All of the issues raised by students come up later in this book. Conceptions of good teaching and trust, the difficulties of motivation and engagement, the "irrelevance" of many basic skills courses, and the problems with assessment all emerge from our observations and interviews. The student voices articulate a grim picture of basic skills instruction, but the consistency of their perspectives means that they must be respected.

Some Solutions: The Differentiated College

For an institution like the community college, which by design accepts an enormous variety of students, the persistent challenge is to differentiate its offerings enough to meet the varying needs of its students. Community colleges already have a wide number of mechanisms to provide differentiation. Student support services, profiled in chapters 5 and 6, provide varying amounts of help to students with different levels of academic and nonacademic difficulty, though their effects are limited. Colleges typically have special services for students with various disabilities (in California, this is called the Disabled Student Programs and Services; DSPS), and others for various kinds of "disadvantaged" students (Extended Opportunity Programs and Services; EOPS). Many colleges have developed learning communities for distinctive groups of students: African American or Latino students, or older students, for example, though these tend to serve relatively small numbers. The entire basic skills enterprise, including ESL, can be interpreted as a way of meeting the needs of students with varied levels of academic preparation, allowing them to join a course sequence at the levels they need. Indeed, the problem often seems to be that the community college is overly differentiated, with an array of special services and programs that are too complex for students (and counselors, too, unfortunately) to understand, never mind negotiate.

But this chapter has implicitly argued that colleges are still not differentiated enough, since the variety of students and their needs *within* basic skills courses are still too great for conventional courses to manage. Based on these findings, a number of recommendations emerge—some obvious and widespread, some not so obvious—that might enable colleges to better meet the needs of their varied students. They would also reduce the numbers of students in basic skills courses; given the testimony from some subsets of students that such courses are "easy and boring," this would certainly be appropriate.

- Colleges could work more with high schools to alert both teachers and students to the nature of "college readiness," and to the multiple dimensions of what college readiness requires. In our sample of 13 colleges, only two had made serious efforts to work with feeder high schools, and these were necessarily limited because neither colleges nor high schools are explicitly funded to develop coordination mechanisms. Currently, there are efforts in California to administer a common assessment test for basic skills to high school juniors—perhaps a step in the right direction, but possibly a case of "too little, too late" for those individuals whose academic and behavioral capacities are poorly developed. But opportunities to do more exist: high schools have finally been alerted to the pervasiveness of the college readiness problem, and the advent of the Common Core Standards for K-12 education presents possibilities for embedding dimensions of readiness into this academic core.
- Colleges could provide a great variety of services, including College Success courses, explicitly to help students with the behavioral aspects of college readiness. To be sure, some colleges we visited already have a substantial array of such courses—one offered five such courses—but others have many fewer options. And there's the issue of whether to make such courses mandatory, or at least mandatory for some segment of the college population—like those who assess into developmental courses—so that those who are in the greatest need of such courses can benefit from them.
- More accurate assessments are necessary, particularly to distinguish brush-up students from those whose knowledge of basic skills is truly deficient. Refresher courses that students could take before any assessment are another way to distinguish between brush-up students and others, but again, these are relatively uncommon in colleges at present.
- Testing-out options should be available at every stage, to make sure that students have a chance to show they have mastered certain skills rather than simply sitting through an unnecessary developmental sequence. Similarly, students might be tested only in subjects related to their majors, so that

students whose fields of study do not include math (for example) need not sit through the related basic skills courses.

- Individualized options should be available to distinguish students with pervasive basic skills needs from those who need remediation in one or two subskills. These could be developed either with computer-based programs or by modularizing basic skills sequences. For example, the state of Virginia is moving toward a modularized system where each area of basic skills is broken into nine modules; students then take only the individual modules that they need. Unfortunately, developing modules for subskills is likely to lead back to remedial pedagogy. To avoid the most obvious faults of remedial teaching, new methods may be required to develop modules that are oriented to conceptual understanding, real applications of basic skills, and active student participation.

- Instructors could be trained in the use of differentiated instruction (DI). DI is a method developed in K-12 education of allowing instructors to work with heterogeneous students by using different readings or different problem sets for distinct groups of students, or providing different levels of support (including student services). The idea is that any such groupings are only temporary (rather than permanent "tracking"), and that once students master certain skills, they can rejoin the majority of the class. Unfortunately, while DI is a pedagogical method for coping with heterogeneous classes, it is also a difficult technique to master (especially for adjunct instructors with little preparation time), so it would require a new orientation toward pedagogical expertise among college faculty.

- Colleges need greater diagnostic capacities to detect learning disabilities, as well as any mental health problems that might interfere with classroom performance. This could be done either by expanding current services for students with disabilities, or by working through faculty; for example, by providing workshops for faculty to help them learn to detect learning disabilities or mental health problems, and relying on faculty to refer students with special needs. Of course, community college students are still adults, so there are few ways to force them to use diagnostic services, as is true for student services in general.

- The common critique about "not being ready to be college students" must be carefully understood. In many cases, it is literally true of basic skills students, who are missing many cognitive and noncognitive dimensions of college readiness. But this need not lead to "dumbing down" basic skills classes. Instead, it should lead to a variety of differentiated services—workshops, student success courses, instruction embedded in basic skills classes—that prepare individuals to become college students. Such an approach could turn a pejorative phrase into a diagnosis for further differentiation.

Overall, these recommendations suggest an institution that is even more complex and differentiated than the community college is now. It would also mean a more expensive institution since most of these new activities would require additional staff. Indeed, creating ties to high schools, staffing more courses like College Success, administering testing-out options, developing and implementing individual options for basic skills instruction, creating professional development seminars aimed at instructors, and expanding capacity related to disabled students would not be cheap. Policymakers who seek to use community colleges as low-cost alternatives to 4-year colleges would probably not support such changes. But without the additional resources necessary for additional differentiation, community colleges will remain unable to cope with the extreme variation in their students, and developmental education will continue to be a filtering mechanism rather than one that allows students to continue their educational trajectories.

SECTION I

Inside the Classroom

3

INSTRUCTION IN BASIC SKILLS

The Dominance of Remedial Pedagogy

In chapter 1, I argued that understanding any kind of instruction, including teaching in basic skills classes, requires examining what happens in the classroom within the triangle of instruction composed of an instructor, students, and content. Unfortunately, there is relatively little research that describes community college classrooms. Except where individual departments have organized themselves to improve instruction, profiled in chapter 4, there is no tradition in community colleges (and indeed, in most formal schooling) of instructors visiting each other's classes to understand what happens there. As a result, neither in the research literature nor in the community of instructors is there much analysis of classroom practices.

Most discussions of education seem to ignore instruction itself. David Labaree (2010, pp. 109–112) has noted that most discussion about education is *rhetoric*, where most reform efforts begin and end. Some rhetoric is translated into changes in the *formal structure* at the federal, state, or district level; still less finds its way into *teaching practices* in the school and classroom; and *student learning* is the most difficult to improve because it requires student participation as well as changes in teaching practices. Cuban (1990) presents an ocean metaphor, in which waves of attention on the ocean surface (the vociferous debates and rhetoric about educational policy, often prompted by economic and political crises far from the classroom) influence only issues near the surface. Discussions about greater effectiveness, or equity and narrowing the achievement gap, or College for All, have no influence whatsoever on classrooms, as they are buried deep beneath the waves. These metaphors may not be accurate; as I will show in chapter 4, there are bewildering numbers of innovations and swirls of reform in many colleges. But these metaphors clarify that what happens inside classrooms, the dimensions of instruction and pedagogy discussed in the first chapter, are often the last issues to be addressed in policy discussions.

However difficult it may be to get inside the classroom, this is the principal though not the only place where learning does or does not occur. Therefore, the purpose of this chapter is to describe what instruction in basic skills looks like based on classroom observations in 13 colleges, as well as interviews with both instructors and administrators, in order to analyze the institutional and policy effects on instruction. The first section describes how instructors tend to treat students in basic skills classrooms, a crucial element of the triangle of instruction, and documents the evident caring for students that was observed in the majority of classrooms. The second section describes the dominance of one particular approach to instruction that I call "remedial pedagogy," which takes distinctive forms in math, writing, reading, and English as a Second Language (ESL) classes, and also shows up in other instructional tools including textbooks, technology, and tutoring. The third section discusses why remedial pedagogy is so prevalent. Unfortunately, there are many reasons to think that remedial pedagogy is among the weakest approaches to instruction, and that learning and progressing through basic skills sequences cannot improve substantially until other practices become more common.

Concern for Students

One crucial observation in our examination of many basic skills classes in 13 colleges is that many basic skills instructors are primarily concerned with teaching. As one English teacher said,

> I love teaching. I love seeing their results—both on an immediate basis and a long-term basis...and I love it when they come in and they'll say that they don't really like reading, but that [book or reading assignment] was really interesting or really fascinating.

This represents the ideal of a "teaching college," with faculty devoted to instruction and their students. Similarly, most basic skills instructors are enormously respectful of their students. They praise students lavishly, they ask about their lives, and they seem to know a great deal about them. We saw almost none of the belittling or demeaning treatment of students (sometimes called "microaggressions)"[1] that one routinely sees in high schools, or that we have seen in more advanced classes in community colleges.[2] In this sense, basic skills instruction in community colleges rarely becomes the dreadful, destructive teaching that is so demoralizing to watch and is so likely to push students out of formal schooling. Of course, there are exceptions, both individual and institutional; in one college, the student services personnel bitterly complained about the math department:

We had student protests over the math department. They're not very good teachers, and they don't like our students. They are dismissive of them. There are teachers with 70% failure rates, some teachers talk in a whisper, some teachers reject students asking questions.

This was an unusual case; even when instruction is not all that it could be, instructors are still supportive of students. Here's an example of a class that highlights the amount of encouragement and support from instructors:

> This is a class in basic arithmetic, with students seated in rows facing the instructor. He asks them to complete the following: "12 is what percent of 600?" using the formula $A = RB$, or the rate R (percent) times the base B. He walks them through this problem, then changes the problem slightly: "6 is 15% of what number?" Throughout the process, he is praising students for their responses: "Excellent"; "That's it"; "You've got it." Once they complete several problems, he encourages them to do a "sanity check," examining whether their results make sense given the numbers they started with. He then instructs students to work on a sheet with similar problems; he and two tutors walk around and assist students. Students are also discussing their answers with each other and explaining how they arrived at their answers. Several volunteer to work out problems at the board; one becomes quite nervous, but she gets through her demonstrations with his patience and encouragement, and the class claps when she is done. One student told the observer that she loves the class, and this is the first time she has understood math because the instructor pauses, takes his time, and often asks, "Is that right?" "He knows where the hard places are, and gives you support at the right moment." His kindness and patience were evident, and the students showed how appreciative they were of his support.

Many colleges have recognized the extent of student anxiety, especially in math. Some instructors have incorporated topics from student success courses in their classes. Sometimes a department develops a support class for a gatekeeper math class to provide other review and support. One college developed a course in Managing Study Strategies, taught by an enthusiastic instructor with the persona of a caring grandmother, which covered such topics as study skills, test-taking tips, and ways to manage anxiety. Many colleges have adopted student success courses for new students, again to reinforce study skills, time management, and other dimensions of "how to be a college student," a subject I introduced in chapter 2.

To be sure, the concern for students in the previously mentioned arithmetic class, and in virtually all the basic skills classes we observed, has a dark side as well. Out of concern for students and the busy conditions of their lives, many basic skills instructors place very few demands on them. Most writing assignments are one page long; much of the reading consists of a few paragraphs, or one or two pages. Because they are aware of how busy many students are, some instructors arrange their classes so all of the work—problems to solve, reading, essays to write—can be done in class, resulting in virtually no homework. They appear to feel that students are fragile and only weakly connected to the educational enterprise, and that imposing too many requirements would cause them to drop out (which may be true, given high dropout rates). Unfortunately, instructors with low demands are not preparing students for college-level work, and certainly not for transfer to 4-year colleges. Therefore, one of the enduring problems in remedial classes is how to impose adequate demands on students while simultaneously providing the moral and academic support so that they will continue.

The Approach of Remedial Pedagogy

The arithmetic class described earlier is also notable for following an approach I call "remedial pedagogy." This practice varies somewhat in math, writing, reading, and ESL classes, as I will clarify below, but there are some commonalities. The approach emphasizes drill and practice (e.g., a worksheet of similar problems) on small subskills that most students have been taught many times before (e.g., solving a simple equation, subject–verb agreement, punctuation rules, sentence-level writing, converting fractions to decimals, solving standard time-rate-distance problems). Moreover, these subskills are taught in decontextualized ways that fail to clarify for students the reasons for or the importance of learning these subskills.

In some ways, the arithmetic class in question is an improvement on most remedial pedagogy: Students do work with one another in groups and share their solutions, and several students present their procedures at the board (so the instructor can check their logic). But most classes are extremely teacher-centered in that there is no student-to-student interaction and very little public display of work or teacher diagnosis of what students understand. The basic approach has also been called part-to-whole instruction, emphasizing subskills ("the parts") that presumably are assembled into broad competencies like the comprehension of varied texts, an understanding of mathematical procedures and thinking, and the ability to write in several genres ("the whole"). But in remedial pedagogy, these larger competencies—number sense, an understanding of mathematical operations beyond procedures, the ability to see in word problems what information is given and what needs to be determined—are rarely practiced or experienced in any way, so instruction results (at best) in students mastering small subskills.

Here's another example of a class with remedial pedagogy:

> The instructor entered class 5 minutes early, but didn't interact with students. Right on time, the instructor started by saying that the topic of the day (factoring linear equations) is important, but didn't explain why. The instructor commented that students might have forgotten everything

because of spring break, but he didn't review what happened before the break or review the sequence of topics.

The instructor worked through one example from the text, using the conventional approach of writing the mathematical steps on the board while explaining each step orally. When one student asked, "Where did that come from?" the instructor repeated the same explanation; the student still did not appear to understand. The instructor then worked on a second problem from the text, asked for questions, and responded with short answers. These are inquiry-response-evaluation (IRE) questions, rather than questions that elaborate on the mathematical issues.

The instructor put two expressions on the board for students to factor: $16z^4 + 24z^2$ and $12x^3 + 6x^2$, but without instructions. He circulated and provided individual assistance when asked. Several students in the back appeared to understand and were sharing methods, but other students' questions sounded as if they didn't understand at all. The instructor showed no awareness of the extent to which students did not understand the material. He commented that "we need this skill in order to factor polynomials," but again, there was no reason why factoring polynomials might be important.

The instructor then shifted to a textbook example of grouping with four-term polynomials. Most of the students did not have the text with them. At the end of this demonstration, the instructor asked, "Everybody understand how it's working?" Without waiting for any responses, he said, "So, now try it by yourself." He circulated again and corrected students who had done something wrong, but he didn't use such problems to share general errors or misconceptions with the rest of the class.

The instructor then provided an example of algebraic multiplication $(x+m)(x+n)$, again without any rationale. One student suddenly complained that the instructor was explaining as if she already knew the material; she sounded frustrated, bordering on hostile, and asked him to use different colored chalk. Again, the low-key response was to repeat the same explanation, not to ask the student to explain what she did; the student complained, "This used to be fun; now it's moving too fast. Show me how you get the answer."

The instructor continued to present small algebraic procedures throughout the 2½ hour class without any breaks, circulating to provide individual help with getting the right answers but never using students' questions to examine more carefully what they did and did not understand.

This class is almost a caricature of what we saw over and over, a presentation of small subskills without any justification for why such skills might be useful in other contexts or in subsequent courses. The class itself was calm, with only a few moments of students' irritation showing through, but it was also extremely tedious, and a single method, presentation and practice, was used for the entire class. When students asked questions about the procedures, the instructor simply repeated his previous explanation rather than providing an alternative. The instructor periodically asked a formulaic question about understanding: "Everyone understand how it's working?" When students made mistakes or were obviously guessing, however, he provided the right answer rather than engaging in any diagnosis of why students arrived at the wrong answer. Therefore, the instructor had no way of understanding whether students were making mistakes systematically. This approach is contrary to the idea that instructors need to understand students' reasoning in order to correct it (Donovan & Bransford, 2005; Shaughnessy, 1977).

Other characteristics of remedial pedagogy include an emphasis on getting the right answer, rather than any conceptual understanding of why an answer is correct or how to develop alternative "right" approaches to solving a math problem, writing an essay, or interpreting a reading passage. When instructors ask questions, they are usually IRE questions with a single correct answer, rather than open-ended questions that students might answer in different ways. An example of the latter might be to ask about students' interpretations of a reading or an author's purpose, which might vary for conventional literature, an auto repair manual, or anatomy texts for nursing students. Instructors often provide the right answers if they don't get responses right away; an alternative is to rely on the same few students to give the right answers, and then to move on without checking to see whether other students understand.

Very seldom is instruction contextualized with references to how basic reading or writing or math might be used in settings outside the classroom, either in subsequent classes or in the world outside schooling. Math seems to exist for its own sake, and it is obviously a gatekeeper, but rarely are there explanations of why mathematical procedures or mathematical thinking are necessary in occupational or civic settings, or illustrations of how math emerges in daily life. For example, in one class, the textbook was full of ways that instructors could ask students to collect real-life examples of math use, which might have helped them with number sense as well as the capacity known as document literacy,[3] but the instructor ignored these elements of the text. Reading is similarly decontextualized; students usually read short passages or short stories, but the variety of nonfiction reading that students might be exposed to in occupational or academic transfer courses is rarely included. There are well-developed contextualized approaches to basic skills; for example, in learning communities where students take several courses simultaneously, or in linked courses where a basic skills course is paired with a conventional academic or occupational course. However, they tend to be few and far between, and the practice of forging links between classroom learning and the world outside the classroom is rare.

Other common problems include covering material too quickly without checking for understanding, the basis for the student's complaint in the class that was factoring linear equations. This is something that often happens in K–12 education, and that may explain why so many community college students need basic skills instruction. Many instructors also use humor or short games to lighten the class, but these usually have little to do with fostering understanding. Sometimes instructors circulate to provide individualized attention, but without giving other students anything to do; in these cases, students quickly get bored and restless. In general, these basic instructional techniques are often weak, as one might expect of instructors who have no preparation in teaching methods.

One problem with remedial pedagogy is that it violates almost all of the precepts for good teaching presented in the supportive arithmetic class in the previous section. It is the most passive form of learning, with students absorbing material from the instructor. It is relentlessly teacher-centered, with almost no chance for students to participate in their own learning. It focuses on the most basic skills, subskills, really, and regardless of one's definition of "higher order" or "21st century" or conceptual abilities, it is clear that they are missing from remedial classrooms. As a result, these classes are poor preparation for either college-level courses or transfer, which are the goals of most basic skills students. Such classes have none of the characteristics of motivating instruction clarified in *Engaging Schools* (National Research Council, [NRC], 2004), and students "vote with their feet," drifting in and out of these tedious classes and often dropping out of remedial sequences before they finish. The lack of any context in remedial instruction, of any examples of how these subskills are used, means that students who intend to transfer or to move into occupational programs have no coherent answer to the enduring question of "Why do we have to learn this?" For observers like the researchers in this study, who can leave at the end of the day, these classes are painful and tedious; for students who have to stick with them in order to make progress in their education, they must be excruciating.

As one might expect, remedial pedagogy shows up in different forms in different subjects. This reflects the meaning of pedagogical content knowledge; the understanding that general pedagogical practices (student- vs. teacher-centered instruction, using project methods or remedial pedagogy) take different forms in specific content areas.

Math

There is little question that the teaching in basic math follows remedial pedagogy much more than any other subject. Many of the classes we observed were relentless in their emphasis on drill and practice on small skills, without any applications to the world outside the classroom. A great deal of instruction is based on little tricks for getting the right answer without understanding the underlying procedures. For example, in shifting from decimals to percent, students are taught to move the decimal point two places to the right and add a percent sign (e.g., .39 to 39%); in converting percent to decimals, students are taught to shift the decimal two places to the left and eliminate the percent sign (39% to .39). In setting up simple one-variable equations to solve, there is again a mechanical process. Take the problem "35% of what is 21?" as an example; "what" is rewritten as X, "is" becomes an equal sign, and the word problem becomes 35% X = 21, X = 21/.35 = 60. But when word problems are given in nonstandard form, students can't use these shortcuts and they get lost. For example, one problem gave a table of the presidents who had died in office, and then asked students to calculate the fraction of presidential terms in which a president had died; however, since this was not in standard form, one student burst out with an objection: "I don't see no 'is' up there, where is the 'is'?" Unlike the instructor portrayed in the supportive math class in the previous section, there's very little checking for understanding by most instructors, and since students don't have any mechanisms for judging the correctness of their answers, their answers are likely to be nearly random combinations of the numbers they have been given.

The emphasis throughout is on getting the right answer, not on understanding the underlying math. Students may be able to get the right answers and pass tests because the problems they face have been so standardized, but they seem to lack any number sense, or any understanding about what is happening when someone sets up an equation. As someone who needed her students to be facile with basic math, a science instructor in one college mentioned that

> they don't have a number sense, they see symbols but they don't relate to a reality at all, you've got a word problem and how does that relate to a mathematical equation? Because [the student] has just learned patterns and manipulating equations—[the student] doesn't know what they mean, they don't represent reality.

This comment shows that the routine shortcuts used in most math classes fail to teach students the value of math in representing other phenomena, so they can't use the math they have learned in other settings, in this case, science. Math becomes a self-contained subject, a requirement for transfer or for other courses, but not something valuable for its applications in other subjects and in areas of life outside school.

Many of these instructors seem to think there is only one way to teach math. As one instructor commented about working with a student in an electrician program, "That person may have an understanding of his environment, but math is math. He's still having trouble doing the fractions." So, even though there may be ways to contextualize math—for example, to focus on the particular kinds of math that emerge in electrical work, machining, or other occupational areas—"math is math," and the instructor insists that students need to understand fractions in some decontextualized way before they can use them in a class on current, ohms, and resistance. As another math instructor commented, "Our math classes are terrible as far as connecting with anything real-world."

But a clear alternative is to teach math in some particular context so that students start to understand how to take some phenomenon they know and express it mathematically. A great example from a college outside of our sample comes from an applied math course created for heating, ventilating, and air conditioning (HVAC) technicians, where the instructor got her students to move between the heating and cooling applications they knew and the nonlinear multiequation representation of these same phenomena.[4] Wisely (2011) found that students in CTE-contextualized prealgebra are more successful than those in standard prealgebra in passing the course, attempting and passing subsequent degree-applicable math courses, and passing transfer-level course work. However, he only found 10 contextualized courses in the 35 colleges who responded to his questionnaire, so this apparently effective and well-known method[5] is hardly used at all.

The effect of such mediocre math teaching on students was quite obvious: In many math classes, students arrived late, drifted in and out, had off-topic conversations in the back of the classroom, and continued to text and check e-mail while the class was going on. The contrast between effective and ineffective approaches was particularly stark in one particular college whose English department had developed a coherent, nonremedial approach to reading and writing (profiled in chapter 4, "Innovation in Basic Skills Instruction"). In that college, students in English classes were on time, engaged rather than off-task, and displayed none of the signs of disengagement that (roughly) the same students showed in their math classes.

A final problem, which will be deferred until chapter 4, is that math instructors are the least likely to participate in college efforts to reshape instruction, even as English, ESL, and counseling faculty try new approaches to basic skills. "The people the least on board are the math instructors," said one of the faculty members associated with a basic skills initiative. "We haven't had as much participation from math as we would like," noted another. The result is that when initiatives come along to improve instruction, from foundations, Title III, the Fund for the Improvement of Post-Secondary Education (FIPSE), or the Basic Skills Initiative in California, math instructors are the least likely to get involved: "We've had no leadership in math to really connect with basic skills initiatives," so "it's a black hole."

It isn't clear why math is so uniform in its adherence to remedial pedagogy. Textbooks are surely part of the problem, since most of them are relentlessly remedial in their approaches, with page after page of routine problems with no effort to develop any mathematical understanding. In a system where adjuncts are often handed a textbook and a syllabus, textbooks often determine what teaching looks like—these are less teacher-centered classes than they are text-book-centered classes. In addition, math instructors typically have a master's degree in math without any preparation in teaching methods. While this is also true of most other college instructors, there are traditions of discussion in English that encourage more student-centered approaches, but this is not the case in math. Also, many math instructors in community colleges come from Eastern European countries and Asian countries, which have particularly rigid, teacher-centered approaches to instruction in all subjects—although U.S.-born math instructors were just as guilty of remedial pedagogy. Finally, as I will clarify in chapter 4, there appear to be fewer innovations in math and fewer organized groups promoting alternative approaches; on the contrary, examples from English instruction include Reading Apprenticeship and the writing process approach championed by the National Writing Project. Even though the American Mathematical Association of Two-Year Colleges (AMA-TYC) has written about math instruction being "meaningful," "relevant," and a "carefully-balanced educational program" combining problem-solving and collaboration with skill acquisition,[6] it hasn't developed curriculum materials or teaching guides that instructors use—the math innovations I describe in chapter 4 are all developed by individual departments. Instead, there seems to be a pervasive belief that "math is math," and that the only way to teach it is through remedial pedagogy.

Writing

One of the oddest aspects of basic skills instruction, to an outsider at least, is the division of language competencies into separate reading and writing courses. This approach assumes that reading and writing are different "skills" to be taught in different ways, rather than viewing speaking, reading, and writing as alternative forms of communication, as in the whole language approach. The separation of reading and writing, in turn, means that readings—including ones from different genres, disciplines, or subjects—cannot be examined for their writing conventions, and that writing exercises cannot follow models from readings. By now, the separation has been institutionalized in separate reading and writing courses, sometimes even separate departments. To be sure, several colleges are now experimenting with combining reading and writing courses, or offering several reading-writing combinations alongside more conventional separate courses. But, just as remedial approaches break complex competencies like mathematical understanding into small subskills, the common practice is to break communicative competence into different courses in reading and writing.

Remedial pedagogy in writing instruction is often a part-to-whole exercise following strict procedures—just as it is in math. As one instructor noted,

"We find that the only way to address that [low skills at the third or fourth grade level] is to break it into parts." These classes typically follow a predictable trajectory. They start with grammar rules (many colleges have courses called simply "Grammar," or workshops in "Spelling") and move to sentence-level writing, stressing correctness in grammar, usage, and spelling. They then move to combining sentences into paragraphs while following rigid rules (e.g., there must be a topic sentence introducing the paragraph, two or three sentences of elaboration and evidence, and a concluding sentence), and continue to the five-paragraph essay, where (again) each paragraph serves a particular role. The final focus is the "research paper," where much of the material stresses the correctness of citation styles and the rules governing plagiarism, rather than the communicative aspects of writing. Each of these steps may be broken into further sub-kills; for example, one writing class for ESL students uses a checklist that students have to follow for the paragraph they write:

1. The paragraph starts with a topic sentence that clearly states the main point of the paragraph.
2. The paragraph gives relevant details to describe/summarize the news story.
3. The paragraph includes at least two time transitions.
4. I use the passive voice at least once.
5. I use at least 2 words or idioms from Unit 1.
6. I include 1–2 sentences about my opinion of the news story at the end of the paragraph.
7. My sentences are clear. I have chosen my words carefully and punctuated my sentences correctly.
8. I have edited my sentences for grammar (tense, word forms, number, verb form, etc.).

So, writing becomes essentially an exercise in following a specific script or procedure for producing error-free sentences and paragraphs with topic sentences and supporting sentences, rather than a way of communicating to different audiences in which the form might vary depending on the purpose.

If students get this far in a sequence of writing courses, the next step is to conduct research, which means collecting some kind of information and then arranging it in a logical order. However, when instructors get to research, they spend a great deal of time explaining what plagiarism is: Many students think that "research" means going on the Internet, looking up a topic on Wikipedia or some other source, and then copying great chunks of Web material into their essays. Of course, high schools are at least partly responsible for students' conceptions of writing: since high school English instructors face 150 to 180 students a day, very little writing is done. In classes that focus on research and writing, a great deal of time is spent on the correct forms of citations—according to the Modern Language Association, Chicago Manual of Style, American Psychological Association, etc.—and this practice returns a class to the study of correct forms and avoiding errors. The notion of a writer constructing an independent argument, marshaling evidence from a variety of sources, and both identifying and resolving disagreements about controversial points is not emphasized because the part-to-whole approach spends so little time on what the (multiple) purposes of writing are. In other words, the kind of writing that is required in college-level courses or for transferring to 4-year colleges is simply not part of this approach.

Like math, the teaching of writing tends to be decontextualized. More precisely, the contexts are confabulated, or made up for the purposes of teaching. Thus, the topics for writing tend to be personal essays about students' lives or their reactions to small segments of writing. But students in basic writing classes are in college because they want to transfer and need to pass a series of academic courses, or because they want to enroll in nursing or business or some other occupational field. The writing requirements in different fields of study are quite varied, and occupational areas in particular usually require forms of writing that are quite different from academic writing—medical diagnoses for nurses or descriptions of automotive problems for mechanics; precise descriptions of procedures undertaken for medical technicians; and business plans and budget descriptions in various business courses.[7] These specific forms of writing are not taught in most basic writing classes, unless there has been an attempt to link a writing course with another academic or occupational course. (The award for the most ingenious course title in a community college goes to a basic reading and writing course developed for auto technicians called "Reading, Writing, and Wrenches."[8]) So, students are learning how to write in a particular format, one with a certain logic and structure, to be sure, but not necessarily the forms of writing they will encounter in their subsequent education or work.

By and large, these writing classes are teacher-centered, in the sense that instructors (or instructors relying on textbooks) provide all the information about what appropriate writing is. In turn, students receive individual feedback on their writing from the instructor correcting their essays or circulating during class time and responding to questions about writing. Students also receive feedback from tutors in writing labs and workshops (see chapter 5), but again, most tutors follow remedial pedagogy and its emphasis on "correct" forms of writing.

Only a few instructors have attempted to incorporate group work into their writing classes—this is based on the student-centered assumption that students can learn from each other as well as the instructor, and that students may be more willing to accept correction from their peers rather than an instructor who will grade them. Here, one of the central difficulties of teaching in community colleges often emerges: students are not accustomed to group work or to providing feedback and correction to their peers. Here is an example of such a class:

A writing instructor in a class with about 12 students presented the schedule for the coming weeks, including a sign-up sheet for individual conferences about writing; as an additional 6 students came in late, he repeated the instructions each time. Some students were texting and he had to repeat the instructions for them; others seemed confused by the schedule.

The instructor then asked for students to form groups of three without telling them the purpose, and many students were confused about the activity. The instructor handed out a rubric by which each group of readers was to assess drafts of papers written by their peers; the rubric was a series of yes/no questions like "Does the essay have a thesis statement?" It was unclear from the directions whether students should engage in discussion about the answers to the questions, or about the rubric and its use. As the groups went to work, there were very few comments or questions about the essays themselves, and many students were chatting off-task; the group the observer focused on was more engaged with a student's sister's wedding, sharing pictures, fingernail length, and hair problems in the wind. The instructor was circulating, but he didn't hold students to the task, and his nonspecific questions, "How are you doing?" and "Do you have any questions?", elicited nonspecific answers. At the end, he told the students to give the essays they were reading a rating, though the scale of the rating was unclear. Most groups provided scores without much discussion, and students were very resistant to scoring each other's work.

So an exercise that was intended to get students engaged in discussing and critiquing each other's work according to a rubric, thereby helping them understand in the context of their own work what good writing should be, fell apart in practice. This occurred partly because of the instructor's unclear directions, and partly because the students were not adequately prepared to work in groups and give each other constructive feedback. In chapter 2, I presented numerous examples where instructors complain about students not being "ready to be college students," and an instructor might claim that these students were "not ready" for the kind of academic discussion normally associated with college seminars. However, in this and other cases, the instructor and the college have done little to introduce students to the need for more active participation, or to provide them with models of what such engagement with the subject matter should look like.

Unlike math, where the vast majority of classes we observed follow remedial pedagogy, there is somewhat more variation in the teaching of writing. Some instructors have taken their own approaches, and in chapter 4, I will describe the efforts of instructors who follow the writing process approach championed by the National Writing Project. In other cases, English departments have developed their own unified approaches to writing, just as a few math and ESL departments have done. But unless there is some structured method that can help English instructors teach writing, remedial pedagogy is likely to dominate.

Reading

Reading is a subject that, in some colleges, is only reluctantly included in developmental education. Instructors are likely to believe that students' problems with reading are less widespread than math or writing problems, but many reading instructors believe that there is increased need for remedial reading despite the marginal status of the subject. In several colleges, for example, instructors bemoaned the static number of offerings in remedial reading despite growing need. Indeed, the high and apparently increasing rates of referring students to developmental English courses that concentrate on writing are almost entirely due to assessments of reading, since the most commonly used assessments include reading comprehension but do not require writing samples.

If there has been an increase in the need for basic reading, it may be partly due to the weaknesses of K-12 education and the failure of American culture to support reading.[9] But there have also been demands for more sophisticated reading abilities in society as a whole (Deshler, Palincsar, Biancarosa, & Nair, 2007, p. 18), as well as within community colleges. Transfer students need to be able to read at "college" levels, of course, but even occupational programs require high levels of reading because of the complexity of the textbooks. In subjects like nursing ("in the nursing program, you can't get away from not having those reading skills"), business, electronics technology, and automotive technology, textbooks are written at the 13th or 14th grade level.

As in math and writing, there is a distinctive remedial pedagogy in reading that follows a part-to-whole approach. One college we visited illustrates a typical approach: A three-course sequence in remedial reading starts with Basic Reading for College Success, which covers phonics, dictionary skills, study skills, and vocabulary. The second course, Reading Comprehension for College Success, focuses on vocabulary, reading speed, comprehension skills, and study skills. The third course, Critical Reading and Study Skills, emphasizes analysis, vocabulary, comprehension, and study skills. All students must also enroll in a Reading Lab focused on computer-based practice of the skills they are learning in the classroom.

Within each of the subjects covered in remedial reading, there is (again) a tendency to use drill and practice. Staples of these classes are vocabulary drills, in which long lists of words are reviewed with no more context than a sentence illustrating a word's use. Instructors also teach little tricks and procedures to extract meaning from texts, such as finding the topic sentence, identifying supportive ideas, and identifying the thesis statement. (The similarity of this approach to methods for writing a "correct" essay suggests why reading and writing courses might be combined.) One college used a series of texts called *Reading for Thinking, The Effective Reader,* and *The Skilled Reader,* with tricks for comprehensionlike graphic organizers, study maps, and "blue boxes of strategies of how to do things," as one instructor described them. The advantage of these approaches to comprehension is that many college students have never been explicitly taught earlier in their schooling how to derive information from texts; their teachers usually assume they can pick up this skill on their own. This may happen, particularly for students from well-educated and well-read families, but it leaves students at a disadvantage who are from families with low levels of schooling, including those who are the first in their family to go to college, certain racial minority students, immigrant students, and those with learning disabilities (Deshler et al., 2007, pp. 24–25).

One problem with the part-to-whole approach of remedial pedagogy is that each of the early steps in the sequence is necessary but not sufficient to increase comprehension, especially sophisticated comprehension. It's difficult to read without an adequate vocabulary and fluency in reading individual words, but being able to perform these subskills does not lead automatically to comprehension. And simple comprehension—being able to get the main idea of a text correctly, or locating ideas within a text—does not mean that the student possesses higher level capacities like summarizing, predicting what will happen, inferring what a text has said when it doesn't state something directly, understanding the conventions of different genres, and analyzing and critiquing a text.[10] So, if instructors have not placed sufficient emphasis on comprehension strategies, or if students have not gotten to the end of a remedial reading sequence, then they may not have mastered the more sophisticated reading abilities necessary for college-level coursework. One consequence is that subject matter instructors, such as those who teach history, the social sciences, or general education requirements, complain about the reading skills of students who have managed to avoid taking the appropriate developmental classes.

In addition, there is a good deal of variation in what kinds of texts are used. One problem is finding motivating readings at the appropriate level; one instructor commented, "There's nothing out there at fourth grade [reading] level for college level students." Another problem, and one that also affects ESL instruction, is the goal of remedial reading. Presumably, the purpose is to prepare students for college-level classes that might follow. But many classes focus on nonacademic material—"modern topics, like the Healing Power of Humor," mentioned one instructor, or autobiographies of well-known individuals—and it's hard to know how these materials will help students with academic reading in the future, even if they are more enjoyable in the moment. Another issue involves different genres of reading: While the texts in many basic reading classes are drawn from literature, one department we visited has decided that they should use nonfiction only, because their students are unlikely to be lit majors and nonfiction is more likely to prepare them for the transfer courses they hope to take. But no one uses automotive manuals or texts for medical technicians—unless there is some paired course like "Reading, Writing, and Wrenches" or a learning community with basic skills along with some other academic or occupational focus—so even in the best cases, students are being prepared to read a narrow range of "academic" material.

As in writing classes, many reading instructors have tried to move away from lecture and teacher-centered classes to more student-centered discussion and presentation. This is part of a pattern within English, in which debating different interpretations of literature is common. Such debate is quite uncommon in the sciences and occupational subjects, where precision and a single correct interpretation of scientific findings or X-rays or business procedures are stressed. Not surprisingly, classes vary not only in the amount of such student participation, but also (as in writing classes) the extent to which students embrace these activities. In one example, the instructor of the lowest-level reading class in one college arranged the classroom seminar-style (she stated that she uses some cooperative exercise in every class). In one class we observed, groups were assigned prefixes (like intra-, intro-, inter-, circum-) and were then asked as a group to create other words with the prefix, using the dictionary if needed. But the students were confused about the exercise; there was little instructor enforcement of collaboration; and students by and large worked individually on the exercise, with some students working together only after 10 of the allotted 20 minutes had passed. So, what was intended as an activity where students might learn from one another turned into conventional individual seatwork, partly because the instructor's good intentions were not reinforced during the 20 minutes, and partly because students seemed unfamiliar with cooperative procedures.

However, in another version of the same course at a different college, student participation was higher, and it was evident that participation varies depending on how the instructor directs the class. The instructor started by passing out an article, explained her expectations, and then had students read the article and write down their individual answers to seven questions by locating answers in the text—a standard comprehension exercise. She then had the students discuss their answers with one another and then present them to the class; this increased engagement and participation markedly. Then, the instructor took over with an animated discussion of effective reading strategies, moved to a short lecture on the seven common patterns of organization, and ended with a handout for students to fill in main ideas, major supporting details, and minor supporting details. Even though most of the class was instructor-centered, with short articles and conventional fill-in-the-blank comprehension exercises, the period of student discussion and presentation was much more engaging to students, although it was also comparatively brief.

At the other end of the spectrum, another reading instructor broke the 90-minute class into three segments. In the first segment, she had the students read a nonfiction article about a prep school, and then had them discuss connections between the article and a character in the fictional story they were reading. She then segued into four student presentations on the novel the class was reading in which the students summarized what they had read, provided quotes to back up their interpretations, and gave the class a question to answer in their journals. In the final segment, the instructor moved to an exercise in which students scored an essay written by a classmate, based on a rubric for rating the organization and the development of the paper. Unlike the writing class in which students were asked to assess drafts of papers written by their peers, the instructor had clearly taught her students what student participation and critique should look like, so there was very little off-task talk and refusal to participate.

Once again, more student-centered approaches are possible, but they depend on the skills of the instructor in managing class activities and preparing students for participation. Many innovative instructors follow a whole-to-part strategy—reading entire books that are carefully selected to appeal to adults, and then using these texts to examine more sophisticated literary issues. For example, one instructor used a mix of novels and nonfiction readings to explore multiple points of view, multiple themes, characterization, symbolism, literary devices, and ethical dilemmas, and to examine the "ways in which the fiction illustrates the nonfiction, and how the nonfiction informs your reading of fiction," which was a far cry from "blue boxes of strategies." Chapter 4 examines classes that follow the methods of Reading Apprenticeship, an approach to reading that can be used in a variety of subjects in addition to basic reading. Indeed, there are many alternatives to remedial pedagogy in reading instruction.

English as a Second Language (ESL)

Instruction in ESL seems more varied than in math, reading, or writing. To be sure, there are many "traditional" classes following remedial pedagogy. Many courses are focused on grammar: identifying nouns and verbs; using the passive voice, irregular verbs, and the many different tenses in English; and learning about the structure of independent and dependent clauses. As in other forms of remedial pedagogy, there are a lot of decontextualized little rules: "If you use *how*, you have to use *get*, as in 'How am I going to get there?' If you use *what*, you have to use *take*, as in 'What are you going to take to get well?'"—a rule that seems incomprehensible even to a native English speaker. Vocabulary exercises are also staples of ESL classes that follow a remedial approach. Sometimes these are dressed up as games: one grammar-focused class played a version of "Jeopardy," which was really a word-recognition game without any context (and without the excitement of money being at stake), and the instructor warned that the exercises would be on the test. Other exercises included standard CLOZE drills, such as filling in blanks with the "correct" words, though sometimes the correctness seemed doubtful. One sentence involved choosing one of three possibilities: "I (*get*, *am*, *have*) a headache," where the correct answer was *have* "because headache is a noun"; but, of course, *get* and *am* create perfectly appropriate sentences, albeit with different meanings. A class full of these rules and drills is almost unbearably boring, and it's hard to imagine that students can learn a new language merely by learning a set of rules. Such classes tend to neglect speaking and listening, so students' English language development can become somewhat lopsided.

But large numbers of ESL courses do not follow remedial practice, and instead have students engage in wide variety of speaking, reading, and writing activities; that is, *using* English in a variety of ways rather than *memorizing the rules* of English. In these classes, oral activities sometimes engage the whole class and sometimes take place in small groups; different kinds of reading tasks often include read-alouds so that students can practice speaking as well as reading; and different writing exercises are (again) often linked to reading or oral presentations. This is the ESL equivalent of the whole language approach, which stresses the *use* of language for various social and academic purposes. For example, one class we observed moved in 15- or 20-minute chunks among a series of oral, written, and reading exercises, each leading to the next. The instructor claimed that

> I think it's pretty typical for ESL, because of the nature of language learning. I think we tend to think in, like, 15- or 20-minute blocks in different activities to keep people engaged. I can tell you it's very labor-intensive prepping for our classes.

Unlike some of the classes described above, this instructor (and other ESL instructors in this particular college) had introduced their students to group work and active participation early on, as a *necessary* element of ESL:

> I think, for language learning, it's speaking a language in relationship with somebody, and so I really stress in my class their responsibility when they get into groups.... For some of my students, the classroom is the only time during the day when they're really using English.

As a result of this group work and preparation, there is extensive use of English among the immigrant students in the class. This instructor has also created a link with a global studies class where native English speakers interested in other countries speak with the ESL students: "My students want to have conversations with native speakers, so we just started experimenting with it."

We even uncovered two examples of bilingual classes, rather than the conventional English-only ESL classes. One emerged when an ESL instructor, who happened to be bilingual in Spanish, was teaching in a college where the vast majority of recent immigrant students came from Mexico (as is true in California as a whole). In another case, an employer hired a number of skilled Mexican craftsmen and then asked the local college to provide them with English instruction. One of the ESL instructors was fluent in Spanish, and he created a two-semester sequence where the first semester was bilingual, gradually shifting to English-only instruction in the second semester. Although community colleges stress the enormous variety of languages spoken by their students as the reason for English-only instruction, in fact some colleges serve pockets of Spanish-speaking students, or Mandarin- or Vietnamese-speaking students, and they could create bilingual programs with a little additional effort. In general, bilingual programs are more effective than monolingual programs,[11] and experimenting with bilingual approaches might help the progress and the English fluency of immigrant students.

Thus, ESL classes exhibit a greater variety of instructional approaches than other basic skills courses. However, according to our observations, the previous statement that "it's pretty typical for ESL" to use varied and participatory activities is not always correct, and the reasons for the variation that does exist seem to be departmental. In that particular instructor's college, virtually all the ESL courses we observed were lively and varied, so that was "pretty typical" for her college. But at a college not 20 miles away, one with an exemplary English department that developed its own vision and pedagogy, virtually all ESL instruction was grammar- and drill-oriented. Even here, however, there were pockets of innovation; in particular, one ESL instructor had students read an entire novel and used that reading to develop grammar lessons—whole-to-part rather than part-to-whole instruction. In yet another college, some of the liveliest classes in the entire college were ESL classes, but we also observed a class focusing on articles (a, an, the) and worksheets with blanks to fill in individually. In that college, there had been no full-time ESL instructor for several years, so the adjuncts hired to teach ESL were entirely on their own. The result was an incredible hodge-podge of ESL courses, with no effective assessment, no coherent sequence through the courses offered, no effort to develop a common pedagogy, and very little communication among ESL instructors. This is a good example of what I call a laissez-faire college in chapter 9, with instructors and students left to their own preferences for teaching and learning.

Another issue, somewhat independent of whether instructors use remedial pedagogy or not, is the content that instructors emphasize; this is one way to distinguish *adult* ESL classes, which might take place in adult schools, from *academic* ESL classes in community colleges. The former emphasizes life skills—how to read a financial document or a rental agreement, how to fill out a job application—while the latter emphasizes the oral, reading, and writing competencies that will be necessary in subsequent academic and occupational courses. Some community colleges have respected this division by assigning the lowest-level ESL courses focused on life skills to their noncredit divisions—"the majority of students who come here are looking for survival skills, job skills you do through non-credit." In another case, a college created five levels of ESL classes, with "Levels 1 and 2 like adult ed, and those people go away when they've learned enough English. And then we get another group for the high levels [3, 4, and 5] who go into academic English." At the other extreme, in another college, the ESL department has organized ESL around Learning English for Academic Purposes—"Content as early as possible, support as long as possible," as one instructor described the vision. (I will also profile this department in chapter 4 on departmental innovations.) But in many other cases, college ESL courses emphasize life skills. In part, this is based on a construction of what ELLs (English Language Learners) need, but it may also be the result of perceived difficulties with overly academic approaches; as one instructor asserted, "That kind of personal topic is approachable. If I give them vocational or too academic a topic, many of these students will struggle even more." Classes that combine remedial pedagogy with a life skills curriculum are therefore not only deadly in terms of student engagement, but they also fail to prepare students for movement into college-level courses, which is presumably the purpose of incorporating ESL into community colleges.

ESL raises many other issues that I will reserve for subsequent chapters. These include the role of departments in creating coherent approaches (mentioned previously); the extremely long sequence of ESL courses required in some colleges, presenting almost insuperable barriers to getting into college-level courses; and the low status of ESL instruction on some campuses, where ESL seems to be ignored relative to basic English and math. In terms of developmental education, instructional approaches represent only one of several issues that must be confronted in order to improve the effectiveness of community colleges.

Remedial Pedagogy in Other Forms

There are several other instructional settings in community colleges aside from classrooms, since virtually all colleges have adopted support services for students who need additional help and attention—especially labs for math and English where students have access to tutors, as well as computer-based programs that provide additional ways of reinforcing what takes place in class. Each of these instructional settings can be examined in terms of the "triangle of instruction" (in Figure 1.1 of chapter 1), where an instructor (or lab assistant or computer program) and a student interact around content. Each of these alternative settings has its own pedagogy as well, though almost no one talks about the pedagogy of computer-based instruction[12] or the pedagogy of tutorials and workshops—and this is unfortunate because remedial pedagogy can show up in all these other instructional settings.

In the tutorial sessions we observed, including the help students receive in math and English workshops, a great deal of the interaction between tutor and student is essentially remedial pedagogy—helping students to get the right answers in math problems and to construct grammatically correct sentences and paragraphs. As one dean of student development recognized,

They [a TRIO program] also had a tutoring program, and it took us years to get them not to "do tutoring," which was actually to give them the answers, and instead to have those tutors be trained through the Learning Center.

As is true in most classrooms, there are few efforts in tutorials to engage in diagnostic mechanisms to determine why students are getting the wrong answers, or why they are making the same grammatical or spelling errors; therefore, errors are corrected but without the student knowing why. The tutors are usually upper-level community college students (in rare cases, they are upper-level undergraduates from local 4-year colleges) with only a little training in teaching methods, so they can hardly be expected to master the range of instructional approaches that might be useful, especially for students who have failed to understand a concept in the regular class. For some purposes, this kind of support may be all that is necessary, particularly for "brush-up" students who have been out of school for several years and only need to refresh their rusty academic skills, or for students (including those in ESL classes) seeking additional drill in order to achieve fluidity. But for students who are still fundamentally lost in basic skills, tutors replicating remedial pedagogy are unlikely to provide much help.

Of course, this need not be the case, and several colleges have invested in tutor training, which could presumably provide tutors with approaches that stress conceptual approaches as well as procedural methods, and diagnostic practices in addition to giving students the answers (see chapter 6 for a description of one such college). But such an approach would essentially have to replicate with tutors—whose own content knowledge is necessarily limited and whose educational experiences are limited as well—the kinds of pedagogical preparation and professional development that would be required to change faculty approaches to instruction. As I will document in chapter 9, "Other Institutional Effects on Instruction and Innovation," professional development is quite limited in most colleges. If the purpose of tutors and workshops is to develop relatively low-cost supplements to classroom instruction, then it seems unlikely that colleges would invest as much in tutors as they might in faculty, and tutors and labs are likely to fall back into remedial pedagogy.

Similarly, many basic skills classes provide computer-based instructional packages for their students, particularly in math and ESL; for example, ALEKS, ACCESS, PLATO Learning/Academic Systems Algebra, Carnegie Learning, Kurzweil/Smartxt, Hawkes Learning Systems Basic Mathematics, the Lindamood-Bell system for reading, MathXLß, the Universal Learning Design project. These tools are part of an almost interminable list of computer-based programs, all bought from outside purveyors. No one has reviewed these programs for their pedagogy or effectiveness, though most of them come with "research" of low quality[13] asserting they are "proven practices!!" However, looking at these materials even briefly makes it clear that they are largely drill and practice, with decontextualized examples and simple word problems. They certainly provide additional practice, and they can *manage* the process of learning in the sense that they keep track of student progress through a sequence of problems and issues. As one math instructor, a nationally recognized author of textbooks and activities, said about these computer programs,

> The other thing that worries me is that with computers, the emphasis now is on the computer programs to grade homework. Those are all skill-and-drill.... It turns the curriculum into, well, very sort of dry ... so my personal mission is to try and build some courses that are more challenging at the other end, the nonskills, the conceptual and the applications and stuff.

Even as a form of practice, computer programs may encourage unthinking approaches. The same instructor continued:

> I notice the way students do their homework on the computer.... They're just randomly trying things, just a sort of hacker approach. So, they're not really thinking about how to do the problem, they just keep trying until they get something. So that, I think, is a drawback of the computer drill thing.

While computer-based programs may be fine for review (for brush-up students, for example) and for certain low-level testing purposes, they cannot *instruct* students, or diagnose why students are getting the wrong answers, or even provide practice in a way that encourages real thinking, so they largely replicate remedial pedagogy.

Again, this does not have to be true. As noted in chapter 4 on innovations, one math department uses statistical analysis packages with powerful graphics to have students analyze data sets developed by the instructors. Students are therefore doing the work that statisticians do with these computer programs, not simply engaging in drill. But without being careful about the pedagogy of computer-based learning, it is all too easy to fall back on the techniques of remedial pedagogy.

Finally, textbooks also have their own pedagogy (in addition to embodying the content of the triangle of instruction). Textbooks are particularly important given the large numbers of adjunct professors who teach basic skills; these instructors are often handed a textbook and a syllabus, and without more guidance or professional development than adjuncts usually receive, the easiest course of action is simply to follow the textbook. But too many textbooks—particularly in math and in writing, and in grammar-based approaches to ESL instruction—have a series of decontextualized problems to solve, or lists of grammar rules and examples.[14] Sometimes the texts are somewhat comical in their lack of understanding: One math text asserted in the introduction that it would teach students not only *how* to carry out mathematical procedures, but *why* they worked. However, once again, the text had many decontextualized problems without much explanation about why the procedures work. At one point, the text stated, "Of course, we have a base-10 number system," which assumes that students remember what a base-10 number system is. But when students are converting decimals to fractions and vice versa, a staple of prealgebra classes, it's clear that many students have no idea of place value or (by extension) the base-10 system. Textbooks like these *assume* what they should *teach*. As supplements to instruction, or sources of practice for students, such textbooks may be quite useful (as are drill-oriented computer programs), but when they shape basic instruction, they lead right back to remedial pedagogy.

Again, there are clear alternatives, and I will review some of them in chapter 4. But the point for the moment is that remedial pedagogy is insidious, affecting not only classroom instruction itself but also the textbooks, computer programs, and certain support services that shape and supplement the classroom. Given the many reasons for thinking that behaviorist approaches are less effective than more constructivist or balanced approaches, improving instruction should be one of the ways to enhance the success of remedial education.

The Dominance of Remedial Pedagogy

The community concerned about basic skills might ask why remedial pedagogy is so common. There are at least seven reasons why this is true, some of which are particular to community colleges and some of which are more general:

Remedial pedagogy seems "natural": if English instructors find that students cannot construct a coherent sentence, or if math instructors find that students cannot solve a one-step problem, then the obvious "solution" is to reteach these basic skills. This may work with brush-up students, but for those with more fundamental motivational problems or misunderstandings, it is likely to be ineffective.

Instructors in community colleges have no formal training in instructional methods. Sometimes they discover constructivist methods on their own through trial and error (Grubb & Associates, 1999, ch. 1), but at the outset, they are unfamiliar with multiple approaches to teaching.

Many instructors teach as they have been taught, particularly if they have no formal preparation in pedagogical alternatives. Most often, this means using teacher-centered approaches. If they come from Asian or Eastern European countries, as many do, their only experience is with rigid and behaviorist teaching.

Adjunct instructors, who teach the majority of basic skills courses, often have no time for preparation. They are often handed only a textbook and a syllabus, both of which are likely to guide them to remedial pedagogy. There is very little time for reflection around instruction, particularly for adjuncts.

There are exceptions, of course, including the departments examined in chapter 4 and the faculty-oriented Teaching and Learning Centers described in chapter 6. But unless there is a specific place and time for discussions about instruction, they do not take place on their own.

In most colleges, there is no culture of appreciation for instruction. Often, administrators dominate the culture of community colleges, and they are more concerned with money, enrollments, board relations, political survival, and cost issues than with instruction (Grubb & Associates, 1999, ch. 8). Textbooks, computer programs, and student services like tutoring all reinforce the remedial pedagogy of the classroom.

In every way, then, remedial pedagogy is the default position. Unless there is a concerted effort to the contrary, instructors are likely to fall into this approach to basic skills instruction despite the numerous reasons for its ineffectiveness.

4

INNOVATION IN BASIC SKILLS INSTRUCTION

The Landscape and the Locus of Change

The previous chapter presented evidence that the approach to developmental education that I call remedial pedagogy is dominant. The emphasis on small subskills in part-to-whole instruction, the absence of nonbasic competencies (like analytic and conceptual abilities, or "21st century skills"), the technique of drill and repetition, and the lack of any applications to the world outside the classroom lead to classes that are quite conventional. Clearly, only the most motivated students could stick through semester after semester of such teaching. Given what we know about good teaching (summarized in chapter 1), inadequate instruction may be partly responsible for poor progress in basic skills sequences.

At the same time, community colleges are full of innovation in developmental education. Such variations constitute evidence that remedial pedagogy is not inevitable and that instructors working either individually or collectively can overcome the forces leading to its dominance (reviewed at the end of chapter 3). Indeed, the problem for outsiders (like our group of researchers) is often to make sense of the blizzard of transformation—to understand what is widespread from that which reaches only a trivial number of students, and to distinguish potentially enduring innovations from ones that last only as long as the attention of a single instructor. Even the least innovative colleges have some individuals who are trying to do novel work; often, they band together into a group of anywhere from five to a dozen people who think of themselves as fellow travelers, and refer outsiders (like our researchers) to the rest of the group. Very often, a college will have three or four major innovations taking place; one college we visited was engaging in at least a dozen. Sometimes, the innovations seem to be purely symbolic. At one college, nearly every administrator mentioned a learning community (LC) as evidence of experimentation.

However, quite apart from the fact that LCs are by now well known, the one they mentioned was in its first year, was struggling with an enrollment of only 7 students, and even if it achieved its target of 25 students, would reach only a tiny fraction of the student population. Unless this LC was intended to be the first of many—and its continuation was very much in doubt—it could not possibly affect more than a handful of students.

Thus, the innovations in colleges are both numerous and varied, symbolic and substantive, large in scale as well as small, and I could not possibly cover all the innovations we learned about in our investigations. This chapter reviews several types of innovations: (a) the efforts of individuals to develop their own approaches, often through trial and error, which remain individual and idiosyncratic because other instructors do not adopt them; (b) departments that have, over time and usually with a succession of external grants to support their work, developed a coherent approach to developmental education that includes many faculty; (c) LCs and linked courses (which were, unfortunately, less common than we hoped); (d) reforms following K-12 initiatives, represented here by Reading Apprenticeship and the methods of the National Writing Project; and (e) the formation of Faculty Interest Groups (FIGs), to stimulate discussion that might lead to reforms.

These are innovations that we saw in California. There are, of course, many innovations in other states as well, and some of them are widely cited: the I-Best program in Washington, other places with constellations of learning communities, Virginia's modular approach, faculty teaching and learning centers, and experiments with student services. But we decided to profile just innovations in California partly for logistical reasons, and partly as a way of surveying the innovations in one state with a single set of laws and state initiatives. In particular, the logic of our inquiry would have required observing classrooms in other state innovations, and this would have proved too much for both our budget and our stamina.

Evidently, there is no dearth of good ideas about how developmental education might be improved, no lack of models and pilot programs and exemplars for aspiring innovators (and researchers) to observe, and no shortage of faculty energy and enthusiasm for experimentation. But many of these innovations are idiosyncratic and are not replicated by other instructors; other innovations have taken more than a decade to develop, and cannot be readily imitated or implemented on a larger scale. The most familiar innovations come and go, and seem to be less prevalent than they have been in the past—LCs and linked courses, with some obvious advantages for basic skills classes. The most enduring and promising innovations, departmental developments that create coherent alternatives to remedial pedagogy, emerge from a complex process that we call "innovation from the middle," where senior faculty and middle-level administrators combine forces first to develop and then to promote alternative approaches. So, the real issue is not why there is so much innovation, but rather why so much of it does not spread and then become permanent or institutionalized. I will attempt to answer this question more specifically in the last section of this chapter about the locus of innovation; that is, where innovation starts within these colleges and why it either endures or fizzles out.

We have sought out innovations that are departures from the remedial pedagogy described in chapter 3, an instructional approach that violates so many of the precepts for effective instruction that we assume it to be relatively ineffective. Although the innovations I describe in this chapter are more consistent with effective practices, they have not—for the most part—been carefully evaluated. Therefore, we cannot be sure that they are more effective than standard practices, either at the course level (the extent to which students learn more, or pass courses) or at the program level (the extent to which students are able to enroll in and pass subsequent courses up to and including earning credentials or transferring).

Despite the lack of direct evidence, there are still powerful reasons to examine what innovations emerge and how they emerge. The success rates in basic skills are so low that all alternatives need to be considered. Even if there are many other dimensions of developmental education that might account for success—like the contributions of student services (examined in chapter 5), the alignment of courses (see chapter 7), and individual characteristics of instructors (like charisma and liveliness) that are unaffected by pedagogical approaches—conventional approaches leave much to be desired. The fact that they are both uninspiring and in violation of the precepts for high-quality teaching presented in chapter 1 highlights the need to search for alternatives. And community colleges are excellent sites of experimentation since there is so much innovation to examine.

Individual and Idiosyncratic Innovation

In virtually every community college we visited, there are a few individuals who are widely known (even outside their departments) and whose efforts are widely praised by others as being exemplars of good teaching. A developmental English class taught by Ms. Tudor in South Metro Community College[*] was described by our observer as "the best instruction I have observed in over 30 years of observation":

> *The class of 39 students started with a pitch to the English department's essay contest with the comment, "We're all amateurs, but here's a chance to be a published writer"—placing students on the same level as the instructor ("all amateurs") and*

---

[*]   Both of these names are pseudonyms, as are all names (with the exception of Chaffey College) in this and all subsequent chapters. South Metro Community College is where the caricature of remedial pedagogy described in chapter 3 (the math class on factoring polynomials) took place.

inviting students into the community of published authors. The instructor then asked a volunteer to summarize a book, a department-wide reading cutting across classes; her comment was that "Coming to reading is part of the college culture. College is where you make lifelong friends, become part of the community. Don't just come to class and go home." She then prepared students for a composition due near the end of the class, emphasizing that it should be typed, go through an editing process, and follow Modern Language Association (MLA) format since "you will need to know this before you get into English 47" (the next course in the sequence). She was signaling a series of requirements and the expectation that they would continue in the sequence.

The focus of the class was on five sentence types (simple, compound, complex, etc.), and she encouraged students to explain the relationships of forms to one another, and clarify them in terms of intended meaning. When students had difficulty with a sentence, she would ask metacognitive questions ("What do you intend to say?" or "What sentence would say that?") as a way of leading students to better choices, rather than drilling students on definitions and examples. The instructor then sent students to the board to review run-on and complex sentences, requiring students to verbalize their choices; this generated a lot of on-task chatter among students as they went through the process with their neighbors. The process of verbalization itself required students to articulate their reasoning, and served as a diagnostic device as well.

Then, the instructor broke the class into groups to work on five sentences reflecting different types, circulating to connect what they were doing to past performance in the class. Students also discriminated among inappropriate, satisfactory, and especially good uses of transition words and phrases, rather than simply identifying sentences as correct or incorrect. Finally, the instructor passed back drafts of a composition with an initial evaluation related to comments on the composition itself. "If you have a problem [with my corrections], go to a tutor in the lab; if you're still confused, come see me," clarifying the multiple routes for added feedback.

While the subject was a familiar one from writing courses, the instructor went through four or five different exercises to keep motivation high. She required both individual work at the board and group work where students explained their writing. She also provided a great deal of ancillary encouragement—about the department's essay contest, about being a college student ("Don't just come to class and go home"), and about making progress in the department (in an institution where progress through basic skills courses seemed confusing). All in all, what could have been a conventional class was highly motivating, and all students engaged with material that might otherwise have been routine.

Ms. Tudor is well known in the department for her teaching; as her students have shown greater success in common exams, faculty have begun to seek her advice and counsel. She claimed that there has been "major, major change in the department," and that the chair was committed to "building a solid basic skills program. It was not embraced with open arms in the beginning, but as more people joined in, it became more of a departmental activity." At the same time, another instructor mentioned, "There's no consistency [in teaching]—things happen [only] with little pots of money," and another noted that professional development "is not effective, but you get what you pay for—the activities are not centered on teaching." Furthermore, there were no signs of departmental institutionalization, as we saw in other departments (see "Innovative Departments" below). So, in a college with a good deal of mediocre instruction, an outstanding individual has started to change practice through the force of her example, but it remains unclear how far this will go.

A somewhat similar example in ESL comes from Barkham College, where ESL is dominated by vocabulary and grammar drills. However, one instructor, Ms. Biran, has organized her class as a series of exercises, some of them explicitly didactic but most involving the kinds of speaking and listening skills that ESL students need:

> The class begins with presentations by two students, quite poised, with PowerPoint slides about their home country and why they came to the U.S. Other students wrote on score sheets during the presentations, and asked questions and provided feedback on the presentations. She requested students to formulate five homework questions to ask classmates next time, responding to them as "too easy" or "too hard" if they seemed inappropriate for the level of the class. She commented about online postings for the class and handed back a quiz, with conversation prompts for a new, experimental type of oral quiz. Then, she gave directions for conversations that slipped in grammar comments about tense and provided examples of correct pronunciation. Students proceeded to work in pairs with these conversation prompts, switching pairs from time to time while the instructor circulated and responded to individual questions. At the end of this conversation, the instructor asked several students the meanings of colloquial expressions they had used in their talks.

About midway through the period, half the class went to a neighboring global studies class, while some global studies students entered this class. Again, students chose partners and discussed a series of questions on global developments, providing a shift in topic as well as in classmates and their backgrounds.

> When the class reconvened, she asked about the following week's research presentations. She encouraged students to attend lectures in English, and then switched to a didactic segment on two-part verbs (like "turn on") and the different ways they can be expressed. This was followed by a textbook exercise on four types of apology, followed by group practice where she called names for a request first and then another name for an "interesting" apology; the class worked together to correct language. The class ended with reminders of a forthcoming quiz and instructions for the next class.

In a 60-minute period, the instructor provided some direct instruction, presided at formal student presentations, organized several different segments of conversational pairs, changed topics with the global studies class, and incorporated many informal comments about forthcoming work, correct pronunciation and usage, and other opportunities to practice English. The instructor explained, "For language learning, it's speaking a language in relationship with somebody, their responsibility when they get into groups." The variety of language use was quite broad, and included both oral language and writing (on quizzes and forthcoming papers). The interest level in the room was consistently high, without the distracted behavior—text messaging, checking of cell-phones and e-mail, wandering in and out of class—that occurs in so many classes following remedial pedagogy.

In Parson College, an innovative philosophy instructor illustrated what it might be like to have a wholly individualized approach to remediation—instead of the "batch processing" that we usually see, with groups of 15 to 40 students going through precisely the same course whether they need it or not. There, the faculty has developed a series of "essential skills" courses; one instructor, Ms. Accela, saw the need to teach the course because students were so poorly prepared for critical thinking, collaborative learning, and presentations. She focused her essential skills class on critical thinking, writing skills, learning and study skills, and reading for philosophy. She used a reading response journal—a diagnostic device—to determine where students have problems and then tailored her approach to what she saw in individual students' journals. She also used a tutor to lead student-focused discussions, much like the Supplemental Instruction I will describe in chapter 5. So, there were certainly collaborative and collective dimensions to her class, but in terms of improving student writing, the writing response journals gave her access to individual errors[1] rather than covering errors as if they were generic. In her class, we can catch a glimmer of what it might look like to individualize basic skills instruction.

In examining instructors who depart from remedial pedagogy, the departments in which they work often play very little role in their innovations. In Choctaw College, the ESL department has taken a relentless grammar-based approach to English-language learning, leading students through a series of grammar rules, vocabulary drills, and other elements of a part-to-whole approach to speaking and writing. But one instructor within the department, a part-timer and someone who (like most adjuncts) admitted she didn't have time to attend many department functions, took precisely the opposite approach. She had her students read an entire novel, and used the novel to teach grammar—a whole-to-part approach that has the advantage of providing a context for grammar, punctuation, and the other nitty-gritty mechanics of English. But there was no sign that other members of the department learned from her example.

Furthermore, we uncovered a math department in which there were four distinct and independent approaches to math teaching. At Chisholm College, a divide existed between the traditional textbook and lecture centered approach to math instruction, and what proponents called a more "student centered and technology based lab approach," where students took a lab-based course instead of a lecture-based course. (However, both approaches followed the precepts of remedial pedagogy since so many computer-based programs—while allowing students to proceed at their own pace—still require drill on subskills.) In addition, three members of the department taught "Applied Math," which used a great number of examples—some of them drawn from CTE courses taught on the campus—to provide some context. The applied math course we observed also made much greater use of student demonstrations and inquiry about math, rather than information transfer. Finally, one part-time instructor taught a course on the mathematics of water management, which incorporated the mathematical procedures required in this occupational area—the importance of units, unit dimension analysis, calculation of horsepower and kilowatt hours, the geometry of spherical water storage containers—and used examples from the occupation. So, one department had four different approaches to teaching basic mathematics, but aside from the three applied math instructors, who conceived of this approach together and shared some examples, there appeared to be no communication among instructors using different approaches. Moreover, there were no mechanisms for alerting students to the differences in teaching approaches in case they might favor one over another.

We saw many other departures from remedial pedagogy, particularly in instructors' efforts to provide a few examples of applications, as well as efforts to have students verbalize their procedures in math or writing classes as a way of diagnosing their thinking. We observed other classes that followed the patterns of remedial pedagogy, but where instructors were extremely clear and organized—presenting the material to be mastered in a logical sequence and engineering the pacing of the class so that students were engaged throughout. According to Figure 1.2 from chapter 1, such classes are examples of point A (i.e., high-quality behaviorist instruction) as opposed to point E (i.e., mediocre hybrid instruction); they are also as uncommon as pure departures from remedial pedagogy.

But the main conclusion about all these examples of strong teaching is that they are idiosyncratic, not institutionalized. In other words, instructors have developed their own approaches, often through trial and error,[2] rather than being influenced by members of their department, professional development (which is relatively weak, as I will argue in chapter 9), relevant literature, or examples provided by disciplinary groups. As one of the applied math instructors at Chisholm College noted about his efforts to develop "stories" through trial and error to go with simple algebraic expressions, "I've been trying one thing and another throughout my whole career ... I guess I'm gradually getting better. But I'm obviously nowhere near where I want to be." It's just not possible to rely on this kind of idiosyncratic innovation as a way of improving instruction in basic skills; it is too individual, too isolated from the practice of other instructors, and too limited in scope to influence instruction for more than a small number of individuals. To see innovation with a greater chance of enhancing teaching for larger numbers of students, more collective approaches to pedagogical change are necessary.

Innovative Departments

In a small number of cases, departments have developed their own particular approach to teaching a developmental subject. The advantage over idiosyncratic innovations, is that while not all members of a department may buy into the innovation, it influences the teaching of many more instructors. Furthermore, when a department develops its own pedagogical approach, it can institutionalize that approach through the selection of new generations of sympathetic instructors, through professional development designed to pass on that approach, and (often) through curriculum materials that embody the approach better than available textbooks do. We uncovered three or four examples of such departments in the 13 colleges we examined,[3] and I will profile three of them here because certain similarities in their histories illustrate the necessary elements of widespread innovation.

The English Department at Choctaw College

The reform story at Choctaw College began in the late 1990s, when the college received feedback from the University of California at Berkeley that its students were not prepared to write effectively in upper-division courses. At the same time, there was dissatisfaction within the department because there were

> multiple pathways to English 1A … but it felt really inconsistent, and it felt like there was a lot of churning happening from teachers and students: students weren't making it here, so they would go over there [to another course]. So, we got together and had a 2-year-long discussion that started with values: what do we want to see happen? What do we call learning?

Simultaneously, innovations were fueled by collaboration with another college through a federal Fund for the Improvement of Postsecondary Education (FIPSE) grant focusing on reading and writing instruction, and by the opportunity to hire a number of new faculty during the 1990s. One faculty member in particular, who received his doctorate from the University of California system, was widely cited as a strong instructional leader, providing articles and intellectual stimulation, promoting instructional improvement through an evaluation process, and informally mentoring faculty who subsequently played leadership roles.

The department was assisted in its deliberations by a series of activities and practices that were helpful in developing collaborative norms. One was the availability of grant funding—first from FIPSE, then from a federal Title III grant, and then from foundation funding supporting Faculty Inquiry Groups (FIGs; see p. 98 below) that provided instructors with release time to develop new teaching approaches and materials. One result was the development of course outlines, periodically revised, that provided guidance to those instructors who bought into the department's philosophy. Another helpful activity was the invitation of outside experts to provide support through workshops, which served as a form of intellectual development for the entire department. The practice of a "college hour," an effort by the college to set aside time for full-time faculty to collaborate on common issues, served as a mechanism of collaboration for the English department. Finally, for a period of time, a coordinator position was funded—someone responsible for organizing professional development and mentoring for the entire department. Subsequently, the "college hour" and the coordinating position were lost due to funding cuts, and many members of the department lamented the decline of collaboration and community that these endeavors had helped foster.

However, the departmental efforts did not depend particularly on the college's administration. One dean was perceived as being supportive, and would alert members of the department to sources of political resistance; another dean was remembered as supportive only in the sense that she did not interfere with the department. In general, however, instructors felt that middle and upper management at Choctaw was "not strong," and they did not look to deans for guidance, support, or leadership.

The result of all these internal discussions was the development of a particular approach to teaching reading and writing—embedded first in a set of "Articulated Assumptions" and then in an "English Division Throughline"—describing what all English courses in the college should do. One of the first assumptions is that "the hierarchical model of English where skills progress from words to sentences to paragraphs to essay structure is not favored in this division"—a blunt repudiation of remedial pedagogy. As one long-time member of the department clarified,

> The discrete skill style of teaching English was not effective because students couldn't transfer those skills…. It's what I call a workbook mentality—they would master the workbook, but that's not what happens in a college classroom…. So, we thought it was better to model, early on, the real tasks, the authentic tasks.

The department stressed the integration of reading and writing at all levels, as well as the reading of full-length texts rather than short excerpts or passages, and using nonfiction sources (which student are more likely to read in subsequent college-level courses) rather than fiction. The department also emphasized critical thinking (rather than basic subskills) at all levels of instruction, and it relied on the assumption that students bring knowledge to learning on which they can build—a fundamental tenet of constructivism. There was also an explicit emphasis on collaboration among students, and between students and instructors. Classes were to focus on analytic writing rather than personal reflection—again, in anticipation of what college-level work requires. Finally, there was a clear acknowledgment that developmental students often need to improve their "studenting skills"—the study skills and habits of mind often taught separately in Student Success courses. Our observations of classes at Choctaw confirmed that, by and large, instructors follow these ideas in their classroom practices, and as a result, their classes typically avoid the pitfalls associated with remedial pedagogy.

The Mathematics Department at Median Community College

As I clarified in chapter 3, the emphasis on remedial pedagogy, drill and practice, and mastering computational algorithms without conceptual understanding is particularly prominent in math teaching. We had to seek out a department where something else was taking place in more than idiosyncratic ways (as it was at Chisholm College). Through the grapevine, we were led to Median Community College. There, as at Choctaw, developments started in the 1990s, with an internal "math war." One group of faculty, discouraged by low progression rates into college-level math, visited Harvard College and its efforts to reshape calculus, and they came back with reform-oriented visions of what basic math could be. The "traditionalists" who had not visited Harvard battled with the "reformers," with ugly results including formal challenges and lawsuits, until most of the traditionalists went off to teach at a neighboring campus. Another development was the requirement of Student Learning Outcomes (SLOs) by the accrediting association, starting in 2002; unlike many departments around the state, which treated these as compliance requirements only, the Median faculty tried to develop some genuine outcomes. These were similar to the ones in *Beyond Crossroads* (2006), a publication of the American Mathematical Association of Two-Year Colleges (AMATYC) with a reform orientation. But, as there were no curriculum materials or textbooks available, the department started to develop "activity packets" as its own version of texts. The early versions are described as "horrible," with inappropriate problems and a lack of flow, but the department has persistently worked to improve them over time.

A series of funding opportunities, one after the other, helped sustain these reforms. A 1998 task force from the college's Academic Senate produced a report on developmental education; this, in turn, led to a Title III grant in the late 1990s supporting the rewriting of curricula and the development of partnerships with counselors. When this ended in 2004, another grant to develop

FIGs came along for another 3 years; then, two other college funding sources materialized: a line item for basic English and math courses and funding from the state's Basic Skills Initiative. By this time, members of the math faculty had moved into institutional positions of power, so they were well placed to participate in college-wide discussions about priorities, the role of basic skills, and funding allocations.

Leadership for these efforts came from one well-known and widely respected faculty member, bolstered by other new hires who supported the "reformist" effort. The process of innovative senior faculty becoming more visible on their campuses has taken place at a few other colleges, and is another dimension of "innovation from the middle." In addition, the administration was accommodating. The math department received institutional funds for basic skills, as well as college-controlled funding from the Basic Skills Initiative, but the faculty leaders described the administration as providing "hands-off support"— they provided some resources, but they did not interfere. The vision, the hard work of curriculum development, and any efforts to further the agenda of the "reformers" has come exclusively from faculty.

From these activities emerged a series of beliefs and practices that constitute a distinct alternative to remedial pedagogy. The instruction and activity packets are based on recognizably real-world problems, from which the standard skills—solving simple equations, understanding linear and nonlinear functions—are derived, in whole-to-part teaching. A great deal of group work takes place in classes, the idea being that students will help each other move toward solutions—in place of the usual teacher-centered approach where instructors present students with solutions. Instructors consistently ask students to verbalize their approaches to problems, and to present their solutions at the whiteboard—this is partly an effort to get them to be precise about what they have learned, and partly a diagnostic of how they think about these math problems. In a number of ways, instructors include elements of Student Success into these courses, recognizing that many students are math-phobic and that resistance to math needs to be overcome before they can succeed. Finally, the instructors use a computer program called TinkerTools, a simple data analysis program, to examine a couple of simple data sets (e.g., one on breakfast cereals, another on high school test scores in the region) so that students are carrying out real data analysis, but they do not use computer programs for drill and practice.

To further its practices, the department has activity packets, which are periodically upgraded, as well as a practice of "teaching committees," where all instructors teaching a specific course get together to discuss how best to teach it and to modify activity packets. It also has common mastery quizzes[4] and exams for each course, and the practice of flex days—usually a weak form of professional development—has been successfully utilized for department instructional purposes (e.g., developing a scoring rubric for one of the mastery quizzes). There is no question, then, that the department has developed an approach that is internally coherent and clearly different from the remedial pedagogy of the "traditionalists."

The ESL Department at Sidwell Community College

ESL instruction at Sidwell Community College seems to be bifurcated. The innovative program I describe in this section is called Mastering English for Academic Goals (MEAG; another pseudonym), but the "old" or traditional program of teaching skills in isolation is still available. Faculty who want to teach in the "old" style can still do so—though how students know whether they are opting for "traditional" vs. MEAG courses is unclear.

Like the other departmental innovations, MEAG developed over a long period. It began about a decade ago when the department admitted that their students were not succeeding. The faculty realized they needed a fourth level of ESL, but also realized that "more of the same [ineffective practice] would be inappropriate." After 4 years of failing to come to any resolution, one of the faculty members decided to experiment in evening courses that would not affect most of the faculty. She also investigated other programs and contacted a faculty member from Hawaii. A visit to that college convinced other faculty to move in the direction of a content-based and integrated curriculum; several faculty members began to write curriculum units that were based on work at the Hawaiian college but that were also tweaked in various ways. The dean of the department helped by putting proponents of the content-based approach on the hiring committee, and by providing a grant from Basic Skills Initiative funds (later discontinued when funding was cut). The initial leader also recognized the centrality of adjunct faculty in ESL instruction, and she developed an adjunct program to prepare them in the integrated approach. Like the Adjunct Program at Chisholm College, this has had the added advantage of supporting adjunct faculty and integrating them into the department in contrast to other colleges where adjuncts are isolated. Thus, MEAG developed a supportive hiring procedure, cooperation from adjuncts, innovative curriculum materials, and the support of the dean. Despite these developments, everyone still spoke of MEAG as a work in progress; as the dean of the department commented, "If this was a Michelangelo sculpture, we finally have the marble we want, and we finally are beginning to hit away at it with some kind of an idea, but we have a design in mind."

The design of MEAG emphasizes that ESL must be for academic purposes, not the personal or social goals usually covered in adult ESL or noncredit ESL. A key feature is that skills (e.g., grammar, punctuation, pronunciation, vocabulary) are taught in context, not as stand-alone skills. As one member of the department said,

> If students need to read something or listen to something, and they need to know a grammar point in order to comprehend that, they teach the

grammar then. They teach grammar when they need it to manipulate the material.

As another instructor clarified the necessity of teaching in context, "Students in basic skills can know grammar rules, but if they can't use them in a random text or produce it in different environments, then it's not very useful." She then went on to make a point about Student Success: "And if they don't know how to be good students, then they can't go on and [earn] 12 units. The ESL program therefore integrates content, linguistics, and academic skills knowledge—[it's] well-rounded." This program includes study skills and dimensions of Student Success, just as the math teaching at Median College does.

The faculty no longer use conventional ESL textbooks; instead, they use authentic texts—those that students might encounter in college-level classes. "With activities and scaffolding, they could do it," said one instructor about reading parts of Jared Diamond's *Collapse*. "They could talk about academic topics in intelligent ways." The faculty used newspapers not only for reading and writing exercises, but also to learn about such topics as plate tectonics, global warming, and other hot issues: "Students came back reporting that, for the first time, they could read the news. This motivates students, who are not just confined to certain topics" covered in textbooks. Another component is a commitment to covering social justice issues, particularly those relevant to the lives of immigrant students, like immigration, maquiladoras, and employment. Each semester, ESL courses adopt a theme, which generates some of the readings used in all courses; the department also has common midterm and final exams, to bring coherence to courses. All students must complete a portfolio, a more independent form of learning than simply reading and writing from prompts and books.

Not surprisingly, there has been some resistance, both from faculty wedded to traditional skills-oriented approaches and from students brought up in standard language courses. As one student complained, "We're not learning enough grammar, we're not learning enough rules ... why are we talking about monkeys instead of how to conjugate verbs?" The MEAG approach does contain some explicit teaching of skills (partly in response to this resistance), but again, academic content is presented first, with "grammar and rules" proceeding from reading. Even though most of the department has allied itself with the methods of MEAG, there continue to be conflicts one might describe as "the ESL wars," just as there have been "math wars" and "English wars" in teaching for nonimmigrant students.

Consistency across Departmental Innovations

In these three departments, and in other cases where there has been some partial development of clear alternatives to remedial pedagogy, a number of commonalities emerge. First, these three departments all began their innovations when they realized that students were not benefiting from traditional programs. They then spent considerable amounts of time—at least a decade, by the time we visited them in Spring 2011—coming up with alternatives, devising curriculum materials, and otherwise working out the details of what innovation might look like. Fortunately, all three departments were able to keep working at improvements over this period rather than being forced to stop their developments because of some change in focus or administration. In several cases, this happened as a result of grants supporting release time, the participation of adjuncts, the creation of curriculum materials, and the development of professional development (especially for adjuncts). All of these departments have codified or institutionalized their approaches in various ways: by gaining control over hiring procedures, by developing curriculum materials to guide new instructors, and by engaging in various forms of professional development (again, including adjuncts).

Second, the innovations they have developed share some similarities, too. They all repudiate remedial pedagogy, quite explicitly in the cases of the Choctaw English department and the Sidwell ESL department. They embody whole-to-part instruction in place of part-to-whole methods, teaching subskills in the context of larger tasks. They try to use "authentic" materials that students will see in subsequent classes (or in life outside college) instead of contrived textbooks. They rely much more on student participation, both as a way of getting students to verbalize their reasoning and as a diagnostic device; in this and other ways, they are more student-centered rather than lecture- and instructor-centered. By and large, students are more attentive in these classes, with less off-task behavior (e.g., texting, chatting) and less tardiness and leaving the class. The classes are certainly more engaging to watch for outside observers.

Third, the process of developing these departmental reforms has been one that we describe as "leading from the middle."[5] In all these cases, faculty leaders—relatively senior faculty, with experience in a college and the trust of their colleagues—were crucial in both developing the innovation and persuading their colleagues to adopt it. In some cases (Choctaw is the most obvious), the faculty thought very little of the administration. However, middle-level administrators—usually department deans and program directors, but not upper-level management like vice-presidents or presidents—provided support both indirectly, in allowing innovations to be developed (usually described as "hands-off"), and directly, in the form of grants and some control over hiring. So, the locus of innovation is not the solo practitioner at the bottom of the hierarchy, who can (at best) develop idiosyncratic innovation described in the prior section; nor is it the managers at the top. The locus of innovation is the faculty and administrators closer to the middle of the college hierarchy.

Oddly enough, while those near the middle may be the crucial agents for programmatic and pedagogical change, this level receives little or no training or ongoing professional development for their roles. We therefore suspect that one reason there is so little systematic innovation in basic skills instruction, or in instruction more generally, is that both institutional and individual conditions and incentives need to be just right for innovation from the middle to occur. As one faculty leader noted, reforming departments required both an instructional vision as well as organizational, political, and personal skills—and "how often do these skill sets come together?"[6] We will continue to test this particular hypothesis with other innovations described in this chapter, but for the moment, it helps explain why some departments have created relatively unified innovative approaches while others persist with varying and idiosyncratic approaches to basic skills instruction.

Learning Communities and Linked Courses

By now, learning communities (LCs) and linked courses are quite familiar forms of innovation, even though it remains unclear how widespread they are in community colleges. LCs—where students take two, three, or even four courses at the same time, ideally with content integrated across courses—have been widely described, positively evaluated, and generally appreciated for their role in interdisciplinary work and their ability to teach basic skills in the context of other courses.[7] Linked courses, where one course is integrated with or linked to curriculum material from other subjects, have many of the same advantages on a smaller scale. In California, Wisely (2011) has compared outcomes for students in basic math courses linked to CTE with students in conventional, decontextualized basic skills courses in the same institution, and found that the rates of passing these linked courses and subsequent math courses are significantly higher. These innovations are excellent ways of correcting the tendency of remedial pedagogy to teach skills out of context.

LCs also provide an obvious way for colleges to create a freshman learning experience, where first-year students take whatever basic skills courses they need along with a Student Success course and perhaps another introductory course. One such Freshman Academy we observed emerged from an experiment where one English faculty member first created a small learning community where students took her reading and writing courses together—reflecting the philosophy we saw in the Choctaw English department that reading and writing should not be separated. Then, this small learning community was expanded to include courses in developmental math, reading, writing, and an applied psychology class—really a career planning class—together with a counselor assigned to the Academy. In addition, students were required to spend a certain amount of time in the college's Supplemental Instruction Program. This program is driven by the philosophy of "ask, don't tell"—the "Socratic method" of asking students a series of questions, guiding the students to develop their own solutions rather than simply providing the answers, as is so often the case in tutor–student interactions. (This Supplemental Instruction

Program is profiled in chapter 6 on student services.) In addition, the designers of this learning community believe that one reason basic skills students are not usually successful is that they are "strangers in academia" (Shaughnessey, 1977)—they are unable to figure out the system of catalogs and schedules and course sequences, lacking the language and behavior of formal schooling. The counselor and the applied psychology course provide ways of introducing them to academia, much as student success courses do.

The developmental classes we observed in one learning community followed very different pedagogies. One writing class was relatively conventional and teacher-dominated, with a Jeopardy-like game of answering questions that ranged from the trivial ("How many siblings did the teacher have?") to the useless ("How many verbs are there in the English language?") to the rule-bound ("What is the common structure of a prepositional phrase?"). Overall, there were no opportunities to practice any form of literacy in the class. The associated reading class, however, involved a kind of hybrid instruction, with students discussing quotations they had chosen from reading passages they had brought to class, followed by a vocabulary review and a group activity in which randomly formed groups shared what they learned about the author of a short article called "Cruising Through Alaska." The math class seemed quite conventional: "It's basically a seventh-grade math class," plus linear equations from eighth grade. The instructor assumed that it was the students' responsibility to come to class well prepared, rather than assuming (as the reading and writing teachers did) that such preparation was partly the instructor's responsibility. None of the classes referred to material from any of the other classes, though the reading and writing teachers said that they sometimes collaborate in order to create more consistency between their classes. This variety of teaching approaches illustrates one potential pitfall of a learning community: unless the faculty have enough planning time and the inclination to modify their pedagogical approaches, the teaching is likely to be a hodge-podge of individual and idiosyncratic instructional methods. As a result, the learning community will rely solely on the structure of concurrent courses to build a community of students. Unfortunately, this Freshman Academy proved to be the only learning community we could observe.

In another college, a widely touted LC was struggling to get enough enrollments; in yet other cases, successful LCs had been discontinued because of expense. We heard about plans for other LCs that had not yet started. Our hunch is that, despite the enormous publicity around LCs, there are relatively few of them in California and in many other states some centralized source of support is lacking.[8] Certainly, it is true that in the vast majority of colleges that have LCs, there are only one or two of them—colleges do not rely on LCs for a substantial part of developmental education.[9] The same complaints arise all the time about LCs: they are too expensive, and they require much more planning time—and are therefore more difficult to teach—than conventional stand-alone courses. Also, students are unfamiliar with LCs and are unwilling to take chances on what look like experiments, and it is difficult to schedule students into LCs given the chaotic work and family lives of many students. Therefore, counselors are often hostile toward LCs and won't refer students to them. LCs may have benefits in terms of the learning and progress of students, but it is difficult to compare these benefits to the many types of costs associated with them—benefit-cost analysis is not a very useful framework for evaluating LCs. Note that many of these objections simply reaffirm how unconventional LCs are within standardized educational institutions, where the course (rather than the program) is the basic unit of instruction. We suspect—though we cannot prove it—that LCs in practice are dwindling in numbers, undermined by fiscal problems as well as the ability to sustain innovative structures.

Many of the same issues arise in linked courses, where students take two integrated courses at the same time. Like LCs, linked courses can provide a context for learning basic skills that overcomes the decontextualized teaching in remedial pedagogy. The one linked course we observed—the mathematics of water management—was an exemplar of contextualized learning, using the specific kinds of mathematics required in different water-related occupations to illustrate simple arithmetic, proportions and ratios, and volumetric calculations. But this was an idiosyncratic development connected to the interest of one particular instructor, not an innovation whose central idea had been adopted by other instructors.

When Wisely (2011) confirmed the value of developmental math courses contextualized with CTE, the bad news was how few of these courses he could find. In the 35 colleges that responded,[10] which is approximately one third of the 112 colleges in the state of California, only 10 reported having any contextualized courses. He was able to confirm only 11 such courses in these 10 institutions, indicating that, by and large, only one linked course existed in each college, and therefore trivial numbers of students were reached. Furthermore, these 35 colleges reported no LCs whatsoever! Such figures only confirm our suspicion that these innovations have become comparatively rare.

Borrowing from K–12 Innovations

Community colleges don't like to compare themselves with K-12 institutions; they consider themselves part of higher education, not K-12. However, the idea of looking for innovative ideas across levels of education makes a certain amount of sense; one possibility is that some reforms that have been developed and tested for K-12 education might also work in community colleges, though they might need to be modified for postsecondary students. The advantage is that development, implementation, and evaluation have already been carried out for such programs, so colleges could implement them without the long period of time—up to a decade, according to the testimony of the departments we talked to—required to develop innovative approaches and curriculum materials. We therefore decided to examine innovations in two areas where community colleges in California have used programs initially devised for K-12 education: Reading Apprenticeship (RA), an adolescent literacy program originally developed to improve reading sophistication among middle and high school students, and the National Writing Project, an approach to the teaching of writing, most of whose projects serve K-12 educators.

Both Reading Apprenticeship and the National Writing Project have some real promise for moving instruction away from remedial pedagogy and toward more thoughtful approaches to reading and writing. However, the ways that community college instructors use these innovations reveal how teaching in developmental education progresses—they illustrate how impossible it is to envision simply taking instructional innovations "off the shelf," or borrowing directly from K-12 practices, without modifications.

Reading Apprenticeship

Reading Apprenticeship has developed during the past decade, ever since its ideas were first set forth in *Reading for Understanding* (Schoenbach, Greenleaf, Czicko, & Hurwitz, 1999). It was originally developed to address the reading struggles of many middle and high school students—particularly since teachers typically stop overtly teaching reading after third grade, when they assume (incorrectly) that all students have "learned to read" and can now "read to learn." It has since developed a set of professional development activities, ranging from 2-hour workshops during flex days to the 5-day Leadership Institute for Reading Apprenticeship (LIRA) to 2-day workshops to follow up after LIRA training. These trainings are open to all teachers, and while RA hopes to influence social science, math, and science instructors, where reading is involved, the majority of attendees at RA trainings are middle and high school English teachers. However, the developer of RA received a grant to spread the practice to community colleges. Other community college instructors have found their own way to RA, and one college in California currently serves as a center for the spread of RA by giving workshops around the state, and has developed a substantial portfolio of training materials appropriate for community college classrooms.

To examine developments in RA, a team of four researchers visited five colleges with concentrations of instructors using RA. There, following our overall strategy, we interviewed administrators and instructors, and observed classes that incorporated RA tools and strategies. We also developed a State of Incorporation Scale to measure, for each college and subject area, the extent to which instructors were using RA tools and strategies since we expected the extent of incorporation or implementation to vary—and our expectations were indeed confirmed.[11]

The heart of RA is a set of metacognitive conversations about how we read, why we read, what the author intends, and how different readers interpret a text.[12] This generates a series of questions about what is known and what is unknown, about ways of knowing (and how they vary from subject to subject), about conjectures and uncertainty. Specific questions include those related to the reader's reaction and ways of solving any puzzles that come up during reading, as well as conventional ones like "What is the author's main point?" RA has developed a series of protocols or tools to formalize this kind of questioning; one, for example, asks students to keep a double-entry journal detailing "What do I know?" and then "How do I know it?" from the text. In another protocol, students write down "What I saw in the text," including evidence and quotes, and then pair that with "What I thought," or what they understood at that point. Some of the protocols ask students to think aloud as they are reading a text, giving other students alternative ways of reading and providing the instructor with diagnoses of students' thinking as they read. Note that these questions about texts are much more sophisticated than questions about simple comprehension that we often saw in remedial reading classes. They generate more complex ways of approaching reading than conventional methods like SPQ3R,[13] which doesn't provide much guidance about what kinds of questions might be asked about a text.

However, RA is much more than a method for developing sophisticated questions. The cornerstone of Reading Apprenticeship's instructional framework is a series of metacognitive conversations about how we read, why we read in the ways we do, what we think when we read, and what we can learn from the way others think and process information. Reading Apprenticeship supports the hypothesis that students who may lack strong independent literacy skills can quickly incorporate strategies to help them meaningfully interact with challenging texts. In this way, content instruction and reading instruction are inextricably linked. Sustained interaction with texts helps to strengthen critical thinking, motivation, and confidence. These skills are also transferable to other classes (such as history, social science, and science classes) where students may not have the benefit of Reading Apprenticeship (RA) instruction, but where they can internalize the strategies and easily apply them to other contexts. The overall result helps foster the student's mastery and self-identity as a "reader." This philosophy directly challenges the remedial pedagogy present in most developmental teaching.

RA emphasizes four "interactive dimensions of classroom life." The social dimension stresses literacy as a form of social interaction, and uses students' interests to talk about texts, share reading processes and interpretations, and notice other students' ways of reading. The personal dimension strives to develop students' identities as readers, develop confidence and range in reading, enhance fluency and stamina, and clarify their own purposes and goals in reading. The cognitive dimension involves the development of the specific comprehension and problem-solving strategies that can be applied to academic texts. The knowledge-building dimension stresses building schema through which texts can be understood, enhancing content knowledge, understanding word structure and vocabulary, and developing knowledge of text structures, including the different structures used in different disciplines. In the classes we observed, the social dimension was widely used to frame metacognitive conversations, providing students with opportunities to work in groups; the personal dimension was observed in many cases where students related assignments to their own experience and knowledge. The cognitive and knowledge-building dimensions were less clearly visible, though we could see student-led conversations about such topics as how they approached the homework assignment and the use of prepositions.

In courses that successfully incorporated RA tools and strategies, students seemed fully engaged for most of the class periods—in contrast to the sporadic engagement we usually saw in classes dominated by remedial pedagogy. One reason for increased student engagement is that RA encourages interaction among students, a great deal of talk about texts, discussion of differing interpretations, and more common problem- and project-based work. As described by one instructor, considered an RA expert in the state, her classes are "more active, student-directed, problem-solving and inquiry-based than non-RA classes." Classrooms that incorporate RA tools and strategies therefore look very different from the drill-and-practice reading classes following remedial pedagogy, with their emphasis on grammar, vocabulary and parts of speech, short reading passages examined for literal comprehension, and overall lack of effort to ask more complex questions.

The amount of talk and the sophistication of discussions are important parts of these exemplary RA classes. As one instructor said, "If you have taught low-level students, you know they don't talk. My students talk, they love the routines, the pair-share and think-aloud. They are excited." Along the same lines, another instructor said, "Students are much more willing to ask questions and our discussions are a lot deeper and richer." A third noted, "They [the students] are discussing and consulting with each other regarding what they are learning, relying less on me as the 'giver of knowledge' and are more active learners." Yet another instructor, who (again) noted the increased participation in her RA classes, said, "RA has been my antidote to burnout; I am amazed each day at the connections and perceptions that my class brings to the classroom." The delight that this instructor felt about her students' capacity to engage with complicated text was repeated in many other interviews.

Reading Apprenticeship is also one of the few innovations that, like the writing process of the National Writing Project, can be used in a variety of subjects, not just in developmental reading courses. One biology instructor (and chair of her science department) adopted RA because of her frustrations around students not reading course materials. She said, "Here's what we're trying—this has been pretty successful." She admitted, however, that RA is "pretty far afield" for science faculty who generally have not thought about reading from an educational standpoint; she has to translate terminology such as "metacognition" and try to get them to start thinking about reading. There's little doubt that the use of RA by teachers in subjects other than reading is less common, but that's not surprising as long as such instructors do not see themselves as teachers of reading. The point is that Reading Apprenticeship has the potential to be extended to any number of subjects, including CTE with its demanding reading requirements.

RA is a complex reform with many elements, and it can therefore be used in many different ways. In general, in the classes we observed, instructors used those elements they found the most useful; as a result, there is no one way that RA is implemented across different classes. For example, in one biology class, the instructor interspersed a few RA tools throughout what was otherwise a conventional lecture, illustrating that RA can be used selectively, or in incremental steps. In an ESL class, the instructor used RA to generate more sophisticated questions, but she used them in a conventional inquiry-response-evaluation (IRE) format rather than drawing on the social and cognitive dimensions of RA. And some instructors purported to be using RA but were not; for example, one instructor who told a researcher that she was using RA was in fact practicing traditional (and not very effective) group work assignments. In practice, then, there is a wide range of incorporation of RA perspectives and methods into community college classrooms. It's difficult to know whether this is a positive dimension of RA, allowing flexibility in instructors' uses of it, or a negative dimension in the sense that it's difficult to find "pure" forms of RA. However, this variance illustrates an unavoidable aspect of teaching in community colleges, where instructors must be intrinsically motivated to change their instructional methods and are much less accustomed than are K-12 teachers to having their instruction shaped by external influences.

Just as instructors have used RA in different ways, colleges have also taken different approaches to incorporating it. One college sent 30 instructors to RA training, about half of whom continued to use it. Another used RA as one strand of its overall approach under the state's Basic Skills Initiative, with 12 to 15 faculty receiving training. The incorporation of RA seemed to be strongest at Choctaw College, with a supportive dean and an English department that has developed its own innovative approach. In two other colleges we visited, there is now little institutional support for RA, though a number of faculty continue to use it individually. The initial dissemination of RA has been driven almost entirely by funds from the state's Basic Skills Initiative and from federal grants through Title III and Title IV. But two types of problems arise: one when the funding runs out, as it inevitably does, and colleges no longer pay for training (a problem common to most innovations); and another when instructors return to their colleges and look for support at their own college, a problem more specific to RA. Several colleges have developed Faculty Inquiry Groups (FIGs) around RA, which can provide guidance and mentoring for novice instructors, as well as a forum for discussion and recruitment. But wherever FIGs have not developed, faculty are left to implement RA on their own.

The importance of continuing institutional support—through FIGs, or through faculty centers like the Center for Teaching and Learning we saw at Chaffey College (chapter 6)—is well illustrated by the experiences of those new to RA. Through interviews, the researchers learned that a number of individuals who participated in RA training have either given up teaching with RA methods or have not even tried to apply them. The most common outcome was that the RA trainees would return to their college filled with enthusiasm but also feeling overwhelmed. They would try a range of RA tools and strategies as soon as possible and, all too often, discover that they could not make them work; that is, they encountered student resistance or a lack of student motivation. Then, in the absence of any support structure, they gave up using RA approaches entirely. Instructors particularly vulnerable to this kind of "early leaving" were those working on a campus without any kind of administrative support or FIGs. In part, this may be due to the fact that RA and its workshops concentrate on providing individuals with the skills to teach in different ways, but they do not stress the need for ongoing institutional support as well. Furthermore, most colleges have not provided much backing for instructional innovations, except when something like the Basic Skills Initiative or another external grant comes along, and very few of them have all-purpose centers like the Faculty Success Center at Chaffey College. Overall, while RA is supported by FIGs on a few campuses, it is otherwise floating on its own, supported by a few committed faculty leaders but not by any institutional resources.

RA has been evaluated in a formal random-assignment evaluation of ninth graders, with some critical implications for community colleges. The evaluations show mixed results: Over the course of the ninth grade, students who had gone through the program improved from an average reading level of 5.1 grade-level equivalent (GLE) to 6.1, compared to 5.9 for students in conventional English classes, a positive effect of approximately 25%. In classes with moderately or well-aligned implementation and longer duration, the increase was slightly greater, to a GLE of 6.2. (Implementation was somewhat difficult, and 10 of the 34 schools participating were rated poor in implementation—a result similar to our finding of inconsistent RA implementation in community colleges.) In addition, students' grades improved in core subject areas (language arts, social studies, science, and math). However, while reading comprehension improved, the reading interventions did not make any significant difference in the amount of reading students did nor in their use of reflective reading strategies. Furthermore, these improvements did not last into 10th grade, when Reading Apprenticeship strategies were no longer taught explicitly to students.[14] For community colleges, the implication is that when Reading Apprenticeship is implemented with reasonable fidelity, it benefits students in both their reading comprehension and in their reading and performance in other subjects—but the benefits fade once Reading Apprenticeship instruction stops. For students in a sequence of basic skills courses, this means that the consistent use of RA across a series of courses would be beneficial, but that the positive impact would disappear over time if only one course incorporates RA tools and strategies.

Overall, Reading Apprenticeship comes in many forms and shapes, instructors use it in different ways, and community colleges have provided varying levels of support. However, when it is fully understood and incorporated into developmental courses in genuine ways, RA changes the ways that classes are conducted, and it helps instructors move away from remedial pedagogy to more active and more student-focused classes, as well as more sophisticated analysis of texts appropriate for college-level coursework. We think it deserves greater consideration in community colleges as one way to address the inadequate reading preparation of students, in ways that are consistent with the efforts to prepare them for college-level work.

The National Writing Project and the Writing Process

The National Writing Project (NWP) has been devoted to the improvement of writing, principally in K–12 schools but in 2- and 4-year colleges as well.[15] The Writing Project has developed a peer-to-peer approach where writing instructors learn from other instructors who have been through various trainings and workshops—"Teachers are the key to improving education, and the best teachers of teachers are other teachers," as one of the NWP principles says. The projects themselves are regional; for example, we interviewed instructors from the Central California Writing Project, with a relatively large number of community college instructors. In general, however, we had a relatively difficult time finding community college instructors who had attended NWP workshops and who continued to use its ideas. There are few incentives for writing faculty to participate unless they want to improve teaching on their own.

The NWP has a series of principles, much as Reading Apprenticeship does, but they do not formally specify a particular approach to writing; as the principles state, "We promote no set formulas or packaged plans, though we are committed to an underlying philosophy." As one of the instructors we interviewed said, "We are not like a program. There is no binder that can tell you what's happening." However, they do stress the need for consistent and copious writing, a belief that "meaningful change happens over time," and that "teachers of writing must write"—indeed, NWP workshops involve actual writing, not just talk about writing.

In practice, however, the NWP is often known for the writing process approach, the very antithesis of remedial pedagogy. As one NWP instructor noted, in other classes, "Students have to memorize mechanics and MLA" (i.e., Modern Language Association formats for references). Instead, the writing process approach stresses writing as a form of communication among people and as the expression of ideas, emphasizing the social dimension of writing from the outset. The writing process tends to break the process of writing into discrete steps that lead to a finished essay: first, brainstorming ideas, then writing freely without undue concern for correctness, and then a crucial process of revision and editing (sometimes by peers or peer groups, sometimes by instructors) and creating multiple drafts. The steps that instructors use seem to vary from person to person, but the idea of breaking the writing of an essay into several stages seems nearly universal. One instructor said, "Once you see how the writing process works both for yourself and for students, there would be no way you would teach it any other way." It is a fundamentally different way of breaking down the process of writing since students are always producing essays; as another instructor noted, "I would never break things apart and say, 'Let's write a sentence or a paragraph.'" The mechanics of writing— grammar and punctuation, MLA (or any other format for citations)—are then taught in the course of writing essays, in whole-to-part teaching, rather than as stand-alone exercises.

Rather than simply making their students memorize grammar rules, NWP instructors seem to assign more writing than do others because of the belief that good writing takes practice and time to develop. This may be reason enough for community college instructors to avoid NWP approaches, since the conventional emphasis is usually on "covering" the greatest amount of material in the smallest amount of time. In addition, many English instructors, and particularly part-time instructors, have limited ability to read large quantities of student writing because they have large classes and no teaching assistants.

We learned from the instructors we interviewed that there is a great deal of self-selection among the faulty who choose to attend NWP workshops. First of all, while the NWP process (like Reading Apprenticeship) could be valuable to a wide variety of instructors with writing in their classes, virtually all of the community college instructors who have been through the NWP are writing instructors. Most were attracted to the NWP by its principles; the workshops then provided further reinforcement, as well as specific techniques to use in the classroom. Furthermore, instructors use a variety of methods they have picked up from several sources; most had difficulty articulating what they had learned from the NWP and what came from other sources. These characteristics imply that the NWP approach could not be forced upon writing instructors; those wedded to remedial pedagogy would simply refuse to go to workshops, and those who went and failed to accept the principles of the NWP would simply not use its methods. This is yet another illustration that innovation in basic skills instruction has to start with the faculty and spread outward; it cannot be imposed in any way as reforms within K-12 education have been.

The workshops provided by the regional groups of the NWP are crucial forms of professional development. This is where individual instructors meet other more experienced NWP instructors, see the principles of the NWP in action, and practice both the writing and revision procedures crucial to the writing process. In addition, by joining these groups, instructors get access to the entire regional and national network of the NWP. On occasion, this provides information about an approach that has been developed some distance away. For example, one of the instructors we interviewed used a process developed at the University of California called Improving Students' Analytical Writing (ISAW), which prepares University of California students for the writing exams they must take. ISAW is equally useful for individuals preparing high school and community college transfer students. The idea is that instructors who have been through these workshops and use NWP approaches will, in turn, become mentors in subsequent workshops, replenishing the supply of NWP instructors. Most of the community college instructors we interviewed have continued to work with the NWP in some way—for example, by exchanging lessons and ideas with other NWP participants at both secondary and postsecondary levels, creating a community of practice and support that doesn't ordinarily exist in the community college.

As wonderful as the NWP workshops seem as professional development and as ways of modeling the NWP's writing philosophy, they are focused on developing individual instructors, not departments or groups of instructors. Several instructors we interviewed were isolated practitioners in their own colleges; one had tried to give workshops on RA during the college's professional development days, but "the group somehow didn't survive—it just petered out." At another college, several writing instructors had attended NWP workshops, and they formed a small support group for one another. But while the NWP preaches a social and collective approach to writing, its basic support group is the regional network of writing instructors, not a college- or school-based network. In the absence of a more concerted institutionalized effort—like a departmental initiative, or the creation of FIGs around the writing process—NWP instructors seem like idiosyncratic innovators, following different elements of a well-developed program but essentially isolated from their peers who continue to follow the more familiar remedial approaches to writing instruction.

Like Reading Apprenticeship, then, the approach of the NWP is a promising way to break the hold of remedial approaches. But, to make real inroads into community colleges—as opposed to reaching only a handful of students—a considerably stronger institutional process of support is probably necessary, one at the college level in addition to those at the regional or national levels.

Faculty Inquiry Groups and Faculty Inquiry Networks

Within many colleges, Faculty Inquiry Networks (FIGs) have developed, where faculty meet regularly around issues of common interest. Quite often, FIGs are spearheaded by one or two relatively senior faculty members, who drum up participation among other faculty. The possibilities for FIGs seem endless. Some have concentrated on collecting data to diagnose problems; along the same lines, some have initiated research on specific classroom issues, in a replication of the teacher research that has been practiced in K-12 education for many years. Others have examined students and barriers to their progress; in some cases, this has broadened the understanding of the extreme heterogeneity of students in basic skills classes. FIGs can also provide support for faculty engaged in innovations like Reading Apprenticeship or the writing process. Specialized FIGs have also emerged, liked the Freshman Interest Groups that have formed in some colleges around the "freshman experience"; indeed, one of the enduring benefits of these FIGs has been to initiate freshman-year experience programs, including Student Success courses. And in California, FIGs have spawned a Faculty Inquiry Network (FIN), which has joined FIGs on different campuses into a broader network, helping spread ideas about innovation from one campus to another.[16]

It's difficult to understand precisely what FIGs can and do accomplish, however, since they have varied so much both in the extent of faculty participation and in the activities they pursue. However, one "natural experiment" about the activities and longevity of FIGs is readily accessible. From 2008 to 2010, the Carnegie Foundation for the Advancement of Teaching supported a network of 11 colleges dedicated to creating FIGs in order to address basic skills issues. The project, Strengthening Pre-collegiate Education in Community Colleges (SPECC), served as a laboratory and locus of inquiry for faculty trying to understand and improve student underachievement. To focus on what the most organized and best-funded FIGs accomplish, we interviewed the heads of these FIGs about their continuing activities after the end of the Carnegie grant.[17] We were able to interview 7 of the 11 directors; the others had retired or moved away from the area.

All of the SPECC projects were able to build on previous reforms in the same pattern we saw in departmental innovation, where extensive changes have come about through a series of external and internal initiatives. However, when SPECC funding ended, the problem of transitioning to another funding source arose. Some colleges were able to obtain Basic Skills Initiative funding to continue, but most were not; in those latter cases, the perpetuation of FIGs depended on the ability of their leaders to continue rallying the faculty without stipends for release time or small grants for faculty projects. These small-scale initiatives essentially ended when external Carnegie funding ended; as one faculty leader acknowledged when asked about the funded faculty projects, "It's been quite a while—I don't remember half the projects." Thus, it became clear that many small projects, memorable only to the faculty who had led them, had failed to catch on with other faculty members. (I will return to the weakness of this approach—small grants for individual projects, also called "programmitis"—in chapter 9.) The remaining FIGs seem to fall into two groups: one group examined patterns of teaching and learning, while another continued with inquiry into the nature of students. But while they provided forums for discussion, served as antidotes to the isolation of faculty,[18] and maintained faculty awareness of the basic skills problems, they didn't seem to accomplish anything beyond what had been done under the SPECC grant.

One of the consistent problems mentioned by the heads of SPECC initiatives was the lack of administrative support. Administrators weren't hostile to such faculty groupings, and as long as they found outside funding (e.g., from SPECC), administrators were happy to have faculty meeting with one another—the typical description was that administrators were "hands-off." But this kind of "hands-off" approach generated some hostility among faculty leaders. One took a more historical perspective: "There is very little in terms of the academic program that is initiated above the dean level"; another said pointedly, "They're relatively poorly informed about what we're doing," and another said simply, "I'm really disappointed in them." One faculty leader, talking particularly about efforts to get part-time faculty involved in FIGs and requiring stipends of some kind, declared, "I don't think they [administrators] think it's important. I think that they have taken us [adjuncts] for granted, and they take for granted the fact that we will do it for free." She went on to say that recognition by the administration was almost more important than compensation for participation, and that the lack of recognition is a sure-fire way to demonstrate the lack of any investment in innovation.

One pair of SPECC leaders, widely recognized as among the most innovative instructors in the California colleges, developed a sophisticated understanding of what does and does not change when administrators are so "hands-off." They insisted that they can "move the needle"—improve rates of success—in individual courses through instructional improvement, which can be developed through FIGs or through departmental initiatives. But they cannot "move the needle" on larger measures of success; for example, completion of a developmental sequence, movement into college-level courses, and eventual graduation or transfer. This would require so many more practices to change: "You need acceleration, accurate data ... and the administration needs a strategy, they need to ask why there isn't progress and then come up with a variety of solutions." In other words, "moving the needle" on the largest measures of success requires changes beyond the individual classroom, and these need to be coordinated; first by a vision, and then by a "strategy" and a "variety of solutions" that can only come from administrators, or by administrators in concert with senior faculty in the pattern of "innovation from the middle." Another FIG leader admitted the same thing, in a less complex construction:

> We often assume that faculty development impacts faculty practices and in turn impacts student results and experiences and increases outcomes—but

it's hard to make that connection. It's difficult to point at faculty development as the cause for student success.

Indeed, several FIG leaders noted that there were no data whatsoever that
FIGs had made much difference to outcomes.

In the end, FIGs in California—both under the SPECC grant and, less
clearly, after SPECC ended—have been successful in promoting faculty discussion, in ending the isolation of faculty, and in increasing the amount of
talk about basic skills issues and problems. These are unabashedly good things
in any institution of higher education. They have also made some changes,
notably in supporting some individual initiatives and student success courses.
However, like the idiosyncratic innovations examined in the first section of this
chapter, these are comparatively easy innovations. They fit with the standard
practices of courses taught in a conventional schedule by existing faculty, and
they don't require changes in deeply rooted practices as do LCs, departmental
innovations, and pedagogical changes (including Reading Apprenticeship and
the writing process). For more substantive changes, those that have a chance
at "moving the needle" on overall success rates, something more than isolated
course innovation is required, and that cannot happen without administrative
support.

In many ways, the experience with FIGs confirms our hypothesis that substantial change requires "innovation from the middle," from senior faculty and
from middle-level administrators working in concert. FIGs have managed to
create the first of these, especially since they are typically led by active, senior-
level faculty who command a great deal of respect in their colleges. But they
lack the second ingredient because administrators have been so "hands-off,"
unwilling to learn about or invest in FIG efforts that they see as solely the
responsibility of faculty. It turns out that this is no way to innovate.

The Locus of Innovation

Many other innovations in the colleges we studied are not discussed in detail
in this chapter. For example, one promising approach has been to develop LCs
for specific groups of students with common interests. These include African
American students in programs like UMOJA and DERAJA; Latino students
in the Puente Project and the Digital Bridge Academy (now called the Academy for College Excellence); and older students, especially women returning
to education after childrearing, in the Program for Adult College Education
(PACE). Another innovation, now particularly popular, has been to accelerate
basic skills courses, or to compress work so that completing a series of courses
takes less time—based on the theory that the transitions among courses need to
be minimized because that's when students are most likely to leave a sequence.
We did not investigate acceleration since that practice typically does not change
instruction but merely speeds it up, and a faster pace of conventional instruction

based on remedial pedagogy is not, in the long run, a good solution to the problem of mediocre instruction.[19] There are many more individual innovations than we could possibly cover, including efforts to develop computer-based instructional formats.

The problem is not, therefore, a lack of bright ideas about how to reform basic skills instruction, nor a lack of energetic faculty willing to try new practices. The problem is that what we call the "locus of innovation," the constellation of forces generating innovation, is often weak or incomplete. Evidently, innovation from the bottom, by individual instructors developing their own modifications of standard practice, often looks quite effective—at least in the sense that students appear motivated, and that these innovations usually move away from remedial pedagogy—but it is also quite limited in the numbers of students it reaches. Perhaps as important, such innovation may change one course in a sequence of basic skills courses, but it does not have the scope and power to change the entire sequence itself; changing one or two courses in the end is unlikely to make much difference to overall success rates. As one innovative instructor noted, "If I pass students on to a poor instructor, then all my work is for nothing." Similarly, FIGs, as well as some freshman-year experience programs and student success courses, have managed to generate some idiosyncratic innovations, but these (again) reach relatively few students, rather than the large numbers of students pouring through developmental education.

Similarly, innovation from the top doesn't seem workable, and indeed we saw no examples of innovation that have been initiated largely by administrators, who are reluctant to infringe on academic freedom and instructor prerogatives. As we have seen in departmental innovations, acceptance by relatively large numbers of faculty is crucial for an innovation to become widespread. We certainly think that administrators could fund various programs that would support faculty initiatives. These might include funding for individual faculty initiatives, though this just reverts to innovation from the bottom with its small-scale initiatives reaching relatively few students.

If innovation from the bottom does not work well in several respects, and innovation from the top is largely missing, this leaves innovation from the middle as the most promising strategy. Among the most encouraging innovations are the faculty teaching and learning centers we found on certain campuses. These institutions provide a consistent and institutionalized space for discussions about teaching and learning, support for innovations under development, ways of recruiting faculty to participate in innovations, and methods of identifying and then proposing solutions for various instructional problems—including (but not limited to) those in developmental education. However, a faculty teaching and learning center needs the widespread participation of faculty, and the best example we have seen, the Faculty Success Center at Chaffey College (profiled in chapter 6), emerged from a larger initiative focused on multiple dimensions of student support, with the active participation of both faculty and administrators. So, even teaching and learning centers cannot be particularly effective without faculty leadership and active participation, as well as administrative support—a good example of innovation from the middle.

We have been most impressed by the departmental efforts (reviewed in the section on "Innovative Departments" above) that include the support from a number of faculty members, if not all the members, of a department, as well as the participation of middle-level administrators. These efforts change both instructional approaches (i.e., moving away from remedial pedagogy to department-established alternatives) and the way these changes are institutionalized through hiring practices, mentoring and professional development, and the creation of teaching materials. Such approaches also have the possibility to make sequences of courses consistent with one another, a form of alignment that happens only when faculty can get together to discuss course prerequisites and sequences of courses (I will discuss this in more detail in chapter 7).

But these effective endeavors can only occur under special conditions. The department must recognize that something is wrong with "business as usual," and it must have resources (either outside grants or internal funding) over the extended period of time necessary to develop alternative approaches. The department has to have some control over the hiring process so it can attract like-minded faculty, and faculty need to have the ability and (again) the resources to create mentoring programs for new and older faculty alike. Finally, the best-case scenario occurs when the department can also influence Student Services to provide support in forms consistent with its pedagogical innovations. All of these conditions require the department to have some influence over practices that formally lie outside the department. This is where the administrators come in, with the kind of vision as well as the executive power to make decisions coordinating the many working parts of a community college.

In summary, there is no lack of promising reform; the blizzard of innovation I mentioned at the beginning of this chapter is certainly real enough. Sorting through these innovations to determine which of them might affect a substantial number of students remains difficult, but an understanding of the locus of innovation allows us to review a large number of reforms and the processes that have put them in place—and predict which ones might result in sustained progress. With this understanding, we hope that other colleges will be able to participate in the necessarily long and difficult process of reforming from the middle.

5

STUDENT SUPPORT SERVICES

Their Possibilities and Limits

Community colleges provide an amazing variety of student support services that are designed to help students both in the cognitive dimensions of their work and in the noncognitive dimensions, including "knowing how to be college students." The theory of action behind such support services is usually quite transparent: Students who have trouble in their classes can receive supplemental help complementary to what happens in the classroom so that they can master the demands of coursework, move through a sequence of courses, and achieve whatever goals they set for themselves. If their goals are unclear, then in theory one particular support service, guidance and counseling, can help with this dimension of planning.

The provision of student services has a relatively long history in community colleges (Cohen & Brawer, 2008, ch. 7). Still, it is important to remember that student services cannot cover all students' needs. As noted in an earlier chapter, one of the colleges we studied polled students about what they most needed to be successful. The most common response was a mentor or buddy on campus, but the second most common was providing gas cards so that they could get to class, and the college could not figure out how to do that—just as offering child care, employment opportunities, or family counseling are all extremely difficult. Many of the challenges that make college-going a balancing act—particularly the demands of employment and family responsibilities—are nearly impossible for colleges to address. By the same logic, a lack of time makes it difficult for part-time students in particular to engage in both their regular classes and support services, and, as will be evident later in this chapter, they sometimes decide that they cannot afford the time for services that might help them in the long run.

Under the best circumstances, a rich menu of support services converts the triangle of instruction, presented in chapter 1, into a "quadrangle of instruction" with two centers of learning (i.e., the classroom and supplemental services), as shown in Figure 5.1. Now, students can learn from either or both of these two centers; they have two sets of instructors with whom to build relationships. But the requirements for consistency among all the elements of the instructional quadrangle become increasingly difficult. The consistency between regular and supplemental instructors, the differences in both the content taught and the pedagogy used in the two centers of instruction, and the overall role of student services relative to classroom instruction all pose potential problems. The fact that classroom instruction and student services are generally provided by different individuals, in different organizational units of the community college, with different perspectives on goals has become an issue all its own as the vision of integrating student services and instruction has become more prominent.

One of the special challenges of examining student services is that it's hard to know what happens in these encounters between student and service. Some of them, like counseling sessions, happen behind closed doors; some, like the information instructors provide about specific occupational fields, takes place in the privacy of faculty offices. While a great deal takes place in public

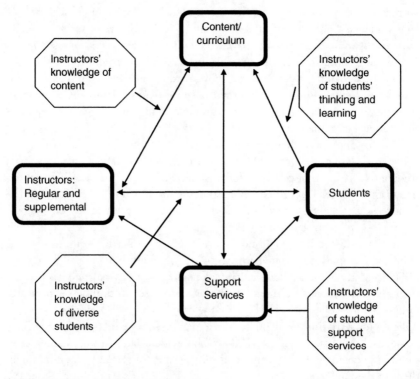

FIGURE 5.1 The Quadrangle of Instruction

settings, such as workshops and writing labs, for example, more of it takes place one-on-one, in interactions between tutors and students that are difficult to observe unobtrusively. And the sheer variety of student services (which will be described in the first section of this chapter) complicates issues enormously. We have therefore relied on a number of sources: Observations in labs and workshops; interviews with student services personnel and instructors; and limited interviews with students.

Given the many student services and the complexity of learning about what happens, we observed a variety of practices. On the one hand, a great deal of student services (and especially tutoring) continue to follow the remedial pedagogy of most developmental classrooms, with tutors concentrating on helping the students get the right answers without the students necessarily understanding why the answers are correct. On the other hand, we have also observed services that dovetail nicely with classroom instruction and move away from remedial pedagogy and expand students' ways of viewing a subject.

The fact that many student services concentrate on noncognitive dimensions of learning, or "how to be a college student," as well as cognitive dimensions, means that colleges vary substantially in *what* they offer and *how* they support students. At one end are colleges either with very few services, or just as bad, with a plethora of services that are difficult to understand and access, and are generally unrelated to classroom instruction. At the other end are colleges with coherent programs of services that are well-integrated with instruction; one of them, Chaffey College, is profiled in chapter 6. In trying to think about which of these services are effective, it is therefore necessary to understand the range of what is being offered, and what exactly these services might accomplish.

The Variety of Student Services

We found an enormous number of different student services. Each college has a slightly different mix of services, so it's difficult to know what people refer to when they talk about support services; similarly, statements applicable to one college's services are often irrelevant to another's, so broad generalizations are often difficult. Here's a basic summary of the services we uncovered in 14 colleges we visited, including Chaffey:

- **Centers for tutoring** are present in almost all colleges, most often for writing and math, slightly less often for reading and ESL, and only rarely for transfer-level subjects like science and social studies. The tutors are sometimes peer tutors, who do have certain advantages. One writing instructor noted, "I think students feel a little intimidated when the instructor is not quite as open, but if you have students [as tutors] who look no different than they do and understand what's being done, it can be very effective." Chaffey College distinguishes between Apprentice II tutors, who have associate's degrees, and Apprentice IV tutors, who have bachelor's degrees. Sometimes tutors are adjunct faculty. Tutoring sessions are usually one-on-one sessions with students who bring in homework, essays, and problems for help. One variant is online tutoring, with various computer-based programs available, largely for drill and repetition.

- **Tutor training** is an activity in its own right. Some colleges select tutors from students who have passed a course, and the amount of tutor training varies from informal on-the-job training to more formalized training sessions. Some colleges have used a good deal of their Basic Skills Initiative funds on tutor training.[1] The existence of tutor training is a tacit recognition that no one should be instructing students without some appropriate preparation—though, of course, this does not apply to conventional instructors, who typically have no special preparation in either instructional methods or in the pedagogies and strategies of student services.

- **Supplemental Instruction** (SI) is quite different from tutoring. It tends to focus on specific courses rather than particular disciplines, and, following the University of Missouri-Kansas City model, instructors engage students in discussions about the subjects of the course but do *not* either work with "products" (like papers or problem sets) or help students get the right answers. The focus instead is on collaboration, the use of tools (like notes, books, and study guides), and studying techniques.

- **Workshops** are typically taught to a group of students by either an adjunct or a regular faculty member. Usually, they are brief sessions (1–2 hours) on specific topics, including specific subskills: fractions and decimals; word problems in math; subject–verb agreement; incomplete and run-on sentences; or the logic of the scientific method. They may function as reinforcement of what is taught in conventional classes, or they are sometimes subjects that the instructor cannot find time for.

- **Student Success** courses go by many names, including Introduction to College, College Success, or sometimes Applied Psychology. They are intended to provide students with information about "how to be a college student" and where to find various services and departments on campus; they sometimes provide career-oriented guidance and counseling, as well as noncognitive capacities like time management (including balancing school, work, and family life). These courses vary enormously, so it's rarely clear what they include; there are some textbooks written for such courses, but the use of textbooks varies widely among colleges.

- **First-year experience or matriculation programs** are, like student success courses, intended to help transition students into college. They typically include assessments of basic skills, counseling about what levels of coursework might be appropriate, academic counseling about putting together a coherent program, and perhaps a student success course or two.

- **Summer bridge** programs take place in the summer before the first fall semester, and are conceptually like freshman-year experience programs moved up earlier in the student's career. Because we visited colleges during the school year, we did not observe any summer bridge programs.

- **Learning communities** sometimes embed basic skills courses into a roster of two or three (and sometimes more) courses; a typical learning community might include one or two developmental courses with a student success or a career counseling course. One variant is a learning community that includes basic skills and focuses on a particular group of students—UMOJA and DERAJA for African American students; the Puente Project for Latino students; and the Program for Adult College Education (PACE) for older adults (usually women) who return to college after years out of the workforce. Such focused learning communities allow different kinds of bonds among students to form, based on one kind of identity or another; they also allow for the exploration of racial, ethnic, or gender identity issues that might otherwise be ignored.
- **Guidance and counseling** are fundamental services offered by nearly every college (though there are indications that, under fiscal pressure, some colleges are abandoning guidance and counseling in favor of computer-based programs). In practice, most counseling is *academic* counseling, helping students determine the courses they need to meet their academic goals. *Personal* counseling may take place informally, though most colleges direct students with serious personal problems to outside help. *Financial* counseling is typically offered by financial aid offices. *Career-oriented* counseling may be given either by a counseling department, in a student success course, or—less formally, but often more effectively—by individual faculty members providing information about the education required in various career trajectories (sometimes as part of courses like Introduction to Engineering or Introduction to Human Services). In theory, all students have access to guidance and counseling, especially when they enter college, though the reality is quite different, as I will detail in the second section below ("The Use of Student Services by Instructors and Students").
- **Early Alert** is a process where students are informed if they do poorly in one or more courses, or if they fall behind in their program of studies. Usually, the point of an early alert system is to direct students to counselors, though how this happens varies widely from college to college. A variant in one of the colleges was a program for students whose GPAs fell below 2.0; the program involved a series of day-long seminars concerned with dimensions of student success. Similar programs exist in some colleges for all students who go on probation, usually as a result of low grades or missed classes.

Some individual colleges may have just two of these—usually guidance and counseling plus some kind of tutoring—while others have almost all of them. One particularly active college provided a rich set of short-term workshops for students; a teaching and learning center with tutors available 12 hours a day so that students had multiple avenues for help; guided learning (i.e., self-paced activities) with materials online for students who could not make it to the teaching and learning center; and conventional guidance and counseling. Chisholm College provided a variety of workshops for students, including a life management course, a human development course, a college and life management class, a math anxiety course, student success courses, and one-unit skills-oriented labs and workshops.

But sometimes the sheer variety of services makes them confusing, and they often appear to overlap. For example, Southern Metro College has guidance and counseling offered by a conventional department, other guidance and counseling provided for students handicapped by different conditions through Extended Opportunity Programs and Services (EOPS), and still other services provided to disabled students through Disabled Students Programs and Services (DSPS). At the same college, both a Learning Assistance Department and a Developmental Communications Department coexist; a Success Center is staffed by part-time faculty; learning communities (UMOJA and the Puente Project) offer some of their own support; a center for students on welfare provides more specific counseling; and a Center for Retention and Transfer serves a small group of transfer-oriented students. It is extremely difficult to figure out all the learning assistance programs available, how they differ, and for whom they are intended. When our observers noted that they were confused by the array of services, a faculty member admitted, "Well, they're [the students] confused, too ... and that's what the counselors are supposed to do [to tell students what resources they can get]. I don't know what the counselor is telling them."

Barkham College has tutoring centers for reading and math, but it also has another separate tutoring center where students are required to sign up for blocks of time, but whose distinctive function is unclear. At Mindano College, a student assessment team shares results with a counselor, who explains to the student what it means; then, the student may be referred to the financial aid office for specialized information, and may then be directed to EOPS. That means four different bureaucratic contacts before the student is even enrolled; if each of them takes a period of time to execute, then there may be a substantial delay between initial application and enrollment. The blizzard of services, and who is eligible for which services, becomes incredibly difficult to understand, certainly for outsiders trying to examine what is being offered, but also for students themselves.

Partly because of this plethora of student services, the major goals of many colleges at the moment are centralization, integration, and coordination. Several colleges have mechanisms in the works that will give students a kind of "passport" that is valid for all services and also provides information about what's available. However, as will become evident later in this chapter, the meanings of integration and coordination themselves vary, and in practice, cooperation and coordination are all too likely to be replaced by competition and fragmentation, both within the set of student services and between student services and instruction.

The Use of Student Services by Instructors and Students

Given the existence of student services in every college, one obvious question is how instructors and students use these services; that is, how strong the links are in Figure 5.1 between student services on the one hand, and instructors and students on the other. As with everything else, there is enormous variation in the use of these services.

In many colleges, instructors are responsible for alerting students to the availability of services. However, in observing large numbers of classes, we found that many instructors never mention the availability of student services. Others mention these services off-handedly, as a source of help if students are having trouble with problem sets or papers. As one staff member mentioned, at a college with a large number of poorly articulated services,

> I think a grand majority [of faculty] just want to teach their classes, they want to leave, they don't want to get involved in student services. I hear the kind of complaints are that faculty are not understanding, they're not sensitive, they're not encouraging. I've even heard that they've never mentioned support services on campus.

This is particularly likely to be true of adjunct faculty, who visit the campus only for their classes and are just as likely as students to be bewildered by the different student services available. On the other hand, many colleges "do have a small cohort of faculty who are highly engaged," who are "more aggressive and understanding." Some instructors repeatedly stress the services available, and at the extreme, some instructors create requirements to spend a certain amount of time in specific services, particularly tutoring or supplemental instruction. The rationale for requiring some participation in these services is, quite frankly, that many students will not participate in anything that is promoted as being good for their intellectual development; they will participate only if something is required, or if their grade is affected (for example, by giving extra credit).[2] But this, in turn, means that relying on students' initiative to get them into support services is unlikely to be effective. In colleges (like Chaffey) that have developed comprehensive systems of student services, course requirements for student services are part of a shift from the notion of a laissez-faire college (where students and instructors behave as they wish) to an institution with definite expectations and requirements of students as well as faculty—in this case, that students will seek out supplemental services as part of their normal work as successful students. Of course, there are other ways that students learn about student services. Sometimes student services staff show up in classes to announce their services. In some cases, tutors attend the classes for which they are tutoring, a practice that is particularly common in supplementary instruction. As one adjunct math instructor noted,

Our goal is to have a better connection between our math tutor and have him come into the classroom so people know him, because it does seem that if there's face-to-face contact, students are more likely to go seek him out.

Student services are also often located in one physical space (in centers for writing or math, or in centers for student success) or in proximity to the library so they are visible on campus. Student services staff try all sorts of ways to alert students: Some have tried using social networking programs, such as "finding students where they are" using Facebook, which "makes it cool," as well as the usual flyers and e-mail announcements. Students therefore have multiple ways of finding out about student services, even if their instructors are lackadaisical about informing them.

But in the end, the voluntary nature of student support creates one of the biggest problems—how students use these services. Particularly in colleges with a laissez-faire attitude, there's widespread agreement that it is impossible to make students use these services, and that the students most in need of these services never show up. As one faculty member in a college that has a particularly rich array of student services commented,

It's always the A students who go, because they're overachievers. If they [the faculty] don't send them, rarely will students go on their own because of the love of learning. And so, we've been really pushing the idea of giving them extra credit, or 10 points a workshop—it's homework, it's part of your grade.

Another noted,

When I used to spend time in there [the tutoring center], the only ones I'd see would be my high-level students, the ones that didn't need it. Low-level students don't take advantage of that stuff ... I think we have fantastic student support, if only students would take advantage of it. It's getting them there to do it [that] is the problem.

But even in a college that has moved to what it calls "intrusive" counseling—where instructors and peer mentors call students to try to get them to come in for counseling and services—a student services staff member reported, "We still know that the motivated students are the ones who come in to SI [supplemental instruction]. The basic skills students, what we call the developmental students, they are not historically the people who seek tutoring."

One of the problems is that attending student services has a certain stigma attached to it. As one instructor noted:

I have a lot of students coming from high school, and they're like, "Free at last!" They don't want to be in anything that seems like special ed, and so I try to make sure they know it's cool here [in the lab], and what amazing services we offer—I want them to know it's so different from special ed. And that's been very hard.

In addition, instructors are fully aware that many students have competing demands for their time. As one adjunct faculty member stated,

The feedback I get, like just this past week, is "Why are you not taking advantage of this free tutorial help with your English paper before it comes to me?" And it's "I have just so much time to get through school, and I don't have any more time. And as long as I can pass, that's all I want." ... And so, even though we have these supportive systems set up around campus, I haven't figured out how we get students to use them.

The result is that a good deal of attendance at student services is crisis- or problem oriented. As one vice-president for instruction noted,

There is not enough utilization of the services. It is only when a problem arises that people begin to take advantage of the services. And it is in part because people are allocating time for the rest of their life—their jobs, other obligations—so they don't really fit in the time necessary for that additional instructional help.

Even an instructor who gave extra credit for students attending a series of Skills for Success workshops complained that "the best we can do is inform them and make them aware of everything and encourage them to go. We can't make them go." This is not precisely right—course requirements (and not just extra credit) *can* "make them go" since students are highly sensitive to what is required to earn grades and pass courses. But in a laissez-faire college reluctant to impose additional requirements on students, the result is that high achievers make use of student services, the students most in need do not, and the concept of student services as a backstop for students who need support breaks down.

We suspect, though we cannot prove it, that one potentially dangerous aspect of student support services affects the students who do show up. Conventionally, with two crucial exceptions in the colleges we visited student services are viewed as programs for basic skills students, or students with deficiencies, "special needs," or problems in completing problem sets and papers. Visits to tutoring centers, the services of early alert programs, student success courses for "students who don't know how to be college students," and short problem-focused workshops all exemplify a deficiency orientation toward students. But this runs contrary to the common convention that such deficiency orientations will stigmatize students, causing them to avoid taking advantage of student support.

An elegant and powerful statement of this problem comes from Claude Steele (2010), who has stressed that there are stereotypes of every kind lurking in our social institutions—stereotypes that racial minorities are not academically able, that women fare poorly in math and science, that White males may be guilty of discriminatory thinking. A vast range of stereotypes exist as part of our social rankings of individuals. Steele and his colleagues have found that when a stereotype is triggered—when individuals or students are reminded of a negative stereotype—their performance is often much worse than in situations that are viewed as neutral with respect to the stereotype. For students in developmental courses, the potentially threatening stereotype is that they are not "smart" since they have flunked an assessment test of basic skills—they are not able students by definition. The language of instructors that "they don't know how to be college students" is a clear and damaging stereotype, and the association with high school special ed noted above is similarly stigmatizing. So, *unless* an institution takes pains not to trigger these stereotypes, they threaten to emerge and undermine the performance of developmental students.

The only good solution to the problem of stereotype threat, then, is to avoid invoking this stereotype—as Chaffey College does when it provides all services to all students (instead of just a subset of "weak" students); the college insists that seeking support "is what all successful students do," not something required only of basic skills students. As the dean of instructional support services stated,

> We place a very high premium on "languaging" our changes because they often influence the culture. That is why we deliberately named our first phase of change our "transformation," and we abandoned "basic skills" as a term for our students.... We also are deliberate about naming EVERYTHING!

Similarly, another college with a wide roster of support services made sure to include all students in them. It moved away from the language of "basic skills" or "remediation" to "foundation" courses in order to stress the commonality of these capacities among all students and subsequent coursework. The conception of stereotype threat, together with the substantial empirical work behind it, provides another way of understanding the poor participation of many students in support services—they simply avoid participating in those services that make them feel inadequate.

The result of all these factors is that only a small percentage of students in basic skills courses show up in student services. One college that surveyed students found that only 10% of students in the two lowest-level English courses attended tutoring. A good guess might be that less than a quarter of students in basic skills use student services, except at colleges like Chaffey and Mindano that have made serious efforts to destigmatize student services and make them more broadly available. Chaffey College determined that the changes they made increased participation rates among developmental students from 28.5% before their "transformation" to 55.9% over a decade.

In addition to tutoring, early alert is another good example of how instructors' and students' attitudes can affect the use of services. In one campus with an early alert system, some faculty like it and make use of it, but some don't: "They're adults; I'm not babysitting. That's usually part of the problem, is that they haven't learned how to do things on their own, and to really go after things." In addition, early alert in that college required faculty to call students, and "teachers feel overburdened, especially adjuncts," who, after all, teach most of the basic skills courses. Also, "Some students don't like it because they feel they're being checked-up on," which is perfectly true. There's a prescriptive element to any early alert system that is inconsistent with giving students responsibility for their own coursework. Finally, "It takes a lot of effort to get students to come into an office"; in other words, the counseling end of the early alert system worked poorly. But if part of "knowing how to be a college student" is knowing when to seek help, then part of *teaching* students how to be college students is pointing out to them when they need and should seek help, which is what early alert systems can do. In this particular college—with instructor indifference, student hostility, and a system that did not provide timely information—the early alert system seemed particularly ineffective.

Overall, when laissez-faire faculty face resistant students, student services are quite unsuccessful. If only a small proportion of basic skills students use support services, particularly compared to the A students and "overachievers," then paradoxically, student services may work to *widen* the gaps among students, not narrow them.[3] At the other end of the spectrum, Chaffey College—with a much more coercive system that relies on course requirements to get students into such services, with a uniform ethos that "this is what good students do," and with a highly visible system of four Student Success Centers where most student services are located—calculates that a majority of all students use student services at some point during a semester.[4] So, it is certainly possible to develop a system of services that are well-utilized, but it requires institutional commitment to linking instruction with services, and to making services more than a voluntary and peripheral part of an education.

The Instructional Approaches of Student Services

All of the student services I described in the first section of this chapter are *instructional* services, in which an instructor of some kind—a tutor, a mentor, a guidance counselor or apprentice counselor, or sometimes just a student services staff member—provides some kind of teaching to students. This instruction could be about either the cognitive dimensions of their schoolwork or, especially in student success courses, about the noncognitive dimensions. This, in turn, means that all student services have a pedagogical method, or a way in which they deliver the content. Just as we investigated the pedagogy of developmental courses and discovered the dominance of "remedial pedagogy" (summarized in chapter 3), we also attempted to determine the pedagogy of various student services.

In our observations within tutoring centers, where tutors (including peer tutors) work one-on-one with students who bring them problems, most tutoring follows the pattern of "remedial pedagogy," with an emphasis on getting the right answers or writing formally correct sentences or paragraphs. Typically, a student will present a question about a problem set or writing assignment, and the tutor will show the way to the right answer, repeating the procedures used in class but not elaborating them or explaining why they work—as instructors by and large fail to do as well. Alternatively, tutors will explain the problem using a different procedure or a different writing approach, which often confuses the student who is looking for the one right answer. This is why some tutors (in math in particular) like to attend the classes for which they tutor so they know how the instructor is teaching it and can use similar procedures in their tutorials. In math tutoring, the dominant approach involves explaining to students why their answers are wrong, and then working out the right answers; in tutoring for writing, students typically bring in writing samples and watch while tutors correct errors of grammar and usage, producing error-free sentences and paragraphs. There should be nothing particularly surprising about the tendency toward remedial pedagogy; tutors are typically students who have been through these courses before, and if the instructor depends on remedial pedagogy, the tutors will, too. In addition, peer tutors in particular, despite their advantages in being about the same age and experience as students, are only one or two steps ahead of the students they are tutoring. They are usually freshmen or sophomores, they have not taken much advanced coursework, and they have not been exposed to anything involving techniques of instruction *unless* the college provides a tutor training program, which is the exception. Therefore, remedial pedagogy in the classroom is likely to be replicated in tutoring.

The division between didactic "remedial pedagogy" and a more constructivist or student-centered pedagogy is most evident in comparing tutoring with supplemental instruction. As developed in the Kansas model from the University of Missouri-Kansas City's Center for Academic Development, the SI leader, who attends all classes, specifically rejects providing answers, and instead leads student discussions about different aspects of a course, providing hints when students are stuck. Materials also clarify that SI is not conventional tutoring, a homework question-and-answer session, another lecture, or a place students go when they miss class; it has its own pedagogy and purpose. Indeed, one SI tutor related a difficult relationship with a faculty member: "I had one faculty member where the professor said, 'Oh, just go to the tutor. They'll relecture you.'" In these cases, SI tutors have to discuss the purpose of SI with instructors, since it is certainly not to "relecture" the material.

Two Chaffey students, reflecting on their experiences as both tutors and SI leaders, expressed a similar distinction: "The tutor [SI leader] does not ever lecture or simply impart knowledge to the students. We guide students using the Socratic method to extract preexisting knowledge from the students and use it as the foundation for new ideas." The difference between the one-on-one tutoring and the SI approach is that "students get results from one another [in SI] that a tutor might have to explicate in a tutoring session." So, unlike the simple provision of correct answers that we have seen in a great deal of peer tutoring, the emphasis within SI is on leading students to discover answers for themselves and with peers—a practice that is both student-centered and constructivist.

Other forms of student services can have varying pedagogies. Sometimes the short workshops covering various subskills—punctuation, run-on sentences, decimals and fractions—are structured so that they encourage remedial pedagogy, but this depends on the instructor. Student success courses vary considerably: Some appear to be highly didactic and concerned with information transfer, including information about the services available at the college; others are efforts to get students to define their own educational goals and programs, and are therefore much more student-focused. As is true for conventional classrooms, there is generally no way to understand the pedagogy of student services without observing the instructional relationships, and sometimes this is impossible, as in confidential guidance and counseling sessions. But the point is first and foremost that every type of student service has a pedagogy, a conclusion that is usually poorly understood and articulated. Furthermore, we fear that in the absence of strong pressures to the contrary (e.g., the philosophy of supplemental instruction; student success and career success courses aimed at getting students to develop their own plans, or writing centers that forego the conventional grammar-sentence-paragraph-essay approach to writing) many student services are likely to revert to remedial pedagogy and information transfer.

One of the most interesting but discouraging conflicts occurs when the pedagogy of student services differs from that of classroom instruction. In several colleges, regular classroom instructors complained that tutoring services followed the approach of finding the right answer, rather than teaching students how to think conceptually. At Chaffey College, the revision of their basic skills program was instigated in part because of a tutoring division mired in a "skills" approach to teaching writing just as the English department was moving toward the writing process approach. At Chisholm College, both reading instructors and the English department had problems with the Learning Center and its "territoriality." But it turned out that the real difference was one of culture and pedagogy. In the English department,

> We're sort of bohemian, liberal, read a lot—and then if the person who's running the Writing Center doesn't seem to be in that cultural space, if it has a schoolmarmish feeling, then right off you're kind of put off.

> There's sort of a cultural tension—the English discipline doesn't see a lot
> of rigor at work.... The Writing Center is very prescriptive, very power-
> paragraph, 5-paragraph model.

Such divisions may lead to departments refusing to refer students to student
services, so that the relationship becomes adversarial rather than complementary. Reinforcing this, learning center faculty are often viewed as not equal in
status to the classroom faculty. With such marginal status, it is often difficult for
them to be "trusted" with the instruction of students outside of the classroom,
or seen as legitimate partners in the learning endeavor. In other cases, students
fail to get the support that they need from learning centers. At Southern Metro
College, an instructor noted that

> Our students struggle with English, and they feel they're not getting the
> support from the LRC, the Learning Resource Center. I think we rely
> too much on these scantrons—these multiple choice tests. But when we
> actually give students critical writing assignments, they really struggle.
> So, we get a lot of students who come back and say, "You know, I need
> more support in this area."

In other cases, differences in pedagogy impede the movement toward centralization. Chisholm College was trying to run all student services through a
learning center so that there would be some semblance of consistency—"You
want to give the Learning Center its due so you don't have people all over the
place." Support from a TRIO program wasn't very helpful: "It took us years
to get them not to do tutoring, which was actually to give them [students] the
answers, and to have the tutors be trained through the Learning Center." This
was a story of barriers to centralization and coordination; but it reinforces the
sense that, in many cases, tutoring uses remedial pedagogy to provide students
help with finding the correct answers, instead of leading them to understand
the material in any deeper way.

In some cases, perhaps not surprisingly, these divisions emerge among different student services. At Sable Mountain College, the Writing Center talks
about ideas about language while the Reading Lab is concerned wholly with
skills and drills on subskills, the five-paragraph essay, and other mechanical
approaches to reading. For struggling students, the differences in approaches to
reading and writing may be confusing, even if observers can understand them
as two poles of instructional approaches.

A second dimension of pedagogy involves the distinction between laissez-
faire approaches and what some instructors describe as "intrusive" student services. For tutoring, this manifests itself as the difference between tutors who
wait for students to come to them with their problems—in which case the
student sets the agenda for the instructional encounter—and instructors who
direct or require students to avail themselves of specific services (for example,

by establishing a course requirement). In the latter case the instructor sets the agenda. If students were sophisticated about their own needs and motivated to use the full range of services, as the "overachievers" are, then the laissez-faire approach would appear to be student-centered. But in circumstances where students are poorly informed about services available, have no incentives to do anything coursework-related that is not required, and fail to understand the benefits of using student services—that is, in cases where basic skills students "don't understand how to be college students"—then the more coercive approach is, in fact, more in the interests of the student.

In addition to voluntary versus required tutoring and supplemental instruction, the "intrusive" label was applied in one college to their early alert system: "We do this intrusively—we call them on the phone, and the peer mentors call them—it's much more effective." Guidance and counseling can also be labeled "intrusive" or "invasive" or "assertive," or "appreciative." As one adjunct math instructor described her ideal setting for basic math students,

> We should put this into a big learning community effort, and where the learning communities are is integrated curriculum, assertive or invasive counseling, intrusive…. It's a horrible name, but a counselor that's there in the classroom—"Let's see what you got on this test. Oh, you didn't do very well. What's going on with you?"—that kind of counseling. It's something we try to do as instructors, but it's impossible when we have 50 students or more.

Or, as another counselor described it, intrusive counseling is "trying to answer the questions students would ask if students knew what to ask,"[5] acknowledging that what one might call laissez-faire counseling, where students come with their own questions, may not be as effective as "intrusive" counseling. To be sure, the whole idea of "intrusive" student services is controversial: If faculty believe that "they're adults—I'm not babysitting," then "intrusive" services seem inappropriate. But if most basic skills students "are not ready to be college students," as the majority of faculty feel, then more intrusive services are appropriate as part of teaching them how college students ought to behave, including seeking out support services when they need them.

Third, the pedagogy of student services is very much a function of the personnel who deliver these services, and the kinds of training they have received. Not surprisingly, the training programs we observed for tutors vary substantially. At one extreme, peer tutors for a particular course are often recruited from the group of students who have passed that course, and they are given little more than on-the-job training. At the other extreme, tutors are required to have higher level preparation in the subject they will be tutoring, as in one college that required all math tutors to have passed calculus—although this guarantees subject matter mastery, not mastery of pedagogical alternatives. Another problem is that content mastery does not guarantee that tutors will be able to understand the dilemmas of developmental students; as one tutoring specialist said, "If you hired someone who assessed at college level reading, they can't necessarily identify with the struggling student … those really low-level students, they need that—they need somebody who understands what it's like." Another tutor commented that "it's the same for writing—I have students who can write a stellar paper, and then a [developmental] student comes in and there's no connectivity between the two—some can talk about Shakespeare, but can you talk with a [developmental] student about a thesis statement or a paragraph?" In this case, the tutoring specialists claimed that "we address it in the initial training—we make them aware that their thinking speed is not the students' thinking speed," with role-playing and other techniques to get them to see the position of developmental students. But in the absence of the appropriate training, advanced students do not necessarily make appropriate peer tutors.

In still other cases—and the training for SI tutors is a clear case in point—the training includes more extensive preparation in alternative forms of instruction, such as discussions, the "Socratic method" of leading students to their own conclusions through questions, and the different perspectives students might come to class with. At Mindano College, tutors must take a two-unit online class, with "lots of worthy topics—it provides the tutor with a venue for thinking about how they are going to tutor, rather than just going in and tutoring." Such courses are typically designed to present a variety of approaches to tutoring so that helping students to find the right answers is not the only option.

Instructors for student success courses often come from the counseling faculty, and they are generally trained for personal or crisis counseling, not in academic teaching methods. Similarly, counselors often follow an approach to career counseling which can be summarized as "test 'em and tell 'em"—giving students interest inventories, then identifying the two or three occupations that seem to suit their interests and personalities, and finally informing them of the requirements for these occupations. So, aside from special cases like SI tutoring and certain forms of tutor training, there's not much deliberation about what kinds of training student services personnel should have.

Ideally (as in Figure 5.1), classroom instruction and student services should have a two-way relationship: Instructors partly determine what happens in various services, and even conduct some of the workshops and tutoring sessions (as is the case at Chaffey). In turn, student services personnel provide information back to instructors about what has happened there—what students' strengths and weaknesses are. But in practice, both of these links are likely to be weak *unless* a college has taken steps to maintain a two-way set of communications; otherwise, each may operate in isolation from the other. Even in Mindano College, which has been trying to centralize its student services, the students who are leading those [basic skills] workshops are supposed to contact the instructor once a week. Supposed to—I have to get on them a lot to do that. The problem is also so much harder in Math 13 and the Math 46 level because we have multiple sections of these courses, and most of these courses are taught by part-time instructors, and you don't even have a way to communicate with part-time instructors.

In such cases, neither tutors nor students themselves, particularly basic skills and evening students, have a way to contact instructors. In all too many cases, therefore, the potential two-way connection between classroom instruction and student services becomes weakened. The result is two independent sources of instruction to students who themselves have to make sense of the overlapping and conflicting information.

Finally, we noted that many student supports, including writing and math labs, use various forms of computer-assisted instruction. (A research project all its own would be to investigate how tutoring centers use technology.) Many of them use computer-based programs for drill and practice, returning to the use of remedial pedagogy that we have found so prevalent with computer-based programs in the classroom. In some cases, however, there is an explicit rationale that routine drill can take place on self-paced computer programs, freeing up the time of tutoring specialists for more difficult and nonroutine problems. As a division of labor between computer-based and in-person tutoring, this makes a certain amount of sense. But in Mindano College, this ended up working poorly for two very different reasons. One was that the reading lab, with its use of computer-based vocabulary drill, "doesn't sync up" because there were five instructors sending students to one lab, and "they would all have to be on the same page for us [instructors] to sync up with them." In addition, they found that the relatively independent work on computer-based programs did not achieve what they wanted:

> We're finding that a lot of students who are in that special group, that they need more interaction. Independent study doesn't work for them because these are people who don't have the skills to begin to know how to organize their time and how to find an idea…. Because they are not strong readers, to give them instructions in writing is not hitting what I felt was the importance of the whole situation [that they were supposed to analyze a reading passage].

This was a long argument that at least for the most basic students, the impersonality of a computer-based program did not work, and the programs could not diagnose what problems students were having. In the end, the presumed efficiency of drill-based computer programs was undermined. A more comprehensive examination of the uses of technology in student services, as well as in the classroom, is warranted, but our examples suggest that the impersonality and drill orientation of most computer-based programs undermine their effectiveness for many developmental students—except possibly for students needing brush-up or those intensely embarrassed by the stigma of attending remedial classes.

And so it appears that a series of factors contribute to a continuation of remedial pedagogy: a lack of training that would provide alternative approaches; direction by faculty who themselves practice remedial pedagogy in their own classrooms; and the interests of students themselves, who are often fixated on getting the right answers rather than engaging in more extensive learning. The short and informal nature of most contact in student services, where the time necessary to establish an enduring personal relationship is lacking, and the use of computer-based programs for continued drill and practice are also important factors. Of course, none of these factors is necessary, and some colleges—Chaffey is (again) the conspicuous example—have been trying to develop student services with a very different model, with longer contact between tutors and students and a greater use of supplementary instruction and other approaches that stress the student's active role. But unless colleges are mindful of the pedagogy of student services, they are all too likely to revert to remedial approaches.

Dimensions of Competition between Instruction and Student Services

The underlying theory of action of student services is that they are complements to classroom instruction—places where students can come for supplementary help with academic (and nonacademic) tasks. But all too often, we found, student services are in competition with regular instruction, and the possibilities for congruence and complementarity are instead replaced by division and discord. We therefore sought out reasons why this should be so common.

In several ways, student services and classroom instruction compete for the time of students. In one college, an adjunct faculty member complained of a difference between adjunct and full-time faculty: The adjunct faculty would refer students to tutoring and workshops, since they had no office hours in which to help students. However, the full-time faculty would not because "they don't want others to interfere, and they think they can do a better job of explaining the material than tutors can." An individual hired as a basic skills counselor began her work by visiting classes to announce her services, "But it became very obvious that every second they had with those students was precious, and my coming into the classroom meant that was taking away some of that time." This sense of competition, and of instruction being superior to support services, is particularly true where there are pedagogical differences between classroom instruction and tutoring or workshops; in such cases, instructors are likely not to refer students to support services at all.

Of course, there are also the usual divisions around money and territory: Any addition to the student services budget is perceived to come from the instructional budget and vice versa; and particularly in a period of tight budgets different divisions of a college are in competition with one another for resources. One faculty member said about a Learning Center, "I think it's just, 'This is my territory. We don't want faculty in here.'" Evidently, one of the strongest mechanisms for integrating instruction and student services—the presence of tutors in classes, and of faculty in tutoring centers—was thwarted by territoriality. Other problems seem to reflect a lack of communication between student services and instruction: One student services staffer complained that "they [instructors] don't know what we do," with the implicit point that they don't care enough to find out. When student services are marginalized—as they are for various structural reasons that I examine in this chapter, they may again find themselves in competition for institutional attention and status, as well as funding and student time.

Competition may be exacerbated by the way college administrations have used student services in the past few years. In many colleges we visited, a substantial amount of Basic Skills Initiative funds were spent on student services, including training for tutors, while as usual much less was spent to improve instructional practice.[6] Our perception of this pattern is that support services are being used as a substitute for improvements in instruction, which are difficult to achieve in any event and may involve "intrusive" policies like required professional development for faculty. On the contrary, adding student support involves simply spending additional funds on one or another of the many services listed in the first section of this chapter. This is consistent with the pattern of "programmitis"—adding little programs as a form of innovation, rather than reshaping important institutional practices (as, for example, Chaffey College did in creating four Student Success Centers to house most student services). If student services were instead seen as complementary to classroom instruction, then one would expect to see investment in both student services and instructional improvement, leading to more efforts to cultivate cooperation between student services and classroom practices. But the focus on student services from new funds suggests that they are being used as an easier substitute for the more difficult task of reforming instruction.

In addition, there are perceived differences in philosophy that create barriers between student services and regular instruction, as well as the differences in pedagogy. Instructors sometimes perceive student service personnel as defending the rights of students no matter what the situation is, and trying to pass them through to completion with less attention to what they have learned. Counselors also see themselves as advocates for students, not facilitators of learning, but faculty see themselves as the protectors of standards—in the long-term interests of the students. As one math faculty member complained,

The counselors got a completely different goal than we do. Counselors want the students to get in, get a C, and get gone. We want a student to get in and thrive, go through a program, and actually do mathematics and not just slide out with a C. Because if they get a C in one course, they probably won't pass the next.

In another college, student services personnel complained about a lack of faculty support in general, but particularly from an "elitist" English department that set standards too high. On their part, the members of the department justified their actions, again, as being in the interests of students in the long run:

If my [English] 99 is more challenging than other instructors' 99s, it is really to prepare them for 101, and we are very proud of the rigor of our courses because we know that the students who go on to university environments know that they have a solid foundation.

But again, more than the complicated question of "rigor" was at stake because of a difference about what tutors were supposed to accomplish. As another instructor said,

The way that the tutors are trained, they're really trained to be more of a sounding board for students—to ask questions of the students—rather than to provide what would to many minds seem like more direct assistance. The Learning Center seemingly wants to set up almost a private-like doctor–patient kind of relationship between the tutor and the student, with the instructor being this odd kind of satellite off to the side, which we [instructors] see as very odd because most of our understanding of tutorial assistance is to assist faculty with their students' responses to assignments. And so it seems to be a bit skewed, where the Learning Center sees itself ... as kind of leading the charge, then we're supposed to kind of adapt ourselves to its rules and approaches.

In other words, faculty saw tutoring as homework assistance, while the tutoring center was trying to establish a more student-centered approach to tutoring. The division was exacerbated because classroom instructors have little or no experience with the techniques involved in academic support. The result was rancor and charges of "elitism," rather than any sense of the two working as complements.

Similarly, in Parson College, there was both a tutoring center and a writing center, but the latter was poorly connected to the English department, so it was unclear how students would find the writing center: "Students would have to come on their own," commented one student services staff member. The tutoring center focused almost entirely on grammatical issues, with a skills bank of exercises and practices described by an English faculty member as "awful."

(Staff working there had to pass a grammar test before being hired.) Once again, differences in approach and pedagogy created distance among departments that might otherwise have worked together.

In Southern Metro College, there has been a long period of uncertainty about centralization and decentralization. There, a developmental communications department vies for students with a learning resources center. As a member of the developmental communications department reminisced,

> Before I got there, they were together. And so then, I joined the department, and when I joined, it was apart. Then, they joined and they split again, and they joined and split. There's been several splits depending on the president coming in, the flavor of the day, whether we should be together or not. And I think we work better together.

Despite opposing forces and widespread evidence of divisions between support services and conventional instruction, the buzzwords of the moment are *cooperation* and *integration* in contrast to decentralized "silos." But integration has several inconsistent meanings. One of them is providing students with complete information about services available, and then allowing students to find their way to the appropriate services; this, of course, will not work if "students don't how to be college students." A second meaning involves sharing personnel between student services and conventional instruction; for example, when adjunct faculty participate in tutoring and workshops in tutoring centers, or when tutors (especially supplementary instruction tutors) attend classes to be sure of consistency between instruction and services. A third conception has led to the development of one-stop centers centralizing all student services, so that students can find all services in one location; in some cases, the personnel working in such centers are cross-trained so that they can perform multiple roles. And a fourth conception is the one developed by Chaffey College, where workshops are provided by instructors, tutors work under the direction of instructors, supplemental instruction is tied to specific courses with tutors attending all classes, and the ethos of student services is that they are activities that all successful students undertake, not just basic skills students or those in academic trouble. So, it's important to be careful of claims about "integration" since the meaning of the word and the associated practices vary so much.

Consistency between regular instruction and student support services is surely a goal to move toward. Otherwise, the "quadrangle of instruction" depicted in Figure 5.1 turns into two independent triangles of instruction— one focused on conventional classroom instruction; the other emphasizing the roster of student support services. But cooperation and integration are difficult goals to achieve, and if they are to be accomplished, they require institutional direction rather than the laissez-faire policies of many colleges.

The Special Challenges of Guidance and Counseling

Conceptually, it might be possible to take each of the support services mentioned in the first section of this chapter and subject them to further analysis. In most cases, this would simply be redundant, and lead to the kinds of conclusions that I have drawn in previous sections of the chapter about student and instructor use and pedagogical differences. But guidance and counseling are different, both in their ambitions in serving students and in the kinds of roles they play within colleges—particularly the "gatekeeper" role in directing students to different courses of study. So, it's worth being more specific about guidance and counseling as one of the central support services.

Guidance and counseling play several roles in community colleges.[7] First and foremost, they are part of the matriculation process when new students come to the college for the first time and establish their educational plans and their programs of study for the next few years. Part of the initial contact is an assessment test, followed by advice on the sequence of developmental courses that a student should take if assessment scores are low. For students who fall behind in their coursework, or who flunk a certain number of courses, counselors may emerge again as part of an early alert process or probationary system. And of course, students may revisit their early choices of direction and major, and wind up seeing counselors several times before they decide on a major. So, counselors play important roles, not only in providing support for the cognitive dimensions of a college education, but in helping students plan for their educational and (sometimes) their occupational futures.

For basic skills students, who often arrive at college without educational plans, or with only the most amorphous ideas of what they need to do, this role of counseling is particularly important. As one counselor explained,

> If a student wants to make an ed plan, they can make an appointment with a counselor, and then they can do one. But otherwise, they're just planning for next semester's courses, which can be very detrimental to math or science majors because they have so many prerequisites to take and so many classes—a little shortsighted [not to have a plan].

Another counselor noted that the advice that counselors give is part of "being a college student": "Some students need help because navigating the educational system is not something they've had experience with." Certainly, the offerings in a typical community college are much more varied and complex than in high school, and the appropriate paths are even more opaque when the long series of developmental courses are considered.

But there are many limits to guidance and counseling. One obvious limit is that the resources in counseling are low, and probably dwindling. In one particular college, there were only six counselors for 14,000 students, and the number was being reduced to four because of budget cuts. In other colleges, the ratios were better, but not by much. One college was moving to online counseling because of the lack of resources; while this may seem like an appropriate efficiency measure, it also eliminates the personal contact that, most basic skills practitioners agree, is necessary to help students develop and complete their programs. Indeed, as one college was moving toward online counseling for fiscal reasons, another college in our sample was eliminating online offerings because it found them ineffective.

The result of shortages of counselors is that meetings with counselors are rushed, particularly at the beginning of the semester when matriculation takes place: "It's basically been an assembly-line process," said an instructor in Southern Metro College. Another noted that because of counselors' lack of time, "students will formulate life plans in 15 to 30 minutes, which is a joke, to me anyway."

A second problem is a variant of one I have already examined: The students most in need of counseling and guidance don't show up. In one institution, the counselors were quite uniform in asserting that "most students don't do a plan—only a few in special programs do." One of them went on to clarify that part of the problem is the pressure students feel to get on with coursework and credit accumulation, rather than taking a course in career planning, or other student success courses:

> People don't want guidance. People want to get on with it, even though we can show them all kinds of statistics…. What I'd like to tell them is that this is what all the smart kids knew about in high school—that you didn't know, that I didn't know. So, you can find it out on your own 2 years from now, or you can take a guidance class.

This is similar to the view at Chaffey that student support services are for all students, and that successful students know they should utilize such services.

A third issue is that there is a tremendous amount of negative talk about counselors from instructors, particularly with respect to their knowledge about basic skills courses. A common complaint is that they just don't know enough about the sequence of courses to help students find the right courses; as one developmental English instructor noted, "They [students] do not know enough [to place into the right class], and the counselors are useless as far as advising goes. The counselors don't know, and we try to teach them but [it doesn't work]." The result is that students find themselves in different courses partly by happenstance. In yet another college, the tension between instruction and student services was partly due to the fact that "the counselors will not change their way of doing things," and the small number of counselors could not handle the overwhelming numbers of students, so an online program was the "only alternative."

It's unclear what it means when instructional faculty complain that "counselors will not change their way of doing things," but one of the constant issues in counseling is the dominant use of the trait-and-factor approach to assessment and advice. This involves administering interest inventories and then providing information about the occupations and educational trajectories that seem to fit students' interests. But this approach to counseling, as distinct from "intrusive" counseling, that is, "asking the questions students should ask if they knew what to ask," is very often another form of information transfer, passing on information about various occupations before it is clear that this is the path that a student wants to follow. In the process, counselors implicitly assume that decisions about educational pathways and career trajectories are readily made once students have full information about the alternatives available. But decision making proves to be a much more complex process, involving uncertainties about what students prefer, complex calculations of probabilities and preferences over time, and (unavoidably, it seems) dimensions of nonrational decision making.[8] A semester-long course in career alternatives might enable students to grapple with these complexities, but a 15-minute appointment with a counselor surely will not.

Perhaps as a result, students by and large have negative perceptions of counselors. In our small sample of 22 students, a disproportionate number made negative comments about counselors. One called them "rude and rushed," no doubt referring to the problem that counselors are overloaded at the beginning of semesters. Several mentioned that they were given unhelpful or bad advice; one commented that a counselor had a "bad attitude," and was just there to get paid. In many cases, we know from both students and faculty that counselors advise students to take their general education requirements first, hoping that during these courses, students find something of interest. For the student whose counselor had a "bad attitude," the counselor gave him a sheet of paper with gen ed requirements, but this didn't provide him with any sense of what courses to take over the long run. Others complained about the amount of time it took to get appointments with counselors:

> I would have to, you know, wait in line, like, for an hour at Admissions to ask, like, one question that took, like, a minute … it's up to your mindset, like, how strongly you feel about college, like, how much time you're gonna waste to actually know things.

Others complained about being directed to a website, or about the lack of information counselors had about specific occupations:

> I wish they knew more about the different occupations, 'cuz it's sometimes, like, when I don't know some stuff about what I need to go for, and they don't know about it, it's like we're sitting there researching it together, which isn't really helpful. I wish they knew more than I did so that I could come in there, get the help, and just move on.

Of 15 students whose interviews mentioned counseling, three had positive comments about counselors, including two where counselors were assigned to a particular learning community, a common technique for getting counselors more familiar with programs. Six had negative comments, and six had not yet had any contact with counselors. These numbers are small, but they are consistent with the comments from instructors themselves.

There are, to be sure, ways of getting around the general weakness of guidance and counseling. One is to attend student success courses that are devoted to formulating educational plans and occupational objectives; these provide a substantial amount of time to develop knowledge about the alternatives available and to explore different dimensions of decision making. Furthermore, one study has found student success courses to increase degree completion and transfer in Florida (Zeidenberg, Jenkins, & Calcagno, 2008); another found positive effects in Virginia (Cho, 2010); and a third found positive effects of student success courses specifically in terms of improved guidance (Barr, 2011). Chaffey College has developed the position of apprentice counselor as a way around the lack of funding for counselors: students who are completing a bachelor's or master's degree in counseling, social work, psychology, or sociology are trained to perform counseling roles. In other settings, counselors are assigned to academic departments, or even to individual developmental courses, so they become more knowledgeable about the range of courses available and appropriate sequences. Another tactic is to assign counselors to learning communities, where they can get to know students better and learn more about the future options of individuals in the learning communities. Some colleges with extensive work-based learning have used on-the-job experiences to help students formulate what they want out of potential occupations and which ones might suit them.

At the positive extreme, Valencia Community College in Florida has developed a counseling program called Lifemap—"Life's a journey; you'll need a map." In this program, there are five stages in a student's college trajectory: The transition from high school; the introduction to college, for students just starting out; the period of progression toward a degree; the period of completing a degree and then planning either to transfer or to work; and a stage of lifelong learning after leaving college. A variety of student services and counseling are available for each of these stages, and the entire process is clearly developmental, matching a student's stage in college with services appropriate to that stage.[9]

Of course, instructors also provide counseling, especially in their own subject areas; one mentioned, "I wish that I got paid for all the counseling I do— I'd be a millionaire!" She went on to mention the variety of counseling she used with her students. (However, it should be noted that programs that *require* instructors to provide more counseling have often failed because of the variety of faculty and their perceptions about what their roles in counseling should be.) But without one or another of these innovations, a great deal of guidance involves counselors who don't have enough time with each student, who tend to provide little more than information, and who often lack information relevant to the specific trajectory that a student might want to follow.

Guidance and counseling are important for all students, not just those in basic skills classes. Students frequently complain that high school has not prepared them to think about the alternatives they face, and many students—the so-called experimenters—come to community college in order to find something they are interested in.[10] But guidance and counseling seem particularly important for students directed to developmental courses, partly since the long sequence of basic skills courses may appear to be a waste of time unless someone—a counselor, perhaps an instructor—clarifies why such courses are necessary. As one nursing student complained,

> Sometimes I, like, ask myself, Why am I here?Like, why do I need to be here [in basic skills courses]? I should be out, like, hands-on or something. I don't need to be sitting here wasting my time on these essays that have nothing to do with nursing.

So, if colleges do not develop services that can provide answers to students' questions about future options—the goal of both academic and career counseling—students are left to drift with basic questions about their futures unanswered.

The Structural Problems of Student Services

Student services suffer from some problems that affect regular instruction to a lesser degree. Prime among these is the issue of funding. In most states, the vast majority of funding for community colleges comes from funds generated on the basis of full-time enrollment, so instructors who teach extra sections generate enrollment that, in turn, pay for their costs. In contrast, student services personnel do not generate additional enrollment, and therefore state reimbursements and tuition. At the margin, institutions can be quite precise about the kinds of courses and the classroom enrollments that pay their own way, in the sense that additional revenues from the state plus tuition generate at least as much revenue as the additional costs required. But this means that services and programs, like support services, that do not enhance enrollment and revenue streams are vulnerable to being cut; as one instructor noted,[11] "You can justify anything that has return dollars in the other [revenue] column. But faculty development [or student support] is like planting seeds, and you do not necessarily have a measureable, observable harvest."

However, student services serve students who are already enrolled in a college; in terms of a revenue-based benefit-cost analysis based on enrollment-driven funding, they generate costs but not additional revenues. Only in the situation where funding is contingent upon completion *and* student services contribute to completion can student services be justified under this kind of benefit-cost calculation. So, the funding of student services is precarious, and these services are the first to be cut in times of fiscal stringency. Indeed, in the colleges we visited, we heard many stories of cuts to student services including guidance and counseling, evidence that support services are always under fiscal pressure. In other places, student services under different names have come and gone, increased in boom times and been cut back in recessions. But boom-and-bust funding is not a good way to make *sustained* reforms over time, as I emphasized in chapter 4, so the ability of student services that are funded in this way to make steady improvements in practice is eclipsed by funding realities.

A second structural element in student services stems from the large number of adjunct faculty used in community colleges. One problem this raises is the issue of communicating information to students: Adjuncts who have time for little more than their own teaching are unlikely to be well-informed about the array of student services, especially on campuses where multiple services are poorly organized. In addition, some of the best-integrated systems of student support rely on classroom instructors who provide workshops and designs for supplementary instruction. But adjuncts do not participate in making these connections between regular instruction and student services. Looking at Figure 5.1, this means that the potential connection between instructors and support services is weakened, and consistency between the two is likely to be undermined. The alternative, of course, is for colleges to pay adjuncts for participating in student services, as Chaffey College has, but this is indeed rare.

Finally, the problem of evaluating student services is much more difficult than even the problem of evaluating other innovations in developmental education. Tracking students is a problem as they use student services and then move out of such services. At one college with a remedial system for students whose GPAs fell below 2.0, the tracking mechanisms weren't good enough to distinguish between success and failure:

> About half of them in any given semester get back in good standing, or disappear—we really don't know which. And the other half wind up going into the second semester [of the remedial program], and it's getting worse. By the time we have them hooked up to a counselor, it's already downhill.

So, the lack of longitudinal data as students move among programs is a special barrier to evaluating student services.

There has been relatively little evaluation of student services, aside from the three studies mentioned previously on student success courses. One problem is data: Many colleges have fine data on enrollment, since enrollment drives state funding. But they have poor data on participation in student services since that is *not* required for state funding and because it is difficult to collect data on all the small kinds of student services, and on the intensity or duration of services. But the evaluation problem is also more difficult because of the substantial evidence that only the best and most motivated students show up in student services. Without considering the possibility that these "overachievers" are responsible for any positive impacts of support services—formally, without considering selection effects—it is difficult to know how to interpret any outcomes, positive or negative.

In the end, many fundamental characteristics of community colleges have combined to make student services a difficult area. On the one hand, because of the nature of community colleges as open-door institutions, many students come with a range of cognitive and noncognitive deficiencies, including the fact that they "don't know how to be college students." Even where colleges like Chaffey and Mindano have tried to get away from deficiency language, by stressing that seeking support "is what all successful students do," there is no denying that some students need support much more than others. Responding to these needs, and trying to teach all students "how to be college students," is surely the right response to these corollaries of being open-enrollment institutions.

But, on the other hand, other structural dimensions of many colleges have contributed to the peripheral status of support services. The tendency of colleges to be laissez-faire institutions, making minimal demands on students and faculty alike, means that the use of support services in most colleges is voluntary, with the neediest students least likely to participate and many faculty reluctant to force students to go. The domination of remedial pedagogy has seeped into student services as well, particularly in tutoring and guidance and counseling aimed at information transfer. This is partly because most instructors feel it is the appropriate pedagogy for developmental education, and partly because students are under pressure to get the right answers so that they can get the appropriate credits, pass their tests, fulfill their course requirements, and make progress toward their eventual goals. The separation of instruction from student services—reinforced in most colleges by a bureaucratic division between the two—has put them in competition with one another, and we suspect that services are sometimes being used as substitutes for, rather than complements to, instruction. It is clear that other structural dimensions of community colleges—aside from the issues of funding, adjunct instructors, and data and evaluation noted in the beginning of this section—can undermine the effectiveness of support services.

It is not difficult to see what might be done to improve student services—in effect, to undo the structural conditions that have put support services in such a difficult quandary. As I argue further in chapter 10, one solution would be to move away from the laissez-faire college toward one in which there are more demands on students to participate in such services, under the rationale that "this is what all successful students do." This would also help destigmatize student services, to minimize the possibility that stereotype threat makes students less willing to take advantage of services being offered. Another remedy would be to eliminate the division between instruction and student services that is so common, not merely by erasing the bureaucratic split, but by making sure that *faculty* direct most aspects of student services, including tutoring, short specific workshops, supplemental instruction, and the array of student success efforts that "teach students how to be college students."

A third option would be to address the limitations of remedial pedagogy head-on—as, for example, supplemental instruction has with its insistence that tutors not act simply to deliver students the right answers, but rather that they guide students in discussions out of which their own answers emerge. Tutor training that alerts tutors to the range of possible ways they can work with students is another example.

Finally, many of the complications of student services in institutions with so many adjuncts can be overcome by making sure that part-time faculty can participate in all support services—for example, by paying them for participating in workshops and supplemental instruction.

All of these steps require challenging the conventional practices and norms of community colleges. But the result might be student support services that live up to their promises of complementing classroom instruction, making the entire developmental education enterprise more effective.

6

INTEGRATING STUDENT SERVICES WITH INSTRUCTION

Chaffey College's Long Journey to Success

Chaffey College, a three-campus college with approximately 20,000 students, located in California's Inland Empire, has become a destination for many community college practitioners from around the country.[1] Over the past 10 years, the college has become nationally known as an institution with both a "risk tolerant change-oriented culture" and student support programs that produce impressive outcomes. Visitors to the college want to understand how Chaffey, as a model institution, does it.

As two of those visitors,[2] we learned a great deal, and this chapter summarizes our findings. The primary concern in this book has been to examine the quality of instruction in basic skills. But colleges have increasingly turned to student support services to enhance the success of their developmental programs. The previous chapter demonstrated that some of these services are not very effective, but we had heard that Chaffey had a broader variety of services than most colleges, including those for faculty as well as students. Contrary to the pattern of separation and even hostility between instruction and student support, Chaffey had apparently developed a model of integrating student support and developmental education. Even though our analysis focuses on specific support services, the Chaffey story is really one of developing a broad structure necessary for success both specifically in developmental education and more generally for all students—a kind of "existence proof" that student services can be done in very different ways.

Our starting point is not the present but the past, because the history of Chaffey provides the answers to a few central questions: Why did Chaffey emerge as an exemplar of what a community college can do right? Why has it been so difficult to replicate the Chaffey story in other colleges? And what did

Chaffey do to enable and then sustain a transformation that supports student success?

The Long View

The full story began in the early 1990s with the establishment of the institutional foundations for Chaffey's "transformation." Don Berz, the vice-superintendent of Chaffey from 1989 to 2004, was instrumental in these changes. Berz grew up in the Peralta Community College District, where he spent 20 years as a faculty member, dean, college president, district vice-chancellor, and finally interim chancellor. In the 1980s, Peralta acquired a reputation as a contentious, tough, and somewhat dysfunctional community college district, caused (in part) by decreased funding aggravated by administrative and board leadership that sought to resolve problems by laying off faculty. Nothing worked quite right in Peralta, and this was true of collective bargaining relations, shared governance, and administrative leadership. Berz says that Peralta was a "defining experience" in his career, and he brought many lessons with him when he got the job at Chaffey. Chaffey resembled Peralta in the 1980s, characterized by contentious relations with the union and the Academic Senate, and aggravated by an "out of control" board trying to micromanage the college and by weak administrators. Berz was tapped for the vice-superintendent position because he came with clear views of what not to do and a vision of what could be done.

Berz put in place the enabling factors that set the stage for Chaffey's "transformation." He established collaborative relations with the unions, built a meaningful collaborative system of shared governance, and established a Policy and Budget Development Committee with representation from all college constituencies that, in turn, made all major budget and policy recommendations to the superintendent, the president, and the board. Berz hired a new group of administrators who were not just managers, but also leaders oriented to issues of pedagogy and instruction who were committed to collaborative leadership with the faculty. He had a strong belief in succession building, and encouraged faculty leadership in transformational roles. He developed an expectation, through the position of a coordinator, that administrators and faculty would become working teams.

As contention abated and trust among the various college groups began to grow, Berz directly addressed the quality of academic and student services. This step relied upon an organizational strategy called the "Abilene paradox," in which a group of people collectively decides on a course of action that is contrary to the preferences of any individual in the group.[3] As Laura Hope, Dean of Instructional Support, recalled, "We knew we were broken and we needed a do-over." Consequently, Berz proposed that a group of community college practitioners from other colleges examine Chaffey and produce a report about those problems. They finished their work in 1999, and confirmed what insiders had already acknowledged: the basic skills department and its courses needed to be radically changed.

Berz, with the support of the superintendent and the board, proposed a process to improve student achievement and success. Unlike most other California community colleges, Chaffey's executive leadership did not immediately distribute additional state funds that were available in 1999-2000—so-called Partnership for Excellence (PFE) funds—but banked them and accumulated a total of $5 to 6 million. Berz proposed that all of the PFE funds should be strategically invested in a plan developed by the faculty/staff and driven by a comprehensive vision to improve student learning and student success. This avoided the problems inherent in spending these funds, as so many colleges have, on small changes and little programs. So, a task force of approximately 35 faculty, administrators, and staff spent the 1999-2000 academic year reviewing data, reading the visiting team's report, interviewing faculty in other colleges, and developing the plan that ultimately became the *Chaffey Transformation Plan*. The development and implementation of the plan would not have been possible without a great deal of trust among all the parties, and the trust would not have been possible without the enabling processes in the 1990s. As Laura Hope noted,

> One of the key elements of this task force is that we were the decision makers. Don invested this group with the planning, evaluation, and implementation responsibility. If the people in that group decided that it was good for students, then it became policy. We did not have to seek "permission" outside of that room, beyond occasional consultation with Don. The task force met every Friday all day long, and the larger group divided into smaller work groups to accomplish various tasks throughout the week that would be vetted or refined by the larger group throughout the process. Once we developed a plan, the governing board adopted the transformation agenda, and the president adopted the goals of the plan as part of his personal goals, which then influenced his own evaluation. This was critical for the development of trust and fostering a belief that whatever we did or changed would last, and that it was embraced by the entire institution.

To ensure the sustainability of the plan and to eliminate cynicism about a "here today/gone tomorrow" grant mentality, Berz and the executive leadership permanently allocated PFE funds that supported the plan into the base budget of the college. Following the executive leadership, the college's governing board adopted the budget and consequently made a permanent budget commitment to the Chaffey plan. So, when visitors ask "How can Chaffey afford its programs?" people at Chaffey respond that all the institutional features are part of the college's base budget because the Chaffey leadership and its faculty took the long view 12 years ago and invested strategically in key programs supported by the faculty.

The Chaffey Transformation Plan

The task force took over a year to construct the original *Chaffey Transformation Plan*. Since the process was iterative and collaborative, most Chaffey faculty supported the recommendations, especially because the executive leadership declared there would be no faculty layoffs and the plan would be funded with dollars that would ultimately be included in the district's base budget.

The Chaffey plan substantially reshaped basic skills offerings. Throughout the 1990s, the college had had two parallel basic skills programs—one contained within a basic skills department with its own support labs, and the other embedded in the math and English departments. Students were confronted with a confusing array of choices, many of which did not lead anywhere. Student data from Chaffey's Office of Institutional Research (IR) confirmed that students were failing and dropping out in very high numbers.

Instead, the plan called for a major reorganization of basic skills with the goal of significantly increasing the rates of student success. The faculty dismantled Chaffey's basic skills department; restructured, modified, or deleted 75 courses; and abandoned the term *basic skills* and replaced it with *foundation skills*. In place of the two parallel basic skills programs, one set of courses was offered through the math, English, and ESL departments in three Student Success Centers. The Chaffey centers, unlike those in many other colleges, were constructed in close collaboration with faculties in the departments; they were seen as extensions of the classroom, using activities developed by classroom faculty and implemented by well-trained staff comprised mostly of students with bachelor's degrees and some faculty. The centers used a monitoring system to oversee the progress of each student. Reporting lines between center staff and faculty were also developed, which was another form of integrating success centers and classroom instruction.

Another major breakthrough was the agreement among faculties from all special programs—including Extended Opportunity Programs and Services (EOPS) and Disabled Students Programs and Services (DSPS)—to merge their student support labs with the Success Centers, thereby eliminating redundancies in support services. The department faculties agreed to rewrite their course outlines. In the case of the English department, the faculty also revisited its approach to teaching, moving away from the old sentence-paragraph-essay format toward one based on different types of readings including more nonfiction (since most students encounter nonfiction in most subsequent college courses). Although reading was initially taught separately from writing, the two have recently been integrated in one Success Center—a good example of the integrative power of such centers.

One additional dimension was crucial: The Success Centers were intended for all Chaffey students, not just basic skills students. The faculty felt that the addition of well-constructed cognitive activities coordinated with classroom faculty would be a boon for every student. Furthermore, defining the centers for all students removed the stigma of "special needs" for basic skills students and ended the segregation of basic skills students on campus. Philosophically, it was important that every center serve students at all levels. The centers were devised on the premise that all learning is developmental and that effective support is an integral part of the learning process, not a safety net after a student fails and needs help. Ultimately, Chaffey created four centers at the main campus: An Interdisciplinary Writing Success Center, a Math Success Center, a Reading/Multidisciplinary Success Center, and a Language Success Center that included foreign languages plus ESL. Finally, based on the theory that faculty (as well as students) need support for their success, a Faculty Success Center was established in 2009 to facilitate the reform of instruction.

As implementation of the Chaffey Transformation Plan progressed, faculty and staff received regular reports on student outcomes, and they were encouraged by what they were reading. The most recent 2009–2010 data from Chaffey's Office of Institutional Research provides a snapshot of why:

- Success rates by course in basic skills courses increased steadily to 68.1% in 2009–2010 from 30 to 35% in the early 1990s;
- Success rates for those students in basic skills courses who accessed the centers grew to 72.8%, compared to 53.5% among students who did not go to centers.
- Numbers of transferring students who completed at least one precollegiate course increased from 10% of the total in 2000 to almost 28% in 2010.
- Two-thirds of Chaffey's honor students (800) started in a foundation skill area.

The numbers of Chaffey students accessing all the Success Centers has continually increased over the last decade, from 28.5% to 55.9% of all students, reflecting a significant shift in student behavior. And student satisfaction among the users of Success Centers was at 97% in the spring of 2009. Similar numbers are reported for transfer courses as well as for special populations like EOPS and DSPS.

Chaffey's organizational structure has some distinctive features that reflect its philosophy and student success agenda. The reporting lines for both the academic and student services operations go to one vice-president, rather than the traditional two VPs; consequently, there are many mechanisms to keep the academic and student services leadership working closely with each other. Both President Henry Shannon and Vice-President Sherrie Guerrero have publically stated expectations that faculty and deans lead and contribute; they trust and expect the structures at the college to produce results, but they expect accountability as well.

As Dean of Instructional Support, Laura Hope oversees all the Student Success Centers and the library, a position not often seen in other colleges. She also serves as a keeper of the Chaffey vision, as one of the few remaining leaders from the 1999-2000 Transformation Plan. Hope cochairs (with two others) the Enrollment and Success Management Committee, which is responsible for monitoring the entire student success program, identifying problems, and coming up with innovations. Like many Chaffey committees of the past 10 years, this committee is comprised of 40 faculty, staff, and administrators, and it has been quite productive. The committee is credited with establishing the Early Assessment Program (EAP) with local high schools to get students to judge their college readiness.[4] Entering students can take a 3-week brush-up math course before the ACCUPLACER, since many of them have not taken any math since their junior year. The Enrollment and Success Management Committee is also creating a completion agenda, and exploring what will count as markers toward completion.

This group has also been the impetus for changing the deadlines for adding and dropping classes, in keeping with data suggesting that forcing an early commitment to courses improves success. It is also the motivating force behind the acceleration movement at Chaffey. In the spring of 2011, the College offered approximately 50 accelerated classes, and in the fall and spring of 2011 and 2012, the College offered approximately 75 each term.* This decision was based on efforts from a task force created by the Enrollment and Success Management Committee, which was very much like the Basic Skills Transformation. In addition, the Enrollment and Success Management Committee was responsible for the vision behind the College's Title V Hispanic-Serving Institutions (HSI) grant, and this group continues to provide oversight for the activities for institutional improvement written into the grant.

People at Chaffey College describe all of these projects and activities in particular ways. Laura Hope noted that

> We place a very high premium on "languaging" our changes because they often influence the culture. That is why we deliberately named our first phase of change our "transformation," and we abandoned *basic skills* as a term for our students. We openly discussed the moral imperative that we had to be better, and the term *moral imperative* has stuck with us ever since. We also are deliberate about naming EVERYTHING! We also have a local "vocabulary." For instance, our vice-president, Sherrie Guerrero, is fond of saying, "Go big or go home," and in committees, we sometimes say to each other that it is time to "stare down the fear."
>
> In keeping with that, Sherrie, Henry [Shannon, College President], and I talked quite a bit about what words to use to describe the phase we are in right now. We have begun to use "Completion Counts: Exceeding Expectations." The term *exceeding expectations* is probably the most

---

* Accelerated courses are compressed versions of standard courses, typically meeting more frequently during fewer weeks of time. Thus, a two-semester sequence might be combined into a one-semester accelerated course, for example.

important part to us because it reflects our moral imperative. We are all committed to exceeding our own expectations. The term implies that we are always striving to be better for ourselves and for students. The term obviously implies students, too, in that we want them to be more than even they expected. In short, words are a big part of our story, and we talk about our words together.

Student Success Centers

The focal points of Chaffey's infrastructure are the Student Success Centers. There are four centers at the Rancho Cucamonga campus while the smaller Chino and Fontana campuses have one each. All of them follow a common format, though they may not be at the same stage of development. The Writing Success Center was the first, and is the best developed; the Math Success Center was "late to the table," as two math instructors acknowledged, and is only now developing some of the activities that have become common in the Writing Success Center. According to the IR office, 55% of students access at least one success center every semester; 35% are in two or more; 45% go twice a week or more. In some cases, instructors direct students to attend some of these activities, for example requiring 15 hours of supplemental learning of some kind. In other cases, students come on their own when they feel the need or when instructors recommend further development of specific skills. A recent IR study found that once students have a Success Center requirement, their Success Center participation increases by approximately 20%, even in subsequent semesters when they no longer have requirements.

The materials of the Success Centers are full of pointers about "how to be a college student," a crucial and multifaceted capacity that community college students often lack. For example, the Math Success Center provides "suggestions for success" that exhort students to devote a minimum of 8 hours per week to homework, arrive at class on time, ask questions, seek help promptly, and "don't be content just to know how to do problems, but seek to understand the underlying concepts."

Each Success Center provides four kinds of specific services, and an intake person in every Success Center can direct students to the right services:

- **Tutoring** represents about 30% of what goes on at the centers. Drop-in tutoring is available, but the centers are trying to move to scheduled tutoring sessions where students sign up with tutors at least the day before for half-hour time slots. This is intended to foster deeper investigation of the problems students have and establish more substantial relations between students and tutors. The tutors themselves are either second-year Chaffey students (called Apprentice IIs) or students with bachelor's degrees (Apprentice IVs).

- **Faculty-led workshops** number about 300 per semester in each center. Typically, they cover a wide range of subjects, from small subskills (incomplete sentences and sentence fragments, punctuation, factoring review, logarithmic equations, etc.) to larger and more conceptual material (organizing writing, complex numbers, applications of problems using percent, etc.). These relatively brief (one hour long) activities are always initiated by faculty and taught by faculty, including adjunct faculty, based on the theory that all student support is instructional and should be directed by faculty, and should have some connection to conventional classes. Sometimes the subjects are issues on which students need reinforcement; sometimes they are topics faculty cannot get around to teaching. In effect, they allow for the teaching of modules about specific skills that are much shorter than semester-length classes.

- **Learning groups** follow the College Reading and Learning Association (CRLA) model;[5] they are designed by faculty, with topics suggested by both Success Center staff and faculty. Usually, they are one-hour sessions led by Apprentice IV tutors. Topics might include academic writing style; eliminating wordiness; accent reduction for ESL students; using a ruler to learn fractions; the logic of the scientific method; the use of active and passive voice, etc. The groups typically include three to five students, while workshops are larger.

- **Directed learning activities (DLAs)** are one-on-one sessions, typically with an apprentice tutor, on specific subjects and following a format devised by a faculty member. The topics tend not to be individual subskills, but are more focused on learning processes and metacognitive approaches to learning, in contrast to conventional tutoring which is usually "product focused," with an emphasis on correcting a specific paper or problem set. Students are given a packet of materials, which they work through; at the end, there is a review session with the apprentice tutor. Topics might include think-aloud procedures to diagnose what difficulties students are having; identifying the reasons students are unable to follow the instructor in the classroom; evaluating the credibility of sources (including websites); the scientific method. There was even a linked writing class for an auto repair course, developed by bringing together a CTE instructor and an English instructor. Other topics involve issues of confidence and student identity, such as a student's sense of self as a writer. These topics (again) address the affective dimensions of being students—getting students to see themselves as students and writers, not as failures. Like the other activities, each DLA must be connected back to classroom goals and values. There are many English DLAs, but only one for math—a unit on measurement, using rulers. Another DLA for word problems is being developed.

The personnel of the centers include regular faculty who teach workshops and develop DLAs; instructional specialists (with faculty status associated with each of the Success Centers) who work closely with regular classroom faculty;

and apprentice tutors (with either associate's or bachelor's degrees) who remain at Chaffey for long periods of time, in contrast to peer tutors, for example, who leave when they graduate. Apprentice tutors often want to go into K–12 teaching, and this is one way to establish experience and credentials.

Other Services Supporting Students

Supplemental Instruction

In contrast to the four activities of the Student Success Centers, which are focused on different *disciplines*, supplemental instruction (SI) focuses on particular *courses*—specifically, the 22 courses that have the lowest pass rates, including some introductory courses, several general education courses, and three basic skills courses. The SI coordinators are students with bachelors' of arts or science degrees who direct SI for each specific course. SI follows the Kansas model from the University of Missouri-Kansas City's Center for Academic Development, which stresses that SI should be attractive to high-performing students as well as those who are behind. The idea, based on the work of Uri Treisman of the Dana Center at the University of Texas, is to get groups of students talking about the course material, problems sets, and tests. The SI leader, who attends all classes, does not provide answers; instead, they lead discussions and provides hints when students are stuck. The materials also clarify that SI is not conventional tutoring, a homework question-and-answer session, another lecture, or a place students go when they miss class—it has its own pedagogy and purpose. For students using SI, course success rates increase as students engage in more SI, ranging from 54.5% among those who attend no SI sessions to 88.7% for students attending 11 or more sessions.

Laura Hope and SI Coordinator Robin Witt have developed a manual for SI leaders as an introduction to the variety of students' learning styles. It includes a social styles inventory, a section on cultural proficiency, varieties of approaches to listening, and directions on conducting SI sessions. In general, the SI coordinator views supplemental instruction as a methodical approach, rather than a place for quick answers; the Success Centers, in contrast, provide a greater variety of tutoring-related activities, with an emphasis on longer sessions.

Two students reflecting on their experiences as both tutors and SI leaders shared a similar approach: "The tutor (or SI leader) does not ever lecture or simply impart knowledge to the students." The difference between one-on-one tutoring and the SI approach is that "students get results from one another [in SI] that a tutor might have to explicate in a tutoring session." So, unlike the simple provision of correct answers that we have seen in a great deal of peer tutoring, the emphasis at Chaffey is on leading students to discover answers for themselves and with peers.

The Faculty Success Center

After the student Success Centers had been in place about 8 years, faculty began to understand that providing centers for students but not for faculty made little sense. Around the same time, the current president/superintendent Henry Shannon arrived at Chaffey, and he spent a great deal of time examining the Success Centers and talking with faculty. He developed a proposal to extend the scope of Success Centers to include all college faculty; the new Faculty Success Center would focus on supporting faculty around teaching and learning issues. Shannon's emphasis on faculty development coincided with the college's self-assessment as part of the state's Basic Skills Initiative. The Student Success Committee took the lead in developing the Faculty Success Center as a result of reflection prompted by the "Poppy Copy" assessment.[6] After review and approval by the faculty, the college invested in a permanent faculty center in 2009 to support professional learning opportunities for all Chaffey faculty. The center is headed by a full-time faculty member who has built a diverse array of activities, including workshops on the psychological impact of growing up in poverty, critical thinking strategies for ESL students, teaching students how to learn, introductions to SI and health services, using technology, and many other topics and workshops that faculty request. Adjuncts are paid to attend these workshops. The Faculty Success Center has also started a voluntary program of classroom observations and feedback for interested faculty, for which almost one quarter of the faculty have signed up—an effort to move teaching from a private to a more public effort. The center also features a 2-week summer institute for 50 part-time and full-time faculty that focuses on an innovative practice or project, where instructors publish their findings in a campus journal. This activity is designed to reinforce the role of instructors as researchers and innovators.

In addition, the Faculty Success Center offers special teaching/learning workshops for faculty who have received critical evaluations from either their tenure review committees or student evaluations. The center also serves as a common venue for faculty discussions about potential innovations, or to recruit faculty to innovations. For example, we observed a 2-hour discussion on acceleration, where faculty who had been involved in acceleration pilot projects spoke with interested faculty about what the innovation entailed. In this sense, any innovation undertaken at Chaffey becomes a visible part of public life, discussed by the entire college, rather than remaining the private responsibility of a few innovators. Center data show that 75% of the Chaffey faculty accessed the center over the academic year, while a smaller number use the center during the summer for special programs.

Centers like the Faculty Success Center, which focuses on teaching and learning issues for faculty rather than students, are one of the most powerful and flexible ways for colleges to enhance the quality of instruction (Grubb &

Associates 1999, ch. 8). At Chaffey College, one of the hopes of the center is that through specific workshops and discussions with other faculty instructors will develop more constructivist and student-centered approaches to pedagogy in place of "remedial pedagogy." These efforts complement those of the English faculty in redesigning courses to move away from the sentence-paragraph-essay approach to teaching writing, those of the math department to stress "understanding the underlying concepts," and those of tutors to move to more constructivist methods of helping students develop their own approaches, rather than simply providing them with answers.

The Early Alert System

Early Alert is the product of a one-year joint instructional and student service faculty planning process involving over 40 faculty from various disciplines and services. The process—like the one used to develop the original 1999-2000 Chaffey Transformation Plan—included the extensive use of surveys to assess faculty views on two major questions about individual student progress: What are the major problems students are experiencing, and what types of outside interventions would be most useful to resolve those problems? The plan called for development of an electronic form easily accessible by classroom faculty with 10 student problem options to check off and a text box to provide additional specific information. The plan also identified specific interventions developed by classroom instructors—in collaboration with the counseling division—that could be applied to help students get back on track. The Early Alert System borrowed an idea from the Success Centers in recruiting a group of counselor apprentices—students with bachelor's degrees interested in going into the counseling profession—to deliver the interventions. Each counselor apprentice is trained by a counselor and provided with a script for contacting the Early Alert student upon receiving the electronic form from the classroom instructor. The turnaround time for Early Alert takes place within the semester in order to ensure that the Early Alert student can successfully complete the course—unlike many systems which track incompletes and low grades, and therefore cannot provide students with information until after the semester is over. The Early Alert system is built upon the idea that a tight linkage between the classroom and the outside intervention will ensure an alignment between what the instructor wants and the support work that the counselor apprentice provides to the student.

Opening Doors

Opening Doors is a support system for students on probation that integrates counseling, Student Success courses, and Directed Learning Activities at the Success Centers (the original program was modified and renamed Enhanced

Opening Doors). The system enables counselors to identify specific challenges facing students and then apply the appropriate directed learning activities used in the Success Centers. Now 6 years old, the Enhanced Opening Doors program has a 43% success rate of removing students from probation.

The Role of Institutional Research

Chaffey has one of the largest institutional research (IR) offices among the California community colleges, with a total of four full-time researchers serving a college of 20,000 students. The IR office was a key participant in the early investigation of the college in 1999-2000, providing longitudinal data showing how many students were failing the developmental education sequences and dropping out. The IR department has continued to provide research and assessment support for faculty and administrative initiatives, and its director is included in virtually all significant projects and issues affecting the college. The IR office also provides accountability reporting, apportionment reports and student enrollments, institutional planning, learning outcomes, and responses to individual instructor requests. Research staff are called in whenever innovations are being considered, and they evaluate all innovations.

The IR staff are currently working with faculty on new approaches that measure student progress and success with both cognitive and affective variables. These include a scale of self-regulated learning behavior, a scale on instrumentality (the extent to which any activity is instrumental to getting a degree), and a measure of learning to learn (the learning strategies that can be applied to any discipline). The IR office is also piloting the "Hope Scale," which addresses various dimensions of student perceptions about their directions and their futures. In these ways, institutional research at Chaffey is moving past conventional measures of success (i.e., courses and sequences completed) to measures that provide better understanding of what and how students are learning.

Chaffey's Office of Institutional Research has also created special databases related to student use of the Success Centers—enabling faculty to track the frequency, duration, and type of services used by specific students. In addition, Chaffey has created a data "warehouse" accessible to all administrators and faculty, whereby they can examine student data by course and program. It is extremely user-friendly, making it easy for instructors to carry out their own research.

Lessons Learned from Chaffey

The trajectory of student support services at Chaffey College implies a number of lessons for other colleges:

- **Taking the long view:** When talking to people at Chaffey, they will tell you that transformation takes a long time; as the president remarked, "We're a work in progress." Many people date the beginnings of the transformation to the plan developed by the faculty in 1999-2000. In fact, the planning activities and the resultant changes could not have happened without the trust-building activities of the early 1990s—including cooperative agreements related to collective bargaining and shared governance, as well as the hiring of a new collaborative administrative team committed to teaching, learning, and student success. So, the Chaffey story is actually 20 years old and is still in progress: The Faculty Success Center is only 2 years old, and the Math Success Center has only begun to develop the activities that have been part of other centers for a decade.

- **An inclusive process:** People at Chaffey learned they could work with large representative committees (35–40 people), always with a member of the research office present, and get a lot done, especially if the planning horizon was long enough. Consequently, almost every major innovation includes a representative planning process with a timeline that allows for discussion and consensus building. In addition, adjunct faculty are encouraged to participate in all activities alongside full-time faculty, and are paid for doing so.

- **Integrated services are more effective and efficient:** At Chaffey, support services are an integral part of instruction, rather than having support services staff who develop their own content. With the addition of support services and their own strong connections to students, classroom faculty, and classroom content, the instructional triangle of instructor, student, and content (presented in chapter 1) becomes an instructional quadrangle (introduced in chapter 5 in Figure 5.1). In this way, student services and classroom instruction are inextricably linked.

- **All services for all students:** Chaffey has sought to erase traditional dividing lines between basic skills students—usually viewed as deficient in one or more college skills—and the rest of the college population. Consequently, the Student Success Centers and most other practices like supplemental instruction serve all students; the philosophy is that seeking support "is what all successful students do," not something required only of basic skills students. The goal is to reduce segregation by ability or level of preparedness among student populations and thereby to reduce stigma. In the analysis developed by Claude Steele (2010), students labeled "basic skills" may feel negatively stereotyped, and if students feel threatened by a stereotype, that by itself leads to lower performance. Many of the actions at Chaffey are designed to minimize stereotype threat and thereby increase the performance of students.

- **Transparency for students:** We heard no complaints about students not knowing where to go for support services. At the beginning of the semester, instructional assistants go to many classes to talk about the Student Success

Centers. Instructors are responsible for alerting students to Success Centers and to SI; some courses have requirements for a certain number of hours of SI or activities in Success Centers. The centralization of many services in Success Centers helps foster transparency, and the intake process in each center can help students find their way to specific services. It is also a huge advantage that all centers now follow the same philosophy, with common training and common activities.

- **Constructivist pedagogy:** All support services use student-centered or constructivist pedagogies, in which students develop their own ways of understanding with the help of peers and the guidance of instructors, rather than having information and procedures given to them by faculty and tutors. For this reason Chaffey has largely rejected the use of remedial pedagogy.
- **Noncognitive strategies are important:** It's important to confront not only the cognitive dimensions of learning, but also the noncognitive and social/emotional dimensions (e.g., seeing oneself as a successful student in the process of development that all students go through, rather than a failure).
- **Leadership is critical:** Strong leadership—especially from the faculty and the deans at the middle level of the institution—is crucial to the success of new programs. Much of what has happened at Chaffey is the result of leadership from faculty members (with and without formal titles) and some administrative deans. This is a good example of "innovation from the middle" highlighted in chapter 4. Executive-level leadership has also played a critical role by using scarce funds to support strategic initiatives that can impact the most students (like the Student Success Centers), rather than small-scale individual programs that benefit only a few students and engage only a few faculty ("programmitis," discussed further in chapter 8).
- **Funding:** At first glance, the system of student support at Chaffey—four Student Support Centers, a Faculty Support Center, different types of tutors and apprentices, and training for all these individuals—seems expensive. However, although we did not audit spending on student services, college personnel insist that they do not have additional funds for student support compared to other colleges; indeed, their discussions were remarkably free of references to foundation or government grants for any of these services. (As Laura Hope explains, external funds create a "grant mentality," where there is a burst of energy when a college gets grants but then cynicism about reform when they disappear and reform vanishes.) Instead, services seem to be funded by using existing resources more intelligently and less wastefully. First, funding from large state grants—first the Partnership for Excellence funds, then the Basic Skills Initiative funds—were spent on substantial initiatives, rather than being wasted on little programs that wind up reaching very few students. Second, the wasteful duplication apparent in other college programs (e.g., similar tutoring provided in reading, writing, and math centers *and* by EOPS and DSPS) is replaced by the four Student Success Centers. Third, some of the services provided aren't very expensive, though they may play a large role in improvement. For example, faculty run work-

shops largely without additional funding; apprentice tutors and counseling apprentices do some of the work done by staff and faculty in other colleges. The Faculty Success Center employs only one director and one secretary, and some of its work is accomplished by convening faculty, not additional personnel (apparently, the cost is about $100,000 per year). A careful analysis of funding would require more accounting work, but probably wouldn't improve significantly on these conclusions.

- **Moving away from the laissez-faire college:** In several ways, Chaffey is trying to move away from a college in which students and faculty are allowed to do pretty much what they want. The college enforces the limit on students taking any course more than three times, and it is trying to replace walk-in tutoring with scheduled tutoring where relationships can be developed better and tutoring can move beyond finding the right answer. Some courses have clear requirements for students to complete work in either supplemental instruction or the Student Success Centers. Faculty are expected to contribute to workshops, rather than viewing this as a voluntary contribution. The college is also moving to require students to drop courses by the end of the first week, rather than the end of the third week—having to commit to a course earlier appears to contribute to success. All of these policies place new expectations on both students and faculty. As the vice-president noted, "You're expected to contribute."

- **Parallels with other innovations in basic skills:** In comparing the Chaffey innovations in student services and basic skills with other innovations explored in chapter 4, a number of similarities emerge. Most lasting and widespread innovations have started with a recognition of serious problems in basic skills, as was true of Chaffey. Reforms have taken a long time—at least a decade, and more like 15 to 20 years in the case of Chaffey—with relatively continuous improvement rather than efforts that stop and start. Reforms have also required a deep sense of trust and responsibility among a group of participants as a prerequisite for reform—what the K-12 world calls internal accountability (Carnoy, Elmore, & Siskin, 2003). Like the department-wide innovations we have seen, the emphasis at Chaffey has been on broad institutional changes designed for all students and all faculty, rather than small-scale initiatives championed by individual faculty.

Above all, the changes at Chaffey illustrate the importance of innovation from the middle. The crucial initiatives have come from faculty leaders and middle-level administrators, epitomized by the large 40-member committees Chaffey has convened, including the Enrollment and Success Management Committee. To be sure, some of the initial support came from an executive-level administrator, Berz, but all the details of the Chaffey plan were developed by middle-level faculty and administrators. In the end, the success of Chaffey College is a story of vision, persistence, trust, and collegial accomplishments.

SECTION II

Institutional Effects on Classrooms

7

ASSESSMENT AND ALIGNMENT

The Dynamic Aspects of Developmental Education

Instruction in developmental education is not simply a matter of what happens in the classroom. The institutions in which classrooms are embedded have their own influences on what happens inside the classroom, and the "triangle of instruction" presented in chapter 1—the instructor, the students, and the content—involves different institutions. This book focuses on the institutions affecting basic skills instruction, including community colleges and the state and (potentially) federal government programs that influence and fund classrooms, of which California's Basic Skills Initiative is one of the most important. If we were examining other roles of the community college—career-technical education (CTE), for example, or economic development efforts—then we would have to consider different external effects, including the labor market and the goals of the business community, but these are less directly connected to the provision of developmental education.

In many ways, community colleges are facilitators of basic skills instruction. Virtually all colleges in the country have accepted the mission of providing developmental education, and in California, basic skills education is one of the three dominant missions (the others being academic/transfer education and CTE). Colleges administer assessment tests and other procedures to determine who might benefit from basic skills instruction. As seen in earlier chapters, they offer a great variety of classes and innovations, and developmental education is connected to larger discussions about instruction and pedagogy that take place in the education system (unlike, for example, short-term job training programs unconnected to education). In general, conceptions of student success (including success in basic skills sequences) have been well defined. In many ways, then, developmental education has been adequately institutionalized within community colleges.

On the other hand, there are ways in which the institutional setting of colleges constrains basic skills instruction, and the purpose of section II of this book is to explore these constraints; that is, the ways that institutional practices lead to basic skills programs that are less effective, or perhaps less varied, than might otherwise be the case. Because these constraints are deeply embedded in community colleges, they are difficult to change, and idiosyncratic reforms undertaken by individual instructors usually do not create such change. However, we saw colleges and departments, and occasional individual practices, where these constraints have been changed. Indeed, the prospects for innovation are alive and well, as I documented in chapters 4 and 6. But it is important to be aware of how institutional limitations operate; otherwise, the prospects for change and reform may themselves be limited.

In the second section of this book, two broad institutional influences are examined first: assessment and alignment of courses (in this chapter), and money and resources (in chapter 8). In chapter 9, I will analyze five additional influences that emerged from our study of 13 colleges: (a) the influence of the course as the basic unit of educational provision; (b) the importance and form of professional development; (c) the crucial role of adjunct faculty, and their isolation from the rest of the institution; (d) the notion of data-driven reform; and (e) the nature of the community college as a laissez-faire institution, contrasted with some policies that move away from this particular model. All these factors shape what happens within the classroom, or alternatively within labs, workshops, and other student services—some of them more than others, some for better, and some for worse. Some are obvious, like a basic lack of resources in community colleges compared to other institutions, but others lead in unexpected directions. At a minimum, an examination of basic skills in community colleges would be incomplete without an analysis of the different effects that college policies and culture have on classrooms.

The Dynamic Nature of Basic Skills Instruction

Developmental education is typically a *program* of study, a dynamic sequence of courses and student services taking place over time. It starts, typically, with an initial assessment to determine whether students need basic skills instruction or not. If the assessment suggests that they do, they then enter a first course, then a second course, in a sequence up to the first college-level course in reading, writing, or math. The presumption is that each activity is linked to the next: that assessment places students in the lowest course they need, that the first course prepares the student for the second course, and so on, with the sequence as a whole preparing students for successful participation in college-level courses. It is common to have three levels of basic skills math, at least three levels of writing, and often five to six levels of ESL, so these sequences can be quite long. But if this sequence is not aligned, if any activity is not coordinated with those before and after it, then there is no reason to think that completing a developmental sequence will successfully prepare a student for college-level coursework. Individual courses may even be well designed and wonderfully taught, but if they are not carefully articulated, then the entire enterprise may be pointless.

In the rest of this chapter, I examine the problems of initial assessment and subsequent articulation in the 13 colleges we visited. Unfortunately, virtually no one at these 13 colleges thinks that assessment and articulation are particularly effective, though a few colleges have tried various methods of enhancing articulation. The problem starts with the accuracy or more precisely, the inaccuracy of assessment, and then proceeds to two types of articulation: horizontal articulation (coordination among sections of the same course in a sequence) and vertical articulation (alignment of adjacent courses in a sequence). In the final section, I return to a basic puzzle: Why, if there is widespread recognition of the problem, is there so little effort to improve articulation and assessment, and what would improved articulation look like? The answers provide additional ways of improving basic skills programs.

The problems of assessment and alignment are good examples of institutional problems, not problems associated with individual instructors. Assessment tests must be chosen college-wide, or at least department-wide; the procedures for aligning courses must take place either for everyone or no one; and no individual instructor can make much progress on articulation. Articulation and alignment are, in effect, collective goods involving research, matriculation, counseling, and instruction, even though in practice only one of these dominates the assessment process. If a college cannot work collectively to address these issues, then developmental sequences will remain poorly coordinated.

The Matriculation and Assessment Problem

The front end of developmental education is essentially the same in all colleges: entering students complete a matriculation process that includes some assessment of basic skills. Then, they (ideally) meet with a counselor and are placed into initial courses—either basic skills courses for the large fraction who do not attain an acceptable score established by the college, or college-level courses for those who do. Orientation to the college is another part of matriculation, as are semester-long courses or shorter workshops like Student Success. The process, on paper, is a rational procedure for deciding where students ought to be placed depending on their levels of preparation, and for ensuring that students start their college education with appropriate information about their academic trajectory.

But right away, there are problems with the assessments used.[1] In the first place, there is no systematic approach to assessment in California; different colleges create their own assessments. As one institutional researcher commented,

> Because we are local control, there is no system-wide way of looking at things. Some of the colleges in the Sacramento area just do self-placement.... Another college in the south, because of where they are located with numerous community colleges around, they [students] take four or five different ones [placement tests].

This, in turn, leads to two issues. One is that, except in cases where there is a dominant local college, high schools cannot know what the initial assessment is, and therefore cannot prepare their students for it. To counter this problem, there are currently efforts underway to define a statewide college readiness standard and to replace the variety of assessments with a single, statewide assessment process (see PACE, 2012) The second issue is that students may "game" the assessment system by selecting colleges with easier placement mechanisms. The same institutional researcher went on to say, "A lot of students were going to other schools, getting assessed, and then coming back because the assessment [at our college] wasn't quite as rigorous or tough. It's sort of a hit or miss operation in some respects."

The entire matriculation process suffers from several problems. One is that, because so many students enroll at one time and at the last minute, the whole process is rushed, with little time to explain the process carefully to students. The result is that many students do not understand what the assessment test is, and how important it is in determining subsequent coursework. As one counselor quoted a typical student, "'I had no idea that test was important.' They are so angry. 'I didn't know it was serious. My friends were waiting outside to go to the beach.'" This problem extends to students who have easily passed their high school courses; as the head of counseling at one college noted,

> We get too many of them that tell me, "Well, you know, in high school, I was in trigonometry; I was in calculus." Well, you just scored in basic math here. So, we don't know why the levels are where they are, but we have to be able to figure out our assessment—Is it accurate? What can we do to make them take it more seriously? ... They're coming here not focused on necessarily getting an education. Some are, but not knowing how intense it is.

This results in students performing less well than they could have if, for example, they had had a period for review—an opportunity that two of the 13 colleges we visited offer—or if they simply took the test more seriously and prepared for it (as students typically prepare for the SAT).

When we talked with students, they were uniformly angry at the results of assessment and placement. They felt betrayed by the lack of preparation—less than for a driver's exam, as one student mentioned—and dismayed by placement in basic skills. "It feels like high school again ... I've already taken these courses, like, why am I taking them again?" another student protested. Many admitted that they had not taken high school seriously, but they were still shocked not to pass. (This might be a good argument for providing high school students with a preliminary version of the basic skills test—to "scare" them into taking high school more seriously.) From this perspective, colleges should do whatever is necessary to reduce the numbers of "brush-up" students and students who are misdirected into developmental programs (identified in chapter 2). Such necessary steps include administering assessments earlier, allowing for test preparation, or offering a summer bridge program.

A second problem, as I clarified in chapter 5, is that students don't get enough time with counselors for an extended discussion about subsequent courses and long-term plans. As one student said, "Trying to see a counselor is, like, impossible; you can't even get the help you need."

A third issue is that there are many ways for students to circumvent the assessment tests. They can do this if they say they are taking courses for personal interests; if they are taking six units or less; or (in several colleges) if they are entering career-technical education (CTE) programs. As one administrator admitted,

> The reality is that as many as possible bail [on the assessment test]. They either don't take it and put it off, or they call on one of the exemptions to say they're exempt from taking the assessment. I have to fix the exemptions, and I haven't fixed them yet. So, at this point, they're pretty lame.

Consequently, many students are simply not assessed. One college roughly estimated that less than one-third of entering students take the initial assessment. The statistics on the proportion of students "needing" basic skills—the widely cited national figure of 60%, or the common California figure of 80%—are, in reality, based on incomplete testing of entering students. The result of all these issues is that what looks like a supremely rational process for entering college is, in practice, undermined in various ways.

The alignment problem is that assessments are poorly linked to subsequent coursework. The assessments are off-the-shelf tests published by testing companies—most colleges in our sample used either ACCUPLACER or ACT's COMPASS test—and are not articulated with textbooks, so the placement test "sort of places people in the right place, even though it doesn't seem to test anything we actually do in class." The available tests are particularly inappropriate for English, since none of them include writing samples; for ESL students, they do not include any assessment of speaking or listening abilities, so the broad facility with English that is typically addressed in ESL classes is not captured by the assessment tests. As one ESL instructor noted, "When you get to the lower levels, there is really not a good placement instrument, and really nothing that addresses speaking and listening. Most colleges have their own home-grown placement system."

The most common complaints about assessment tests are that they are *placement* tests, not *diagnostic* tests—they generate a single score that can then be used for placement,[2] but they don't diagnose what a student's weaknesses are, and therefore generate no information for the instructor on what skills to emphasize. One counselor in a college that uses ACCUPLACER stated, "We don't use a test that's diagnostic. So, we're taking someone who may have had a bad day and making them take three semesters of remediation." Another admitted that she didn't look at the placement test scores because they were not diagnostic: "I just know that they [students] are in my class, and I work with them."

Despite the problems with placement tests, there is little real discussion about replacing the existing assessments with something else. For one thing, the extent of knowledge about assessments is quite limited; it's common to find that the only person in a college who really understands the placement test is the director of placement, while others—including instructors and counselors whose work is affected by placement exams—do not have any idea what the tests contain. One ESL instructor noted that the placement test

> is pretty much a mystery to me. I've heard about it; I've never gone over to testing. No one has ever shown me what the test is … that process needs to be streamlined; it needs to be a lot more clear.

Also, there is a reluctance to get into all the complications of changing the test; as one instructor noted, "They're closed to that—oh, no, we don't change the test." So, despite broad recognition that the tests are inadequate, the pressures to change the core of the matriculation process are weak.

The result of all these problems is that some students are placed in classes that are too low for them—for example, when they do not take a placement test seriously—while others (like those who have used some kind of exemption to escape testing) place into courses that are beyond their real abilities. One ESL instructor noted, in disagreeing with many of the initial placements,

> I've had students at the A level [the lowest level] whom I couldn't believe that's where they were placed. They needed to be at the B or C levels. But there is really nothing we can do about it. And they have to wait 6 months until they take the test again.

The resignation in this instructor's voice is striking ("but there is really nothing we can do about it"). There seems to be disagreement about the direction of misplacement; one basic skills instructor who said, "The assessment is horrible—it places students horribly," thought students should be placed higher in general; other instructors felt that students ought to be placed in lower classes than they were. But most colleges do not allow students to retake the assessment, or require them to wait for a certain period of time, so once they are assessed, students must remain at a particular (and potentially inappropriate) level of basic skills for some time; those are the students I described in chapter 2 as being misplaced. One instructor talked about "students [who] are stuck behind this wall of basic skills" taking too many developmental courses.

One consequence is a broader range of students in basic skills classes. As one ESL instructor commented on her class that we observed,

> I don't know if you noticed, but some people should be in level 2. There are some people who should be in level 4 or 5 [5 being the highest]. So, there is a wide range of people. I kind of try to include all of them in the instruction. But sometimes it misses some on either end.

Similarly, a head counselor asserted that "the assessment doesn't pick up the actual level they should be at; it gives too broad of a range," so that students are likely to be placed too high or too low. One instructor we observed provided multiple assignments at different levels to cope with the variety of preparation levels, but this kind of differentiated instruction is rare in community colleges (though it is well known, if not widely practiced, in K–12 education). When I discussed the heterogeneity of students in basic skills classes in chapter 2, it is clear that the various problems with assessments are partly to blame.

One of the puzzles in the matriculation process as it is actually practiced is what happens to students who avoid the assessment test and then self-place in courses. As one director of basic skills mentioned,

> We also know anecdotally from our faculty who teach in other subject areas that there may be lots of students in those classes who haven't taken the placement tests, and who are also basic skills students. I know there are lots of students who want to remain anonymous and stay under the radar, and maybe take as many classes as they can before they take the placement tests. A lot of it has to do with anxiety, not that they're devious—they are just anxious and they don't know how they're going to place on those exams.

The answer seems to be that some of them self-place in basic skills courses, while others self-place in various college-level courses for which they may not be prepared. Here's one instructor's description of the result:

> They can't get a remedial math class, can't get another class [because they are full], so they [counselors] put them in psychology or sociology. They can't read and write. "Why did you put them in anthropology?" "Oh, well, they needed 12 units to get their financial aid." … So, they get 2 Fs in these classes because they can't read, they don't get financial aid anyway because they're disqualified.

More specific evidence of what happens to these students is not available, though in general, students who need basic skills classes (according to assessments) but who do not complete such classes fare worse than those who do.[3] Once again, the fear factor emerges, causing students to avoid taking assessments and developmental courses—and then to take paths that may not be optimal.

In response to various weaknesses of standardized placement tests, some colleges—though none in our sample—have developed their own placement and diagnostic tests, relying on English and math faculty to devise tests geared toward their basic skills sequence. But devising assessments and then assuring their reliability and validity is not a simple task, and most colleges do not have the capacity to carry this out. As one ESL instructor noted, "What we've found is that different students have different weaknesses, so the general tests don't do a good job. But there's no money, so changing the test looks fairly hopeless at the moment." Indeed, there's no good reason why individual colleges should have to devise different assessments. This is a task that a state could more easily carry out, if there were a system-wide assessment process instead of local control.

The consequence is that existing assessment tests do a mediocre job of placing students. What is necessary is a testing regime that is clearly explained to students, where students can have some time to brush up on academic and testing skills before trying the test; that is, eliminating "brush-up" students from those placed into developmental education. The test itself could be used for more diagnostic purposes and therefore have some educational value, rather than simply being a mechanism of placement. But the elements of this ideal system are rarely in place, so the first step of the trajectory of basic skills is fraught with errors.

Horizontal and Vertical Alignment

The next step in the trajectory of basic skills is the movement from the placement test into a developmental course, posing the question of how these two elements are articulated with one another. I note that there are only three ways that tests and courses in a sequence could be aligned with one another; (a) if a publisher developed tests and textbooks in a sequence with one another, and instructors adopted these textbooks; (b) if a state (or college) specified the elements to be taught at various levels of the basic skills trajectory, and then all assessments and courses were keyed to these elements; or (c) if instructors spent enough time in discussion about assessments and courses, and exit and entrance exams that they could carry out such an alignment themselves. In addition, for any of these three mechanisms of alignment to work well, the entire sequence would have to be aligned with the content and purposes of the first college-level course; in other words, some kind of backwards mapping from a college-level course to earlier basic prerequisites would be necessary.

But while any of the three mechanisms could work in theory, none works well in practice, except under special conditions. Typically, the choice of textbooks is left to instructors, so that using textbooks designed to be part of a series would require restricting the texts that instructors can select. One college in our sample of 13 provided an exception to the multiplicity of textbooks: the ESL department adopted a text that was "sort of a skeleton; it tells them [instructors] what needs to be covered at each level ... we really work from one level to another, and the steps are really important." But this couldn't happen until the college hired one full-time ESL instructor to coordinate the activities of all the adjuncts; before this, a hodge-podge of textbooks was used.

In most of the colleges that we observed, and at the state level as well, no one has yet specified the elements necessary at different levels of basic skills. Thus, no progression from one course to another has been imposed, for example by the state, or has been agreed upon. However, a Student Success Task Force in California has made this one of its principal recommendations. And discussions among instructors about course content are comparatively rare, *except* in cases of departments that have consciously organized themselves to develop more coherent instruction and pedagogy (analyzed in chapter 4 on innovations). As the dean of liberal arts in one college stated,

> I come from the old school where you do pre- and posttests, exit essays, holistic scoring, group reads, great socialization.... And our departments up 'til now generally don't do any of these things. The result is that the alignment of courses is usually haphazard ... basically, these students enroll in our courses and the instructor evaluates each student. But without pre- and posttesting, without maybe a departmentally graded component, there are none of those cross-checks that you frequently find in universities.

The first type of alignment, which is horizontal alignment among sections of courses at the same level (or with the same course number), is actually a prerequisite for vertical alignment, or the alignment between two adjacent courses in a series. If students coming out of a first-level course have covered different material, for example, then they will be differently prepared for the second-level course. Indeed, the instructors we interviewed provided many examples where horizontal alignment was missing. As one English instructor noted,

> The discrepancy between one teacher and another is so diverse. And if you get Claude and you're unprepared, you're messed up, and if you don't get Claude, you're OK. And students use RateYourProfessor.com like there's no tomorrow on this campus.

Aside from testifying to the discrepancies among instructors teaching the same courses, this anecdote suggests that students may search for the easiest professor in taking a specified course, which may serve their short-term goals but at the expense of long-term success. Very often, problems of horizontal and vertical alignment are revealed when students passing one course cannot do well in the next course in a sequence. In this case, several colleges in our sample have put in place common final exams, as ways of making course content more uniform. In one college, the range of textbooks has narrowed to three or four "especially because now we have so many adjuncts, and we find it is better for students to have fewer choices of textbooks if they [students] are going to shift classes." The problem of horizontal alignment is generally made more difficult when there are many adjuncts teaching different sections of a developmental course. Even when adjuncts are given a textbook and a course outline (two ways of enhancing horizontal alignment), the course they actually teach, including how far they get in the outline, varies from class to class; that is, unless discussions among faculty take place, which adjunct faculty do not join most of the time.

One exception to the lack of horizontal alignment came at a college where the reading faculty developed exit requirements for all reading courses. This department required a certain grade in a course, as well as passing one of three tests of reading proficiency. The department also held a series of norming meetings with adjunct faculty at the beginning and end of each semester—and sometimes in between—to make sure that everyone understood the expectations within each course. One of the full-time instructors noted that

> It's a united effort with the proficiency exam because we don't want any one instructor to feel like we're dictating what to do. But we do use the same materials, and we do have continuity across our courses; we all use the same text, and we align so that, hopefully, the student's going to be successful in the next course.

This is a coherent statement of the need for an institutionalized response to the need for alignment, rather than individual actions "dictating what to do" to particular instructors.

For students who face a series of developmental courses, vertical alignment—coordination between adjacent courses in a series—is just as important as horizontal alignment. In some colleges, the problem of vertical alignment starts in noncredit education, since the lowest-level basic skills courses may be offered in noncredit divisions of the college. This means that for alignment to work well, the noncredit and the credit sides of the college must align their offerings. But this does not happen often, and institutional divisions make it all the more difficult for any of the three mechanisms of alignment to work. As one ESL instructor in such a college noted,

> When we started looking at it [ESL], we thought there was a transition. You go through noncredit, you get a little bit of familiarity, and then you go on with the credit courses. There's [supposedly] a path. Well, there's not a path. Noncredit is over here, and credit is over there. [The credit side] started combining classes and eliminating classes, so if you don't have the lower level classes, there's not a link between credit and noncredit.

Something similar happens in one college with an informal "gentlemen's agreement" with local adult education programs, where the lowest levels of ESL courses are provided in adult ed classes instead of at the college. But this, too, creates a problem with articulation, particularly because ESL in adult education tends to focus on life skills rather than academic skills. As one instructor noted, "The more serious ones [students] find that the adult school is not that worthwhile." So, the attempts to develop a rational division of labor between noncredit and credit courses, or adult education and the community college, in practice make the alignment problem worse. One instructor, in a college with a particularly lengthy and confusing set of developmental courses, stated the problem of vertical alignment quite clearly:

> We've got to do something about the way they move from point A to point B. When I came here, they never had any entry and exit skill requirements. What do you expect of your students? If I'm leading [English] 21, what do you expect if you're teaching in [English] 23? And how do you build upon it?—which gets into all our stuff about prereqs and so forth. Those are the types of things that take a lot of work and time that we're working through right now.

In the same institution, however, it was clear that there had been little progress:

> The coordination is a huge issue, as a lot of people are doing different things in one class, and that's not good…. They're using the same book in Developmental Communications 20 as they were using in the online class English 21—that's, like, three levels ahead, and we're using the same book. It made no sense. Coordination is really bad.

In this particular college, the coexistence of a department of developmental communications with a traditional English department made the alignment issue particularly difficult since there were two trajectories of courses to align, but the point was that the process of alignment had just gotten started. An ESL instructor at another college acknowledged that the alignment process had only barely begun:

> What we're trying to do for the first time—of course, we have a description of the classes, but it was a little fuzzy about the course objectives because nobody thought much about what the other person was teaching. We realized that it's really important to establish across the board—by the end of this course, you have to demonstrate these very specific skills.

More generally, while some basic skills sequences are quite clear (e.g., three math courses from arithmetic to algebra), in other cases, there is no carefully delineated pathway. In one college, for example, the ESL program included 6 levels of courses. The problem the department discovered was that

> The continuation or path that students take is not very easy, and the transition from level to level has been very difficult.... There's now an intensive and a nonintensive pathway, and then there's a whole lot of optional courses you can take. And then, the exit and entrance skills between some of the levels are not quite connected.

The same thing happens when there are separate reading and writing sequences that are not carefully articulated with one another, so then, as one instructor put it, "Students are stuck behind this wall of basic skills, and they take these courses over and over ... so, it [the system] is broken."

If courses are not vertically aligned, then students completing one course successfully cannot pass the next course. As one English instructor noted, "Students are passing 105, but they cannot pass 112; students are passing 112—in some cases, with good grades, As and Bs—but they cannot pass 115." This was the college that tried to establish common end-of-course exams to assure horizontal alignment and provide the basis for vertical alignment. "But remember that there's five full-time teachers and 36 to 38 part-time, and they don't participate in all this planning"—so the necessary work is undermined when a lot of adjuncts may not understand what the homogenization of courses is all about.

It is rare to find data on the proportion of students passing subsequent courses, but one college did a careful job of documenting the movement from prerequisite courses into subsequent courses in the basic skills sequence. They found, for example, that 65% of students who placed into Math 70 were successful (passed the course) if they placed into the course through the initial assessment, but only 38% of those who entered by passing a prerequisite course were successful. This suggests that prerequisite courses were not particularly effective in promoting passage into subsequent courses. This pattern was reversed for reading and writing courses, however, indicating that this particular problem in vertical alignment was present in basic math courses but not in basic English courses.

One instructor claimed that his department had discussions about backwards mapping from the first college-level course, but he attributed success more to a required course coding that came from the state: "With this coding, we had to restructure our classes and our objectives and content to fit the coding. The coding actually does a better job of it than we do." The "coding" in this case refers to a procedure called CB21 coding that requires colleges to specify whether courses are 1, 2, or more levels below transfer-level courses—though it does not require colleges to specify the skills required in each one or to align exit skills and entrance skills. This is one step in the direction of a state specification of required course elements, but only a first step.

Part of the problem is that the conventional approach to courses leads instructors to think in individual rather than systemic ways about the courses they teach. One academic support lab coordinator, a person who saw students from many different courses in her lab, mentioned that

> I don't think those instructors have any experience designing *programs*. They're *classroom* teachers, and so the program is not sequential. They've never talked about exit skills from one [course] aligning with the entrance skills of the next level…. They only see the ones [courses] they teach.

She agreed that CB21 coding was beginning to "force the hand of instructors" by requiring them to think more systematically about different levels of developmental sequences. But another part of the problem is that carrying out the requirements for alignment can be incredibly burdensome— "the types of things that take a lot of work and time"—and instructors may not have the time or the personal expertise to do this very well. In one college with five levels of ESL, which had begun to confront the lack of progress through a sequence of courses, one ESL instructor noted that

> Levels 3 and 4 have agreed that they are going to make significant changes so that they are better preparing the students to be there by level 5. They will often say, "Yes, yes, I agree with that idea" publicly, but then we don't see that playing out. This has been an ongoing problem for the entire time I've taught here.

So, unless a department is tightly knit and able to assure compliance with agreements made, it's difficult to move from agreement to implementation of vertical alignment. The same is true of course outlines, which (in theory) are mechanisms of assuring both horizontal and vertical alignment, and which are often used to regulate the teaching of adjuncts. But in one college that had adopted required course outlines, an instructor commented, "It's very sequential. That follows the course outlines, but a lot of people don't want to do that; they want to teach whatever they want." Another way to put this is that the lack of *internal alignment* among instructors so that they hold themselves responsible to group norms and agreements, means that *course alignments* are virtually impossible to develop.[4]

Yet a third problem is that there are institutional rewards for developing *courses*, since they generate additional enrollment and revenue, but not for developing coherent *programs*. As one director of basic skills complained, "It's really true [that there's no real pipeline], and the political economy makes it impossible to have a pipeline … because it looks discretely at access on a course-by-course basis." The college is therefore rewarded with additional revenue when it generates more course enrollments, but when it spends time on the difficult issue of alignment, the resulting coherent sequence generates no institutional benefits since there are no rewards in the funding system for student success—only for course enrollments.

The lack of vertical alignment manifests itself in several ways. One is that students pass one basic skills course, but then are not ready for the next course—this is the most frequent pattern, one that has led a few colleges to set up common course exams as a way of trying to guarantee that students are ready for the next course. (We heard no complaints about students being over-prepared for the next course; the dominant complaint is underpreparedness.) Sometimes students themselves feel unprepared to go on in a sequence; one math instructor noted that "there are lots of gaps in math [in the sequence], and students are retaking courses because they don't feel ready to move on." Both the underpreparedness detected in subsequent courses and that perceived by students cause problems in the trajectory of developmental courses.

At the end of the sequence of developmental courses, students finally move into college-level or credit courses. But if the sequence of developmental courses has not been aligned with college-level courses, students may still be unprepared. As one English teacher noted,

> I do know that the students who come from basic skills classes and say they have been doing average, and have a C, that they probably aren't going to be as prepared … it's going to be more of a struggle when they get into I-A [the first college-level course].

Another instructor from the same college concurred:

> I'm teaching the level below I-A, and there's such a gap, and I complain that the people who have gone through the [basic skills] program are so much less prepared than people who test in at that level. We all agree—there's no way the students can bridge that gap.

The reading faculty in one college had a more precise description of what is often missing from the basic skills sequence:

> The reading folks seem to have a model of what we're trying to do when we're trying to read something that really isn't leading them to 101 [the first college-level course]. The activity seems to be absorbing information rather than critically evaluating the information or asking questions like "Why is this writer writing this to me?" and noticing patterns that are related to the argument. Really, there's a model here where close reading means doing what your employer tells you to do. You're reading carefully to know what the authority figure is telling you, rather than reading with a critical eye.

If just "absorbing information" is inadequate for college-level courses, then even students who complete the basic skills sequence will be unprepared.

When instructors in college-level courses find themselves with many students who still haven't mastered basic skills, then one of their options is to reteach some of these skills; that is, to introduce remedial activities into what are nominally called college-level courses. As one basic skills instructor noted,

Most instructors in humanities and social sciences have incorporated basic skills instruction into their own classes—but I don't think they should really have to do that.... They [students] haven't taken English, but they can enroll in sociology, and by making that impossible through prerequisites, they'd be forced to learn how to take notes and do research and write an essay before even taking the sociology class. And then, the sociology instructors can focus on their areas of expertise, and not have to waste their time teaching such things as note-taking.

Another instructor, in math, talked about what he did with students in his college-level algebra class:

When I teach algebra, I almost assume that they've forgotten everything. It's assumed that they don't know anything from elementary algebra.... So, I do a lot of review within the class, lots of it. In that way, I will review a lot of basic skills in case you've forgotten.

This is, in effect, *hidden remediation* that takes place in college-level courses, not in the developmental sequence. Because we did not observe college-level courses, we did not directly observe hidden remediation, though an earlier study found a great deal of it (Grubb & Associates, 1999, pp. 194–199).

Another option, if students have not mastered basic skills, is to eliminate assignments that would require much of them. A biology instructor noted, "My students don't know how to write, so I'm not going to assign any writing." The biology department is moving away from requiring lab reports and essay questions—precisely the kinds of work students will have to do if they ever transfer to a 4-year college. Another instructor of a college-level general education course was blunt in outlining his strategy:

Here I am, teaching this transfer-level general education course, and I have someone who can barely even read chapter 1 from a textbook. I actually have to dumb down my course and provide a high school textbook just so they can kind of get it.

So, when the highest level basic skills courses are inadequate to prepare students for transfer-level courses, students sometimes flunk, instructors engage in hidden remediation, or they dumb down their courses. Clearly, none of these is a very satisfactory solution.

Therefore, the problem of alignment starts with articulation between assessment tests and the first-level basic skills courses, and continues along the trajectory of courses until the first college-level course. Unfortunately, it's difficult to know how crucial the problem of articulation is, partly because it manifests itself in two different ways. If students are underprepared for the next courses in a sequence, they may fail to pass that course or simply drop out, so misalignment is consistent with the evidence on low rates of completing basic skills sequences. On the other hand, if they are overprepared—as they sometimes are when they are misplaced by assessment tests—then they waste their time in basic courses they don't need, again potentially contributing to dropping out if the basic skills sequence becomes too long or too tedious. In either case, misalignment may lead to failure to complete the basic skills sequence.

Articulation with High Schools

A special case of articulation involves the relationship between colleges and high schools. As I mentioned in chapter 2, the complaint that many students are "not ready to be college students" almost always leads to high school bashing; that is, criticisms that high schools are graduating too many students who are both unprepared for college and who don't understand how unprepared they are. One potential solution is for colleges to reach out to high schools; in particular, to let high school students know what college requires so that students and teachers can adequately prepare together. While it's unreasonable to think that such procedures could eliminate the need for developmental education, they might reduce the demands on colleges for basic skills instruction.

Unfortunately, very few colleges seem to have invested in closer relationships with high schools. Many of the colleges we examined had plans—or good intentions—for collaborating more closely with high schools, but 12 of the 13 colleges hadn't done much to make this kind of articulation concrete. They simply accepted the students who came—"the hand we have been dealt"—with no efforts to warn high schools about the high rates of remediation necessary even for graduates.

The one exception to this pattern was a college in an area where the high schools were known to be in the top 10% of high schools in the state. Nevertheless, 73% of entering students required some level of basic skills instruction in math, along with 88% in English—so it appeared that the local high schools were not doing their job. The college, partly with the help of a nonprofit called Cal-PASS,[5] had established several days during the spring for high school seniors to learn more about the assessment process, take a career interest inventory, figure out the majors and degrees offered at the college, and meet with student leaders and faculty from the college. One might reasonably object that such a program was "too little, too late," that the spring of senior year is much too late to correct fundamental gaps in academic subjects and nonacademic competencies. But at least this effort warns students about the assessment process rather than leaving them ignorant until they actually take the assessment, as is often the case, and it does help with the process of formulating academic plans.

In addition, the college has published a series of reports on the placement rates of students from nearby high schools. These clarify the rather abysmal statistics on placement in basic skills courses, and could serve as a warning to high school instructors and counselors about the inadequacy of their programs in getting students to be college-ready.

Finally, the college maintains an early college high school (ECHS)—a high school taught in conjunction with college instructors. A president in another college remarked that its early college high school "is the reason principals know that students are not college-ready"—presumably because students from the early college high school fail to pass initial assessments. This again could serve as a distant early warning to high school administrators and faculty about the level of preparation *if* information about the ECHS were widely available to other high schools in the district. But in this case, just like the example of reports on placement rates, it isn't clear what the effect on the high school program has been.

Most of these efforts provide more information to high school students, teachers, and counselors about placement exams and about the need to be concerned about basic skills. But there are several other mechanisms of potential articulation between high schools and community colleges that were not being used by any of the colleges we visited:

- Aligning the curriculum of high schools and colleges would assure that students in high schools are being prepared for college-level courses—both academically and in terms of work habits. With the advent of the Common Core curriculum in K-12 education, such alignment should become easier as long as high schools truly implement these standards.
- Another early warning system involves having high school sophomores or juniors take a college's placement exam to make sure they can pass it. If they can't, such a system would provide students with remedial instruction during high school. This kind of warning has already been adopted by the California State University system in the Early Assessment Program (EAP); exams are administered to high school juniors, with a matching basic skills curriculum for those who fail to pass it.
- Coherent counseling in high school about the multiple dimensions of college readiness might help more students become "college ready." Certainly, college-level counselors and faculty would be useful in helping high schools establish what "college readiness" means.
- A mastery learning process, where students are not allowed to proceed unless they have passed lower level courses, might reduce the rate of students entering college underprepared. However, two important caveats must be noted. One is that mastery learning procedures have often led back to remedial pedagogy, as complex competencies are broken into subskills for testing proposes. Second, mastery learning tests might only succeed in pushing students out of high school; for example, the exit exams now used by about half the states, which are weak forms of mastery learning exams, have reduced the graduation rate without increasing the achievement of those who do pass.[6] The creation of mastery learning exams, perhaps as part of

the Common Core standards adopted in most states, must therefore be done very carefully to avoid making things worse or more inequitable.

Local high schools and colleges working collaboratively could conceivably adopt these four policies. However, the lack of much current articulation between high schools and colleges indicates how difficult it has been to get such efforts started. In general, colleges have neither the resources nor the expertise to help reshape high schools, and articulation between the two is perhaps better viewed as a system responsibility rather than the responsibility of local colleges.

Correcting the Alignment Problem

What's puzzling is why there is so much dissatisfaction with assessment and alignment, but so little action to remedy the problem. One issue in all the colleges we visited is that no one is in charge of the entire trajectory of basic skills, from assessment through a sequence of courses to first-level college-level courses. In most colleges, instructors and counselors acknowledged that they knew very little about the assessment itself; usually, only the director of assessment could provide any information about this high-stakes test.

Also, instructors are in charge of their own courses only, and they have no knowledge of courses directly below or above the courses they teach. There are no institutional incentives to determine whether each individual course is aligned with its predecessor and successor—and this is exacerbated by the fact that so many basic skills instructors are adjuncts, with no time or authority to make such inquiries. And the entire basic skills sequence is usually independent of transfer-level courses, so the possibilities for backwards mapping and alignment are difficult to carry out; that is, understanding the skills required in transfer-level courses and making sure they are incorporated into earlier basic courses.

It becomes difficult to coordinate the whole system when there is no one in charge, or more precisely, with different individuals in charge of various pieces of the entire trajectory of basic skills. And of course, there is no one in charge of coordination *among* colleges; when more and more students are "swirling" among colleges (for example, trying to find colleges with the most forgiving assessment system, or moving among colleges as they relocate), then the sequences of assessments and courses become even less well articulated.

A second barrier to alignment is the difficulty of collaboration among faculty, which is again exacerbated by the numbers of adjunct instructors. In general, we found relatively little collaboration among instructors except in cases where departments had organized themselves to improve instruction (as I described in chapter 4). But these are relatively rare cases; in most departments, both adjunct and permanent faculty operate in isolation from one another, and the extended discussions necessary to align courses in a math department or a writing sequence do not take place. Having such discussions requires thinking of basic skills sequences in different ways, with prerequisites specified for the prior course and then exit competencies similarly specified so that students meet the prerequisites of the next course. This is a difficult set of conversations to have, especially when there are many courses in a sequence (as there often are in ESL in particular).

Third, the incentives for alignment are weak. As one institutional researcher pointed out, colleges need to fill *courses* to get their funding, not develop *programs*. Unless there are specific resources for coordination activities, or some form of performance-based funding, there are no incentives to spend additional time in coordination activities, even though that might lead to enhanced student performance. And if there is uncertainty about whether alignment will actually contribute to better outcomes, these incentives are even weaker.

Fourth, the research necessary for alignment is often missing. Few colleges we visited had examined the differences in success rates between students who assessed into developmental levels and students who had taken the prerequisite courses. In part, this occurs because of a failure to build the research capacity even to pose these questions, never mind answer them.

Finally, money and resources are tight, particularly because of the Great Recession and its effects on public funds for colleges. The time necessary for alignment might require additional funds, particularly if adjunct faculty are to participate, and several instructors complained that there is no additional funding to cover the costs associated with alignment.

But it's equally clear, from the experiences of colleges we observed, that practices for improving alignment exist and could be more widespread. To reduce the number of students placed in remedial sequences who don't need them, some colleges have developed preparation programs so that high school students are alerted to the importance of placement tests, and have time to review material that they haven't seen in several years. Others have experimented with their own assessment tests, partly in an effort to align them more closely with basic skills courses, and partly to develop tests with more diagnostic power. Some colleges have added high school grades and transcripts to the information they consider in placement. Still others have moved to limit exceptions to having to take assessment tests, so that unprepared students do not evade being diagnosed. And the process of agreeing upon and then adopting common course exams is an obvious mechanism for assuring horizontal alignment.

One potential mechanism for overcoming the sense that no one understands the entire basic skills trajectory is to assign responsibility for alignment to a basic skills committee. This group could then worry about the alignment of the initial assessment, about both horizontal and vertical alignment, and by including transfer faculty they could focus on the alignment of basic skills sequences with initial college-level courses. Then, individual instructors could continue to be responsible for individual courses, but with some overview of the articulation among them.

In cases where departments have organized themselves as coherent learning communities, one of their primary activities has been the alignment of basic skills courses. This is a kind of existence proof showing that faculty, once they are organized, can indeed address and resolve alignment issues. But this is difficult advice to give since the internal cohesion necessary for departments to act in this way develops only over a long period of time, and does so only with consistent support from administrators as well as senior faculty (see chapter 4 for evidence). The implication is that the development of horizontal and vertical alignment is a long-term project that requires the internal organization and support of departments before it can yield benefits for coordination.

In the end, alignment requires a shift in thinking from emphasizing the improvement of individual courses (valuable as that might be) to focusing primarily on a *program* of courses over time. Clearly, this is not something that even exemplary instructors can do on their own; it is an institutional challenge, one that requires policies that affect all instructors, students, and counselors. It requires a departure from the laissez-faire college where students do as they please, instructors teach the courses they want, and counselors ignore the consequences of misplacing students in the sequence of basic skills courses. However, the promise of taking a harder and more prescriptive approach to the trajectory of assessments and courses is that students will be able to complete these sequences more effectively than is true in the current state of misalignment.

8

FUNDING, RESOURCES, AND THE MONEY MYTH

Effects on Instruction and Innovation

Among the most crucial institutional effects on developmental education, indeed, on all of education, are those of funding and resources, especially in times of fiscal shortages. The issue of funding, and the kinds of resources money might buy, has a long and vexing history in this country. On the one hand, money is absolutely necessary to create institutions like schools and colleges, with their buildings, faculty and administrators, materials of various kinds, and other expenditures that become necessary once education and training are moved out of families and workplaces. This has sometimes been elevated to the principle that money is necessary for improvement and for high-quality education, something I have called the *Money Myth* (Grubb, 2009). As Ellwood Cubberly, one of the first school finance experts, expressed it in 1905, "The question of sufficient revenue lies back of almost every other [educational] problem" (Grubb, 2009, p. 2). In the words of the dean of one college, "Plans are just plans unless you have some money"—as if there is no way to make progress on plans and innovation without new money. Another dean said simply that "innovation requires an augmentation of budget," which is a direct restatement of the Money Myth.

On the other hand, people are sometimes skeptical that the Money Myth is correct, and I will provide many illustrations in this section of when it is suspect, particularly when money may be necessary but not sufficient (NBNS). Wherever the truth lies between these two extremes, it's clear that money and resources are crucial to understanding what colleges can and cannot do in basic skills instruction.

There are several ways of recognizing the relatively low level of resources in community colleges, and in basic skills instruction. Community colleges are the bottom tier in state systems of higher education, with regional or state colleges just above them and public research universities at the top. In California, an especially definitive tripartite division of postsecondary opportunities has governed since the Master Plan was devised in 1960, which delineated the responsibilities of each level of higher education. Specifically, research universities provide PhDs and serve the top 12.5% of high school graduates; the California State University system administers masters' degrees as well as bachelors' degrees, and serves the top 33% of graduates; and community colleges oversee associate's degrees and certificates and serve all remaining high school graduates. This hierarchy has been repeated in spending levels as well: On average, universities spend $21,034 per student on instruction, state universities spend $13,452, and community colleges spend $5,450 (substantially less than K-12 education).[1] So, right off the bat, community colleges, which some might say have the most difficult educational challenges of any level of the system, have fewer resources to respond to these challenges.

Furthermore, in California and many other states, resources for higher education have been dwindling. This has been almost universally true of all states after the onset of the Great Recession beginning in 2007; however, California has suffered from over 30 years of dwindling resources ever since the property tax limitation Proposition 13 passed in 1978. As a result, real spending levels have consistently fallen in the state. While there are no good figures comparing expenditures per student in community colleges among the states, there's little doubt that California ranks near the bottom of the 50 states in both colleges and K-12.

Finally, basic skills instruction is one of the lowest-status missions or roles of the community college. It's impossible to separate basic skills funding from other funding in most colleges, but the widespread perception is that basic skills gets short shrift in internal funding decisions. One coordinator of basic skills noted that 75% of students in his college need basic skills instruction, "but only 5 to 10% of our resources go that way." While the comparison may be a little off—basic skills students usually take college-level courses as well—the sentiment suggests that basic skills is underfunded relative to its importance, a low-status mission in a low-spending state in the institution with the lowest levels of spending per student in all of higher education.

The Role of Money in Basic Skills Instruction

Of course, money makes a difference to the offerings in developmental education. The numerous ways that the problem of insufficient funds manifests itself in basic skills instruction are quite varied:

Many colleges are unable to offer enough sections of basic skills courses, and students complain of being turned away from classes they need. In many ways, the decisions about which courses and sections to offer is a zero-sum game, and offering more sections of basic skills courses to meet demand would require cutting the number of transfer-level courses. As one institutional researcher and basic skills coordinator said,

> There is not enough room in the [basic skills] sections. Everybody wants to expand [the number of sections], but I think it's a trade-off with the other courses—with the transfer-level courses. The dean of English arts, who couldn't be more supportive of basic skills, just feels she cannot cut down on English 1A. Then where would we be? ... We keep butting up against structural issues.

So, neither cutting basic skills nor eliminating transfer courses is an acceptable alternative since both of these fulfill crucial goals of community colleges.

Student Support Services

As discussed in chapters 5 and 6, the potential role of student support services is much greater than the funding available. There are always more effective but more expensive forms of student support, especially individual tutoring and supplemental instruction, and the broad array of student supports that an active college like Chaffey College provides would require additional funding in many colleges (or, at the very least, substantial shifts in funding). Student services also suffer from the instability of funding: They are the first to be cut in times of fiscal crisis, and therefore cannot benefit from the steady development and improvement that stable funding might allow.

Basic Skills: Lack of Resources

In many ways, basic skills instructors experience (and report) a lack of resources because of their perceptions that these students need *more* resources per student than do students who come to college well prepared. As the director of basic skills in one college said,

> We can't touch the actual instructional program [because of the lack of funding]. We can't pay for teachers and courses, and we can't pay for the courses to have fewer students in them, and right now, our classes are just jammed to the walls. So, yes, [funding] is a huge issue because basic skills students need smaller classes and a lot more individualized instruction and a lot more counseling and a lot more tutoring, and we don't have the resources to provide that at the level we'd like to.

So, the gap between basic skill "needs" and resources is widely perceived to be enormous, given the judgment that basic skills students need more resources per student than do college-level students. Even if the effectiveness of some of these more resource-intensive strategies could be disputed—for example, smaller class sizes would make little difference if instructors continued to use "remedial pedagogy"[2]—there's little question that more resources provide many more possibilities both for innovative instruction and additional student services.

Students with Learning Disabilities and Mental Health Problems

I argued in chapter 2 that an unknown number of students in basic skills classes suffer from learning disabilities and others from mental health problems, yet the resources to diagnose and treat these conditions are inadequate on most campuses. The potential solutions to these issues would surely include more specialized diagnostic personnel, since regular faculty are not trained to recognize learning disabilities or mental health problems. Then, with more accurate diagnoses, treatment of some kind would require other specialists.

Part-Time Faculty Working in Isolation

The large number of part-time faculty teaching basic skills in isolation from the rest of the institution, noted in chapter 9, is entirely a fiscal issue. If finances were not constraints, then all faculty teaching basic skills could be full-time faculty, with greater integration into the mainstream college, including access to professional development and ongoing discussions about improvement. But as long as part-time faculty cost roughly 40% of what full-time faculty cost (Grubb & Associates, 1999, p. 332), the incentives under conditions of limited funding will always be to substitute part-time faculty for full-timers.

Lack of Institutional Researchers and Data-Drive Inquiry

The lack of institutional researchers and data-driven inquiry, which is examined in chapter 9, is partly a fiscal issue. While the presence of a serious institutional research capacity is no guarantee that it will be used effectively, the lack of such a capacity ensures that data-driven reform becomes impossible, particularly in efforts to diagnose problems in the trajectory of basic skills.

Faculty-Oriented Centers for Teaching and Learning

Based on the examples of a few colleges,[3] faculty-oriented centers for teaching and learning can improve the quality of instruction and foster innovation in a variety of ways. There are obvious costs, such as paying for individuals to operate the centers and organize the activities (including professional development) that might improve instruction. However, such centers need not be expensive. In fact, they can be operated with as little as one director and one additional staff person—and in an institution of 100 to 200 faculty, this represents a marginal increase in spending. But fiscal constraints invariably limit the willingness of colleges to develop such centers, unless they have outside funding.

The Effects of Layoffs

Decreased funding often results in layoffs, with the remaining individuals taking on more responsibilities, especially when fiscal pressures are experienced over long periods of time, as they have been in California. Over time, this leads to an institution where everyone has too many responsibilities. This happens with administrators as well as faculty—"It's not money, it's all about people" and "We're strapped for people" are common statements in the colleges we visited. The result is an institution without the human resources to engage in innovation: Everyone is so busy keeping the college operating that planning and reform have to take a back seat, or, more specifically, they have to wait until there is discretionary funding to enable the college to hire more individuals. This is one of the reasons that external funding becomes so important to reform, as I will illustrate later in this chapter.

The Limits of the Money Myth

While more funding could be used to make basic skills instruction more effective, many respondents doubt that money is the central issue, or is the only important issue in reform. The chair of a student success committee stated bluntly, "It's not really a money issue—it's hard to get people with the time and interest." As one director of basic skills noted,

> I would say it [streamlining and improving programs] is less about funding than it is about long-term planning, and maybe part of that is this turnover of presidents every so often—and we've had a lot of administrative changes and VP changes and structural changes.

Thus, stability is a resource that is quite different from money but that may be required for greater effectiveness. Later in our discussion, this director rethought the role of money: "Actually, in the end, [the budget] is it: The issues of budget and being organized and having a long-term plan are really tied together." In effect, funding is only one element in being able to improve programs; being organized, adopting a long term plan, and having enough stability for a long-term plan to work are intertwined with budget problems—and all four of these would be necessary to develop meaningful reform. The necessary resource is what I call a *compound* resource: three elements are necessary in addition to funding, so money is necessary but not sufficient (NBNS).

In several other ways, it turns out that money is not necessarily the problem, or not the entire problem. A number of other issues related to funding are just as difficult as the lack of money, and they suggest that the Money Myth is sometimes either wrong or incomplete.

Programmitis, or Funding Small, Uncoordinated Programs

One characteristic of how many (but not all) colleges spend money is that they use new funding, or outside funding, to support a variety of small programs rather than larger innovations.[4] The tendency to search for external funds from foundations and governments is part of this practice. Individual faculty and offices apply independently for funding and then support innovations in one part of the institution, in one department, for example, which are not matched by innovations elsewhere, so the reforms are not systemic. The tendency to do this with outside money has been particularly prevalent with the state's Basic Skills Initiative, in which small grants have often been given out without any coordination. As one director of basic skills said about the way her college spent these funds, "The primary finding [from a needs analysis] was that we lack coordination and integration. So, my concern is that we will continue to fund individual, uncoordinated projects without looking at the big picture, which was the biggest disconnect." This college did, as usual, finance individual projects with its new money.

In another case, a college committee recommended basic skills funds for eight small projects, including pilot projects. But in an institution where the math department was generally thought to have conventional instruction, only one of the eight projects focused on math, and none of them did anything to correct the dominance of remedial pedagogy. The president decided that these proposals were too fragmented, and refused to release funding for them until a basic plan was established. Similarly, an administrator at another college declared, "The other part of it being that when you have a proliferation of projects, at some point when you decide what the sustainability plan is, maybe all of those things don't necessarily continue." Again, planning and spending are ideally interwoven in place of spending on "a proliferation of projects." One college spent its first amount of Basic Skills Initiative funds on smart classrooms and training in how to use them, described as a real waste "because we didn't have anything else to go on"; that is, no overall plan. After that, however, the money was doled out for small-scale programs, partly because equitable representation of all interested parties led to each of them promoting a different approach, rather than a clear plan based on overall priorities.

The tendency to fund little programs without much scale extends to pilot programs as well—initial efforts that presumably could be "scaled up" if they proved effective. But in the college that funded eight pilot projects with its BSI funds, one faculty member commented, "We can try pilots all you want—a pilot doesn't change a culture. No, the conversation will—if you can get people going and doing things in concert," rather than individually.

A chair of a learning assistance program in another college talked about the many programs she would like to see at her college, particularly learning communities for several different groups of students. But then, she backed up:

I would rather us focus on specific groups and moving forward with one thing that works, instead of making us so broad that we have a lot of programs but we're missing the mark. I would like something more focused. [If we have many different programs] it would just get bogged down with so many different things.

One way to avoid the problem of many little unfocused programs is to centralize services in some way, and several colleges have tried to centralize support services, in a Learning Center, for example ("Give the Learning Center its due so you don't have people all over the place").

Lurking beneath the tendency to spend on many small programs are several other issues. One is the difficulty of implementing larger and more centralized ideas. As one director of basic skills asserted, about the innovations in her college, "There are silos of interesting things, but it's not spread around." Similarly, another administrator said, "We don't do what we already know. We're often aware of existing effective solutions, but we don't implement them on a large scale because there's not enough budget allocation, and many proven strategies can't be utilized in traditional classrooms." So, when larger innovations look too daunting, the only alternative is the proliferation of small-scale interventions.

Second, small innovations are consistent with the culture of isolation in some colleges—what I call the *laissez-faire culture* in chapter 9. One instructor complained that

working alone is part of the culture. The college doesn't require instructors to do anything [together], so they become lazy. The administration encourages everyone to remain separate so they can deal with them as individuals, rather than working with a group that wants something. Because our jobs are so easy, why not teach and go home?

The result is that the agreement and coordination that would be required for large-scale efforts does not happen.

A third issue is that of consistency, coherence, and alignment. One director of student support services talked about trying to "run everything through the Learning Center so there is some consistency." In contrast, when small programs proliferate, there is unlikely to be much consistency, particularly in approaches to instruction. This means that student experiences are also fragmented and incoherent. Similarly, with small programs in different parts of the basic skills agenda, creating a coherent pathway through basic skills becomes close to impossible. One college we visited had articulated a Quest for Success program, one which

takes the students and walks them through [a sequence] ... but first, we had to have the shell, and that shell is Quest for Success because that was what was missing. We had this piece here, that piece over there, but we didn't have anything coordinating all of those efforts. And that [Quest for Success] will produce a paradigm shift.

So, the common notion of clear pathways for students to follow represents "a paradigm shift" in the words of this educator, but it cannot be accomplished with individual programs that are uncoordinated.[5]

The final and perhaps most important issue is that of scale: "little programs" (by definition) do not reach many students. One director of basic skills described the process of soliciting proposals for basic skills programs on her campus ("I'm not sure the process ... is a healthy one"), and then acknowledged,

I worry sometimes that programs like this [little programs that emerge out of soliciting proposals] focus on small groups of students. I have 60 to 65 sections of basic skills math—that's a ton of students. Can we touch them all? I would like to somehow see where lessons learned could be scaled up and incorporated right across the board because that's the only way we're going to be able to benefit students.

When colleges invest in many small programs, each of them is really a "boutique" program, and none of them has the ambition or the methods to "scale up," with the result that very few students are "touched" by the innovation. This is, of course, a problem with many innovations, including learning communities and contextualized courses, but it is driven, in part, by the way that many colleges allocate funding.

In contrast, Chaffey College—with its exemplary student support services described in chapter 6—has avoided programmitis by investing in larger initiatives like Student Success Centers that then house smaller efforts. That's what the motto "Think big or go home" means. The result has been a set of services that are more transparent, operate with some consistency in their basic principles, and involve large numbers of students, in contrast to what individual programs typically accomplish.

It is tempting to claim that programmitis leads inexorably to the waste of external resources, but that is not always true. Many small-scale programs funded in this way surely do some good while they are in existence; many of them have been chosen through a competitive process, so they must be superior in some ways to the alternatives. But these types of programs, particularly those tied to individual faculty members, the kinds of idiosyncratic pedagogical innovations profiled in chapter 3, usually don't survive, so any benefits are only temporary. If the point of innovation is to develop sustained changes for the long run, then programmitis looks like a waste of money. These programs may also lead to cynicism about innovation—or "innovation fatigue," as in K-12 education—if faculty watch one innovation after another evaporate after investing in them.

The Volatility of Funding

In addition to relatively low levels of funding, California's funding for education—as well as that in many other states, which are subject to roughly the same business cycles—has been quite volatile. Increases in funding during good years (like the late 1990s) have been followed by sharp cuts when the economy plummets, as in the recession of 2000 to 2002 and in the Great Recession since 2007. Volatility also comes from specific grants being expanded and cut because of colleges' dependence on small outside grants for any innovation. Volatility creates its own problems, quite independently of low levels of overall funding: It becomes difficult to plan, and programs vary from year to year. As a tutoring specialist complained,

> I have memo after memo from, like, 10 years, saying, "Hey, I need money." If you're asking me to function on federal work-study and Cal-WORKs work-study, the pool [of students to hire] is going to vary quite a bit from semester to semester. And one semester, I might have a stellar program, and the next semester, I won't be able to find very good tutors.

In addition, volatility means that the kind of decade-long but steady improvements we observed in some departments (profiled in chapter 4 on innovations) are not possible because of periodic cuts in resources. The previous statement from the basic skills director that "it is less about funding than it is about long-term planning" is a clear indication of the effects of volatility on planning efforts. This represents another example where money is necessary but not sufficient (NBNS); where more funding *and* stability of funding would allow planning and steady improvement, but where instability undermines the effectiveness of whatever funds are available.

The Problems with Soft Money

Like most other educational institutions, community colleges devote the vast share of their resources, perhaps 90%, to salaries, which cannot be reallocated without the bloodshed and political difficulties involved in letting people go. As a result, virtually the only discretionary spending comes from outside grants—from foundations and government discretionary grant programs, also known as "soft money" (in contrast to the "hard money" in a college's basic allocation from government funds and tuition). But soft money suffers from several problems, the principal one being that it is almost always of limited duration; therefore, when the funding ends, the program it supports is likely to end as well. The result is that soft money, while it might be the basis for later permanent changes supported through hard money, largely supports temporary programs. As one director of student services said, "There's a cynicism that sometimes grows up around soft money because we've all watched soft money projects come and go," with the implication that when they go, they leave no trace of themselves in the organization.

Similarly, a vice-president of academic services expressed his dismay at funding student services from soft money:

> I'm uncomfortable using the level of soft monies—grant monies—to support services so essential to student success. I want us to be able to step up to the plate and be able to provide a guarantee to our students.... In terms of them planning long-term and short-term project development, it's much more advantageous if we know that there's a stable base of funding there.... Consistency is another piece we need to have—that what we provide our students, they need to know that next semester, it's still there, and the semester after, it's still there, so it's not something they will be worrying about.

This VP highlighted the importance of transferring the funding of student services from soft money to hard money. In another college, a dean of basic skills forced the vice-president for instruction to fund a basic skills coordinator out of hard money "to institutionalize it," rather than using the state's basic skills grant that would surely disappear.

Most colleges ardently seek out soft money from any source they can find. However, it clearly undermines the Money Myth-related notion that money can solve all problems because it may not be effective in creating long-lasting change and effective planning—as hard money can be.

Creating Constituencies for Programs

Another funding issue is the tendency for specific programs to generate political constituencies, making it more difficult to create rational budget allocations, particularly in periods of economic distress. The constituencies come both from the student side and from the faculty side, and make it difficult for colleges to develop new priorities. Here's a dean of students talking about the power of existing constituencies, when it became clear that her college needed to place more emphasis on basic skills:

> I saw the BSI initiative as a way of taking those best practices that were identified, and bringing them in and see how we can produce change. Will they allow us to make change? And what can we do with resources that we currently have? And the different ways of how can we do that by doing a paradigm shift with the players that we have.... And what are we going to shift to? ... Even our president has said very clearly that there are three initiatives that we're going to have, and when we cut classes, he said that the three we're going to work toward are basic skills, transfer, and general ed. We lost some programs that the kids are screaming and hollering [about], and I screamed on some things. We lost the applied

music program, and the kids are hollering and screaming. We lost work experience for the nurses—they came 75 strong at a board meeting. We lost our GED and a lot of programs—I can't believe the pressure he took for dropping that cheerleading class.

So, even programs that are peripheral to important missions of the college develop constituencies, and cheerleading is surely a good example, which makes them that much more difficult to cut during hard times. Of course, these constituencies include faculty and administrative deans as well as students. A dean of language arts recounted the internal battles during a period of scarcity: "Then it becomes competitive with other disciplines, and especially in a time of scarce resources, administrative deans are advocating for their own areas—so they fight one against the other, and then we can't [decide]—we have to choose." There's a general tendency for deans to come to view funding as "theirs," and they become unwilling to give up "their" funding even if, from an institutional perspective, it makes sense to reduce one program to sustain another. The problem with this perception is that it forces planning and innovation to become issues of personal sacrifice, rather than institutional issues where priorities are clearly defined.

These are the conditions in which the zero-sum nature of funding becomes most acute—with any improvements in one area needing to come from other areas (with their constituencies) being cut. So, the power of constituencies leads right back to the Money Myth: It is infinitely easier to innovate and change when there are increased funds to do so, but the notion that "innovation requires an augmentation of budget" is simply untrue, not when colleges can set priorities and plan accordingly.

The Neglect of Complex and Abstract Resources

When most people in our sample talk about innovation, they refer to what I call simple resources, such as more full-time faculty, fewer adjunct faculty, more sections of tutoring or supplemental instruction, sometimes smaller class sizes, or more counselors. These are resources that are arguably effective* *and* cost money in obvious ways. But these are not the only kinds of resources that might be effective. Two other categories include *complex resources*—resources that are complex both to understand and to change, particularly those related to instructional approaches; and *abstract resources* describing abstract features of a college like stability, its climate, and the extent of cooperation and trust within it (Grubb, 2009).

---

* Whether they *are* effective is a more difficult question, one that has usually not been asked (let alone answered) at the community college level. In K-12 education, some favorite and expensive resources turn out not to be effective, like smaller class sizes and classroom aides.

The importance of highlighting complex and abstract resources is that they cannot be bought directly—there's no way to simply buy improved instruction or greater cooperation, the way there is for simple resources. Instead, faculty and administrators must work together to *construct* abstract resources using nonfiscal resources like vision, collaboration, and trust. Most of the time, when people talk about the Money Myth, they neglect abstract and complex resources, and the ways they can be enhanced without spending much money. For example, here's a dean of student services talking about some of the weaknesses in his college:

> We do a lot of research, [but] we don't follow our own research…. We're still doing chalk and talk for the most part in a lot of our classes. We are not doing a lot of student engagement, not doing anything new and different. We have an older campus as far as staffing goes, so people are set in their ways. And a lot of the things that we say [about] how students learn best—different learning modalities, how to present it differently, different mediums to give students information—we don't know. We are in the classroom and we talk; you be quiet and you write down what we say, and that's it. And so, engaging the students—there's not a lot of that going on.

But all the dimensions of change he calls for don't cost that much money; for example, actually using the research the college produces, trying innovations with older faculty who are "set in their ways," moving away from remedial pedagogy to forms of teaching that are more motivating for students. However, they do require vision, leadership, and trust, which are precisely the qualities we saw in the few departments that have collectively reformed their approaches to instruction. Many of the innovations profiled in chapter 4 have the same characteristics: They may require funding for dissemination, but their adoption in any one college depends more on existing resources (and especially faculty) working in different ways, rather than additions that require increased funding. Until faculty and administrators recognize the centrality of complex and abstract resources, they will consistently underestimate the amount of innovation that can occur with existing resources, rather than the increased funding dictated by the Money Myth.

Waste

Finally, in virtually every organization that we can think of, a substantial amount of waste takes place, and community colleges are no exception. Waste takes many forms (and sometimes is virtually invisible), but within educational institutions, perhaps the dominant forms of waste are embedded in practices that are ineffective. In the colleges we visited, some of the important forms of waste include professional development following the approach of flex days; the dominance of remedial pedagogy, or the failure to develop approaches to instruction that are "engaging the students"; and the lack of articulation among basic skills courses in a series, causing students to have to repeat courses. Other forms of waste are related to the inaccuracy of basic skills assessments, causing some students to take developmental courses they don't really need; ineffective guidance and counseling, with an overwhelming amount of criticism of counselors for being poorly informed; and (again) spending money on individualized programs without any overall plan or coordination among them, or programmitis.

What is particularly upsetting in educational institutions, especially low-spending ones like community colleges, is the simultaneous existence of great need and great waste. Although it is relatively easy for individuals to identify waste in their own organizations,[6] these forms of ineffective spending are usually neglected when it comes to thinking about the role of money and outcomes. Waste weakens the relationship between spending and outcomes, and thereby undermines the Money Myth in important ways.

Overall, the belief in the centrality of money as a precondition for reform and improvement, the Money Myth, is alive and well in community colleges, as it is in most educational institutions. Moreover, some of the time, the Money Myth is right: There are many innovations that are sorely needed in developmental education that would indeed require additional resources, and both the low levels of funding and the volatility of funding in many states undermines the ability to invest in these programs. But the Money Myth is not wholly correct, either, and there are many examples where the barriers to reform and innovation involve other characteristics of colleges aside from their relatively low spending levels. These examples—particularly instances of waste, as well as generating and utilizing complex and abstract resources—provide opportunities for innovation without spending large sums of money. Until colleges recognize such possibilities, they will remain trapped in the mistaken belief that only simple resources with obvious high costs can lead to improvement.

The Effects of Funding from California's Basic Skills Initiative

So far, the institution of the community college has been examined as if it were independent and autonomous. But that's not true, of course: In every state, community colleges are dependent (in part) on state policies, including funding decisions. Therefore, a complete account of the institutional conditions affecting any classroom or affecting developmental education requires an examination of state policy as well. It might also require an examination of federal policy, too, but because there is so little federal funding in community college basic skills education,[7] this aspect of institutional influence can be ignored for now.

In California, a major influence of the state has come through the Basic Skills Initiative (BSI). The state has funded this program since 2005–2006, providing about $30 million in the first year, slightly higher amounts in the next 3 years, and then only $19.1 million in 2009–2010 and 2010–2011. The

BSI is important because it illustrates how colleges behave when they are given an injection of funds specifically earmarked for developmental education.[8] The most significant issues concern the effects that new funding has and how new monies are spent, especially with regard to the kinds of innovations they support.

The effects of the BSI can be divided into three categories: the symbolic value of funding, the effect on planning mechanisms, and the actual effects on expenditures. First, it's clear that the BSI had a symbolic effect in highlighting the importance of basic skills. As one vice-president stated, after years of "having felt so marginalized and sort of having to justify ourselves, to have the state say 'We're going to give you this money' was just phenomenal...Thank you—you are noticing that these are who our students are." Another noted the role of external funding in signaling the importance of basic skills: "Basic skills became important on this campus when we got money for it. If all the money disappeared this year, we'd stop talking about basic skills next year." In a third college, the English department had left basic skills to a Learning Skills department, and wanted as little to do with it as possible. When BSI money came along, however, the English department got interested in basic skills again, and the two departments merged. As one participant described the process, "It was that kind of politics—'We [the English department] don't want anything to do with it. Oh, there is some money attached to it somewhere? Now, we want to get back into it.'" Of course, symbolic effects do not support real programs, but there was still a pervasive sense that the mere existence of the BSI signaled the importance of basic skills in a way that no internal efforts could.

A second value of the BSI has been its role in convening important constituencies, and planning. Virtually every college we visited (except one) convened a planning committee to decide how to spend the money. This then led to discussions across departments about priorities for the use of funds—discussions that would not have taken place without external funding. As one vice-president of instruction explained,

> The whole Basic Skills Initiative is causing everyone to look at how they do things. It wasn't just another grant; it really required assessment and accountability. Because we want that money, the requirements have forced us to look at what we are doing. Without the BSI initiative, we would probably have ignored the idea of basic skills—"Well, there are always going to be these students that don't read and write at the right level." I think we would have kind of ignored that, but this has, in a good way, forced us to look at it. [The BSI] has forced us to recognize that there is a problem. That's been a wake-up call.

Several colleges discovered the need for greater coordination; as one dean said, "The primary finding is that we lack coordination and integration" of the many parts of the basic skills program.

In addition, what might be called the convening function of the BSI led to other discoveries. In one college, the basic skills committee included faculty from disciplines other than math, English, and ESL. These faculty began to understand what a crucial role basic skills play in getting students prepared for other courses: "If they [students] can't read a textbook, how much synthesis, how much mental synthesis and mental maturity is there in understanding the bigger concepts?" Then, the instructors in the various disciplines began to understand that some of these demands were beyond what many students could do: "There was a very big disconnect between what I was assigning and what that [BSI] advisory committee was geared toward." Another instructor said, "That's what this grant is doing, giving us opportunities to get the faculty from different departments together, where we don't always find ways to do that." There is indeed some irony in relying on an external grant to convene internal participants, something that a college could do on its own: "It's kind of funny that the Basic Skills Initiative has given us the platform for having conversations that we wouldn't have had otherwise," commented yet another participant. But there's no question that the function of an external grant in stimulating planning and convening has been one of the real benefits of the BSI.

Partly because of the widespread finding of the need for coordination and integration, virtually all of the colleges spent some of their funds to hire a basic skills coordinator. (There were a couple of exceptions, as well as cases where one individual has performed the function of the basic skills coordinator along with other administrative tasks.) However, the dominant pattern of funding was to develop an Request for Proposal (RFP) process to invite the submission of individual ideas for funding, and then to support a number of individualized programs—what someone called an "ATM model" of handing out money—rather than supporting one or two large objectives. For example, in one of the colleges with the most careful planning process, a committee was convened. It held a series of meetings, developed a document that remained unpublished because of the contentious things it said, distilled a set of principles and goals ("We developed a couple of things we know we want to keep, no matter what"), and created a great deal of faculty participation. In the end, however, the first year's money was spent on a series of smart classrooms, which everyone recognized as a waste (as mentioned above). From then on, funding was spent on little programs according to an RFP process, and the committee's hard work in distilling principles and goals went for nothing.

In one college, a learning specialist said that "everybody's just grabbing money," even though the basic skills coordinator was trying to think of new ways to coordinate and prioritize. In another college, a participant noted,

> a lot of talk and still not a lot of coordination. On paper, it may sound like there's a lot going on, but I think nothing really substantial and significant has gone on, even though all this money has been thrown in during the last couple of years.

In this sense, the BSI process replayed the tendency for colleges to spend money on the types of small-scale programs that I reviewed in the previous section. In the end, the majority of colleges funded a basic skills coordinator—reflecting the pressures for coordination and planning—but spent most of the money on small programs, reflecting the difficulty of getting agreement on a smaller number of larger priorities.

To be sure, a few colleges did not follow the path of investing in individualized programs. One college decided to invest in a full-time ESL instructor, since a problem for many years had been the lack of coordination among ESL adjunct instructors; the college also invested in professional development for instructors. Another college began with an RFP process, but after seeing the fragmentation that would emerge from this approach, it decided instead to hire five full-time faculty members in basic skills. (Note the importance in these two colleges of hiring full-time faculty members—who can, in turn, create some coherence—in place of adjuncts who teach classes but never have the authority to plan or coordinate.) A third college began to develop a program of spending on small programs, but the president intervened and declined to sign off on spending unless the basic skills committee developed a coherent plan. Similarly, Chaffey College has consistently used new sources of revenues to develop substantial practices like the Student Success Centers, with presidents and deans refusing to support little programs (as mentioned in chapter 6, Vice-President Sherrie Guerrero described the approach as "Go big or go home"). So, once again, a small number of colleges are able to use resources for large, overarching practices that create a more coherent basic skills system, but most have spent their resources on small innovations that don't emphasize effective practices much beyond the immediate classroom.

Finally, in at least two colleges, funds were spent in ways that represented a simple substitution of BSI funds for other funds. In one college, the director of matriculation bemoaned the lack of counselors: "That's because they [the college] cut matriculation. And the only way they get counselors back is from Basic Skills Initiative money. And if you have a Basic Skills Committee that does not want to fund counseling, then they don't." In other words, the proposal in this college was to use BSI money to backfill money that the college had cut from matriculation and counseling. Similarly, tutors in another college reported that when BSI money came, the district funds for student services dried up—rather than BSI money adding to what the district was already spending. This was a substitution of BSI funding for district revenues, another case of backfilling. Of course, grants like the BSI are always susceptible to the phenomenon of substitution; the result in these two cases—and possibly in other cases[9]—was that BSI money did not fully add to the spending on basic skills.

Finally, some data are available on the kinds of spending under the BSI.[10] By far the largest amount, almost 53% of $19.5 million in 2010-2011, went for student services—advising, counseling, supplemental instruction, and tutoring.

The second largest amount, 15.6%, went for program and curriculum planning, and another 13.6% went for coordination, which is consistent with our observation of the effort spent on convening basic skills committees to develop priorities and coordination. Four percent went to the development of assessments and 3.6% for research. But only 11% went to instructional materials and equipment and professional development, so the funding for instructional improvement was small compared to that for supplemental services and for coordination and planning. Indeed, in one college, the coordinator of the Writing Center reported that he stopped attending the BSI committee meetings. Although he was interested in the improvement of instruction, the committee stressed study skills, social skills, role models, and the alleviation of stress, aspects of teaching that could all be incorporated into existing instructional approaches ("Why not make these part of classroom instruction?"). But actually *reshaping* approaches to instruction is difficult, and it requires professional development of a particular sort. In contrast, spending money on support services is much easier, it seems more directly linked to students' academic troubles, and it identifies the locus of the problem in the students rather than in college-wide problems of instruction. It appears that even given the dominance of remedial pedagogy, very few of the additional resources available under the BSI were spent to develop alternative approaches to instruction.

In some ways, the story of BSI funding is an account of what happens when a state spends money without any clear guidelines, and with pressure to spend money quickly, but without a lot of time spent on thinking about how it could or should be allocated. Two things inevitably happen: the responses of individual colleges vary considerably, and colleges do not necessarily spend the money on good practices. Indeed, one director of matriculation was quite cynical about the process that the state has followed in the BSI and in other community college grant programs:

> When you throw money like Partnership for Excellence money at a community college and say, "Do something good with it"—yeah, right. Basic skills money, same thing. "Do something good. Point it toward this, OK? Let us know how you're doing. Good luck." As far as I can see, there are no demands for anything.

This director blamed the lack of directives from the state—or accountability mechanisms—for the inadequate use of BSI funds. Other states have been more directive in providing additional funding to basic skills; for example, Washington's I-Best program restricts funding to learning communities incorporating basic skills instruction with career-technical education. California's laissez-faire approach maximizes local discretion, but probably not the effectiveness of spending.

Overall, then, the results of the Basic Skills Initiative seem distinctly mixed. There's no question that the BSI has had substantial value in highlighting the importance of basic skills, and was also a shot in the arm for those who felt marginalized and neglected in developmental teaching. There's also little doubt that the planning and convening role of the BSI has been important in fostering conversations about developmental education that would not otherwise have taken place. But, at the end of the day, the additional funding supported by the BSI largely followed the familiar pattern of being doled out in small amounts for individual initiatives, rather than substantial efforts to reshape basic skills. And the majority of funding has gone for student services, not for instructional improvement. Until colleges are able to spend discretionary money in other ways that are consistent with a vision for what strong instruction and support services should be, additional resources for basic skills, contrary to the Money Myth, are likely to have only marginal influences on their offerings. Once again, money itself is necessary but not sufficient (NBNS) for improvement in developmental education.

9

OTHER INSTITUTIONAL EFFECTS ON INSTRUCTION AND INNOVATION

In previous chapters, I examined two broad institutional influences: assessment and alignment of courses in chapter 7, and money and resources in chapter 8. In this chapter, I analyze five additional influences that emerge from our study of 13 colleges: (a) the influence of the course as the basic unit of educational provision; (b) the importance and form of professional development; (c) the crucial role of adjunct faculty and their isolation from the rest of the institution; (d) the notion of data-driven reform; and (e) the nature of the community college as a laissez-faire institution, in contrast to the possibility of moving away from this particular model. All five influences shape what happens within the classroom, as well as in labs, workshops, and other student services—with both positive and negative effects. Certain institutional influences are obvious, like the basic lack of resources in community colleges compared to other institutions, but others, like the laissez-faire nature of many colleges, are not so clear. But any comprehensive examination of basic skills in community colleges must include an analysis of these types of institutional influences.

This examination, in turn, leads to a number of recommendations, though I won't be explicit about all of them. Some are simple to articulate but politically difficult to accomplish, like the need for more resources. Others are politically easier to achieve but conceptually much harder to envision, such as the call for more individualized instruction, for example. But all of the recommendations in this chapter have the potential to improve the quality of basic skills instruction and the progress of students, despite their roots in rigid institutional practices that are often difficult to change.

"Batch Processing": The Course as the Unit of Instruction

One aspect of community colleges, indeed, of all educational institutions, which is easy to overlook is the dominance of the course as the basic unit of instruction. Most educational institutions package their offerings as courses, with specific constraints for duration (e.g., one semester or one trimester long, starting at the beginning of each semester); frequency (e.g., meeting two to three times a week); and format (e.g., one instructor and many students). Any pressure for new offerings or innovations is likely to find its way into courses. For example, the need for instruction in "how to be a college student" is usually placed into student success courses or courses like Introduction to College.

This means that, with the help of assessment tests, students are formed into groups and go through each course together, which is a form of "batch processing" where students are treated in batches or groups. As mentioned in chapter 7, opportunities to test out of a course are rare, so once students are directed to a place in a sequence, they usually must complete that sequence with other students. As cited previously in chapter 7, one counselor lamented, "We don't use a test that's diagnostic. So, we're taking someone who may have had a bad day and making them take three semesters of remediation." Another complained about students "stuck behind this wall of basic skills" taking developmental courses over and over again without getting free.

To be sure, there are widespread practices within developmental education that do not follow the conventions of courses, and many of them are in student services. Several colleges offer brief workshops, which range from a couple of hours to several sessions, on particular basic skills. Labs and centers allow students to come in for varying periods of time and varying or individual purposes. But many of these practices are course-driven; indeed, I argued in chapter 5 that it would be an improvement to make them more course-driven by requiring certain labs and workshops in courses, particularly as a way to get students who are most in need of student services to use them.

There are, of course, good reasons for the domination of courses in educational institutions. For example, courses are more efficient than certain practices like tutorials since there are more students per instructor. Also, it is bureaucratically easier to keep track of students and instructors in courses than it would be if all instruction were individualized, and it's easier to articulate longer courses than a sequence of smaller modules. Furthermore, having a class of students that meets regularly allows for some of the student-centered pedagogical practices that move away from remedial pedagogy and that treat learning as a social rather than an isolated activity. Similarly, the popularity of learning communities comes (in part) from the fact that students can get to know one another better when they have more contact, and students can then learn from one another. Some of the ways of moving away from courses are too expensive, some are too difficult, and some lead to inappropriate pedagogical practices, such as adult education with its drop-in/drop-out practices, in which instructors are often forced to use individualized workbooks to accommodate student schedules.

The alternative to batch processing is some form of individualized instruction. In the many classrooms we visited in 13 colleges, we saw only two examples of individualized instruction. In one case, an instructor used reading logs to diagnose her students' reading levels and difficulties, and modified assignments accordingly; in the other case, an instructor prepared several assignments, at different levels of difficulty, for different students. Both are versions of differentiated instruction; that is, instruction tailored to the needs of individual students or small groups, which is widely recommended but less often practiced in K–12 education. Otherwise, all the classrooms we observed were dominated by batch processing, or the similar treatment of all students within the class.

But there are two other approaches, aside from differentiated instruction, that allow for more individualized instruction but which are discouraged by an emphasis on courses. One is a modularized approach, where colleges offer modules (which are much shorter than traditional courses) focused on specific skills. Then, using *diagnostic* assessments, students are required to take only those modules they haven't mastered. In fact, the state of Virginia is moving toward a modularized system, where all courses will be split into nine modules and students will complete modules as needed (Asera, 2011). This would get around the problem of students having to take entire courses when they don't need them. The only problem is that smaller modules lead quite naturally to remedial pedagogy; that is, drilling on the small subskills of each module without much understanding of how they fit together into a comprehensive competence. One could readily argue that as long as most instruction follows remedial pedagogy, modules will make no difference to this practice; they would have the decided advantage of individualization without changing instructional approaches. But the best approach in this case would be to develop modules with more conceptual or constructivist pedagogies, and that was something we didn't see in the colleges we visited.

A second form of individualization would be a mastery learning approach, in which individuals can test out of any sequence, course, or module once they have mastered certain skills measured by a series of assessments. This would allow students to escape the need for completing sequences or courses when they really don't need to; it would be particularly beneficial for "brush-up students" (see chapter 2) who have been away from academic work for a while and just need "brushing up" on basic skills to remember what they have already learned. From the perspective of the students we interviewed, a mastery approach would enable them to escape from long sequences of courses that seem "just like high school." A mastery learning environment requires a series of assessments that allow students to demonstrate their mastery. Unfortunately, like modules, the need to develop mastery learning tests for subskills runs the risk of reinforcing remedial pedagogy.

The conundrum, then, is that different instructional approaches are better at achieving different goals. If basic skills instruction is thought of as a sequence of subskills—relatively decontextualized but useful in many different contexts— then remedial pedagogy that includes small modules and mastery learning procedures is wholly appropriate. But if developmental education is thought of as the early stages of collegiate education—learning fundamental competencies related to mathematical thinking and communication—then small units or modules are weak alternatives to longer courses. Therefore, to reflect the most desirable aspects of basic skills instruction, a division of labor seems appropriate. Longer courses could be structured as they are now, taking conceptual or constructivist approaches to instruction in place of remedial pedagogy. They would be supplemented by short workshops and modules following mastery methods for those subskills where students need more review or drill. Indeed, this is what now happens in the best-developed colleges like Chaffey College (see chapter 6). Short skill-oriented workshops provide access to drill and practice on subskills; supplemental instruction reinforces conceptual aspects of courses; and conceptually oriented classes take advantage of the dimensions of courses—longer periods of time, students learning from one another—that are consistent with constructivist approaches rather than remedial pedagogy. If such an approach also incorporated conceptually oriented (rather than skills-focused) mastery tests, then it would balance the need for individual progress with the need for some conventional coursework.

Moving toward this vision of flexible scheduling requires partially abandoning the course as the basic unit of instruction. To be sure, there are other requirements for such a vision, including different ways of calculating workloads for students and for instructors. But colleges already have methods for incorporating courses with workshops and individualized labs. Coordinating them more systemically would emphasize the advantages of different forms of instruction, rather than depending largely on the course as the basic unit of instruction.

Professional Development

In all educational institutions, including the community college, instructor quality becomes central, especially when we are concerned with approaches to instruction. Colleges (like universities but unlike K-12 education) do not require any preteaching preparation in instructional methods, assuming instead that content mastery—typically, a master's degree in a subject area—is sufficient to know how to teach. If this proves not to be true, then there are only two solutions: to fire weak teachers (say at the point of tenure decisions); or to provide professional development (PD) in the hopes of improving the quality of teaching. The first of these solutions, letting instructors go, is not widely used in colleges (Grubb & Associates 1999, ch. 8), leaving professional development as the only mechanism for improving the quality of instruction. One might reasonably conclude that the effectiveness of developmental education is crucially dependent on the quality of professional development. In addition, community colleges like to think of themselves as "teaching colleges," as distinct from research-oriented universities. Again, being a teaching college requires some commitment to instructional improvement, presumably through PD.

"Professional development" means many different things to different people. In K-12 education, there is a long and regrettable tradition of professional development that takes the form of Friday afternoon lectures from prominent outsiders. Only relatively recently has it become apparent that effective professional development—activities that change teacher practices—require *consistent* action over long periods of time, in *collaboration* with colleagues. Effective forms of professional development also give teachers opportunities to practice alternative approaches to instruction (with feedback from supervisors) and to concentrate on pedagogical content knowledge (Little, 2006)—the application of general pedagogies to specific content areas like basic skills instruction. This approach emphasizes professional learning communities of teachers working together to improve their collective practices. We can see professional learning communities in community colleges in Faculty Inquiry Groups, which convene like-minded faculty to discuss instructional issues. Professional learning communities also emerge when departments organize themselves into cooperatives for the purpose of first defining what strong instruction is, and then reinforcing it through a combination of faculty selection, development of course materials, and ongoing discussions about pedagogical approaches (see chapter 4). So, the nature of PD, and not only its mere existence, is crucial to teaching practices.

We saw an enormous variety of professional development in the 13 colleges we examined. At one extreme, a college required 33 hours per year of professional development, but faculty could qualify almost anything for these hours, such as reading in their discipline, any kind of conference or Webinar, or presentations on technology. This approach to PD was totally individual, with no effort to set a collective agenda or to get groups of faculty involved in coherent activities. Another college supported a number of "achievement coaches" with state funding; these coaches brought basic skills to the attention of faculty, distilled best practices and disseminated them, mentored individual faculty, and worked with departments to support faculty making their own improvements. These practices had the advantage of trying to focus a department on different approaches to basic skills. Yet another college supported PD for 12 adjunct faculty per year, working through modules on topics like approaches to instruction; it proved quite popular not only as a form of PD but also as a mechanism for integrating adjunct faculty into the college. However, there was nothing quite comparable for full-time faculty, though this college did provide an active schedule of workshops for all instructors.

Two of the colleges we visited, including Chaffey College, had centers for teaching and learning focused on the faculty. A third had just gotten a federal

Title III grant for such a center; the administrator described the grant as having "a focus on the faculty and staff development and helping them understand the learner-centered method of teaching, as opposed to 'I taught it, so why didn't they learn it?'" These teaching and learning centers are, in effect, forms of faculty development, since they can provide help to faculty in a variety of ways. At Chaffey College, for example, the Faculty Success Center (examined in chapter 6) offers a series of workshops ranging from the effects of growing up in poverty to critical thinking for ESL students. It operates a voluntary program of classroom observations and feedback, and it also runs a summer institute focusing on innovative practices, with the goal of getting faculty to think of themselves as researchers. In addition, it provides a forum for discussions about innovations on campus and offers workshops for faculty who have had critical reviews of their teaching. A faculty-oriented teaching and learning center can therefore carry out a variety of professional development activities, and serve as a point of focus on campus for instructional issues.

However, by far the most common approach to PD in California is the designation of "flex days," when colleges provide a number of speakers on different topics of interest to the faculty. Unfortunately, almost no one thinks flex days are effective forms of PD. One instructor, asked directly about professional development, responded,

> Well, they don't directly offer anything. We do have flextime, according to our contract. Usually, people find the flextime activity just a waste of time. So, I would have to say that, professionally—all around from every possible angle—the school actually has no professional encouragement. I haven't gleaned anything from [this college] whatsoever.

Another faculty member mentioned that "you get what you pay for—the PD activities are not focused on teaching," and they lack any kind of follow-through: "The faculty like to do their own thing." Another individual, a director of a Center for Teaching and Learning, claimed that "when it [professional development] is left to individual instructors, they like to learn more in their own disciplines, so they learn new content—as opposed to spending time looking at pedagogy." Because individuals choose the flex day activities they attend, and because many activities are not focused on instruction, the possibilities for using flex days as the basis for any collective agenda around instruction are limited. To be sure, the few departments that have organized themselves into professional learning communities have used flex days for collective discussions of teaching approaches, assessments, alignment, and curriculum development. Otherwise, however, flex days represent smorgasbords of topics without any coherence.[1]

From an institutional perspective, flex days serve the individual interests of faculty, whereas colleges with centers for teaching and learning can address institutional and departmental priorities. Only when PD is viewed as a mechanism for collective improvement—as is true in colleges with teaching and learning centers, or when departments have organized themselves into professional learning communities—can PD can be structured so that groups of faculty are committed to ongoing instructional reform. In the process, their promise of being "teaching colleges" can be realized.

Adjunct Faculty and Their Isolation

Despite their high numbers, adjunct (or part-time) faculty in community colleges are elusive. They don't usually show up on rosters of courses, and they often don't list their phone numbers or e-mail addresses, so it is difficult to contact them. As a result, our efforts to observe and interview equal numbers of full-time and adjunct faculty were unsuccessful—we simply couldn't find many adjunct faculty, and many did not respond to our requests for interviews. Nevertheless, in virtually all colleges, adjuncts teach the majority of basic skills courses, even though numbers are hard to come by;[2] in the colleges we examined, the numbers of adjunct instructors in basic math and English far outweighed the number of full-timers. (In community colleges as a whole, temporary faculty represent about 70% of total faculty.) This is partly because of the simple economics of adjuncts: per course, they cost roughly 40% percent of what full-timers do.[3] The need for flexibility also leads to the use of more adjuncts—they can be more easily hired and let go as enrollments in basic skills courses ebb and flow.

Finally, full-time faculty usually want to teach college-level courses, and since their preferences have priority, they leave basic skills courses to adjuncts. At one college, we asked what proportion of basic skills courses were taught by adjuncts, and the response by a math instructor was "most of them…it's the adjuncts that get stuck" teaching basic skills courses. (In this college, the math department had 16 full-time instructors and 70 part-timers.) In this college, as in many others, teaching basic courses was unpopular among the full-time faculty, and there was resistance to teaching them from the "historical transfer culture." Like several other suburban colleges in our sample, this was an institution that had been devoted to transfer for middle-class students, and the full-time faculty dealt with the shift to more developmental education by hiring part-timers to teach basic skills.

One issue with adjuncts is how they develop their courses, since they are typically paid for hours of teaching and not for preparation. The dominant method is for a member of the full-time faculty (often the department chair) to be the contact point for part-timers. The curriculum is created by full-timers and then handed to adjuncts; as one part-timer noted, "I am given the book and then I teach from that. I have never seen anything else beyond that, for me." Of course, adjuncts are free to develop their own approaches, partly because no one checks on how instructors are teaching; this particular instructor engaged in different types of instruction, for "variety—students do well in different situations, and I don't want to spend the whole time lecturing." But another adjunct was more explicit about the process of following a prescribed outline and homework activities:

> At [this college], we're very privileged. We have a class coordinator and they tell us what to teach … it makes our job so easy. They organize—on this day you're teaching this, on this day you're teaching this … it's called the lecture outline, what you're going to cover each day…. They [the full-timers] pick the homework, and they develop, like, which things you're supposed to do so we know what sections to cover.

If the goal were to standardize sections of a course—to eliminate what I call "horizontal misalignment" in chapter 7—this would be one way to do it. But note that the instructor called these materials "the *lecture* outline," suggesting that they would encourage a conventional lecture following the outline of the text. Since the vast majority of textbooks are dominated by remedial pedagogy, any elaboration or contextualized examples or conceptual approaches must be developed by the instructor—so the easiest path for an adjunct instructor (especially the overly busy "freeway flyers" who teach in several different colleges) is simply to follow the textbook. Rather than being a way of creating consistency across sections, this approach looks like a way of "teacher-proofing" the curriculum so that any adjunct could teach it—but at the cost of reinforcing inappropriate teaching.

Of course, some colleges are less prescriptive than this; they merely hand adjuncts a syllabus—what topics to cover in different courses—and then the adjuncts can choose their own textbooks. But since most textbooks in math and in writing follow the approach of remedial pedagogy, this increase in instructor choice still doesn't enhance instruction very much.

The second issue with adjuncts is the extent of their integration into the colleges they serve. If they were really part of a faculty, then they would participate in developing the courses they teach and in all professional development efforts of the college, including experimental or novel approaches to instruction; they would participate in identifying problems in basic skills and then formulating solutions. But except in a few colleges that have made substantial efforts to integrate part-timers, adjunct faculty in virtually all colleges are marginalized in various ways. For example, they have much lower status, and can even seem invisible to the full-time faculty. As one part-timer who tried to follow his department's philosophy complained, "The few times I have gone to department meetings, or when they've asked me to come as a part-timer, I was not well received." Another ESL adjunct at the same college said that "part-timers are pretty much left out in the rain," though at another college where she taught, the adjuncts were encouraged to work with others in the ESL department—so, as with everything in community colleges, there's considerable variation from college to college.

In examining adjuncts, it's worth profiling an adjunct math instructor at one of our urban colleges. His teaching was the epitome of remedial pedagogy, dominated by lecture and demonstrating procedures from the board, with no examples or indications about how math or mathematical thinking might be used in other settings:

> Basically, [my instruction] is the traditional type, which is the lecture. So, I'm out there to present the idea, then go through examples and home-work and ask if there are any questions.... If I had a smaller class, maybe their response would be group study. However, I've got to be mindful that that uses a lot of time, so therefore, is not efficient. So, it depends on how much time I'm willing to expend in order to cover subjects.

In practice, then, coverage and efficiency were most important, and "group study" was nonexistent. While this part-timer admitted that adjuncts have autonomy to bring in supplemental materials, he didn't do so "because I find that the textbook examples, as well as the exercise prompts...[are] sufficient"— though the textbook provided no examples outside of conventional math prob-lems. But it isn't clear what would prompt him to change his instructional approach, since (like most adjuncts) he was quite isolated from the rest of the department. He admitted his discussions with members of the department were "infrequent," and they sounded quite scattered:

> I would have conversations with them when I'm in trouble—for exam-ple, if students need to talk to the chairman or the dean. Sometimes we have professional development days, so therefore, I'm in conversation and meetings with others. This is very rare, but if I see them in passing, we might chitchat. One occasion that comes to mind, I was sitting there and getting ready to leave to go to my parking lot, and I saw another instruc-tor—we just talked as we went to the parking lot. But that was only once in the three semesters I've been here.

Regarding professional development days, he admitted, "I won't say it's been helpful, but it's been informative"—in other words, it had not changed his practice, but "it's always food for thought." So, here's an instructor with con-ventional remedial pedagogy, but he is not integrated into the college in a way that any professional development could engage him or change his practices.

Another adjunct at a different college, an English instructor with a more varied approach to teaching (and also a "freeway flyer"), described his isolation from the rest of the college in similar terms. He had a problem with ESL stu-dents showing up in his class unprepared, but he was unsure whether there was any forum to discuss this with the ESL department. In practice, he had asked his peers (i.e., other adjuncts) about any problems, and then "the full-time faculty I've actually had contact with," and then, if necessary, the dean. But

> In terms of us part-timers as part of the department, speaking with the ESL department—in my years here, I haven't talked to anyone officially from any other department. So, if I go to the full-time faculty or the dean with my questions, it's kind of their ball, and then they run with it from there.

So, instructional issues that come up for adjunct faculty don't have any real resolution mechanism. Similarly, mentoring is haphazard: while adjunct faculty are supposed to have full-time mentors,

> [Contact with mentors] is pretty much voluntary, and it's up to your schedules. Some adjuncts, they know they have a mentor and they've talked with them. Some adjuncts know they are supposed to have a mentor but it was never set up…. So, if adjuncts aren't talking to people about the issues that come up, then they may not know that they have a mentor.

Similarly, professional development is hit-or-miss; as another adjunct said,

> There's not a whole lot of communication from the department to the adjuncts regarding these [professional development] days. Most of the time, I go to meetings and I'm not sure if I'm supposed to be there or if I'm required. So ultimately, I didn't end up going, just because I wasn't sure.

Furthermore, this adjunct continued, "On this campus, I don't see a lot [of teaching support]. In terms of workshops and meetings and things like that, they do offer them, but again, the problem with being an adjunct is you don't have the time." Or, as another adjunct said, "It's the part-timers' problem—a lot of things are scheduled when we're somewhere else."

The unfortunate part of this instructor's story is that his English department has worked hard for over a decade to develop its own approach to teaching writing (profiled in chapter 4 on innovations). But poor communication to adjuncts, uncertainty about how they fit into the department, and the crazy schedules of part-timers all conspire to prevent them from participating in efforts to improve instruction. Also, part-time faculty at many colleges are left out of innovations or pilot programs because of the additional funding required. Somehow, adjuncts are viewed at many colleges as not worth the investment—even though adjuncts often teach for many years at the same institution.

Part-timers are not always so marginalized and need not be. In several colleges, individual adjuncts were full participants in innovations like learning communities, or developing a coherent approach to math instruction (profiled in chapter 3). Such efforts may be due to adjuncts who are particularly motivated to engage in innovative instruction, but they do illustrate that adjuncts can be fully engaged in the instructional life of the institution.

More impressive are the institutional efforts of two colleges to incorporate adjuncts. One of them has developed a professional development program focused on adjuncts with three components: (a) a Teaching Skills Workshop, an 18-hour course for instructional improvement based on microteaching (15-minute lessons on which adjuncts receive feedback); (b) Advanced Teaching Workshops, which are 1- to 2-hour workshops on common teaching practices and techniques (like constructing an effective syllabus, technology, and promoting "active" learning); and (c) Reflection on Classroom Teaching, in which participants plan a lesson with a mentor and then receive feedback. Within this mix, the program covers the nature of community college students. As one adjunct, who had attended the college years before, admitted while reflecting on the program,

> I'm not going to get a student that was like me, where I took initiative and I loved to study—I was home Saturday night studying. I have students who don't have their basic skills sets, they're not motivated, they don't know why they're here. And that was another big thing: understanding the community college student.

Most importantly, the four part-time instructors we observed who were included in the Adjuncts Program were not isolated, as adjuncts usually are, and were all enthusiastically supportive of the program. One argued that "it should be for everybody—as a requirement, part of the job description," and another confirmed that it was rougher than any boot camp but that it had made him into a "real teacher." A third instructor noted its importance in "opening the doors to a lot of things … as a result, I feel even more connected to the college. I feel the sense of community here." So, a relatively small effort—in this case, six Saturdays over the course of one academic year—seems to be enough to reverse the isolation that most other adjuncts feel. The only problem with this program is that it can accept only 12 people a year (down from 20 because of budget cuts) out of 40 to 50 applicants, so it has been unable to accommodate the evident demand. The adjuncts who do not get into the program are presumably in the same situation as adjuncts elsewhere.

Similarly, part of the Chaffey Plan (profiled in chapter 6) is the principle of including both part-time and full-time faculty in every activity of the college. The college pays for adjuncts' time to attend workshops and seminars provided by the Faculty Success Center, to participate in discussions about future directions (like acceleration, the wisdom of online courses, and the fledgling efforts to integrate math into the Chaffey Plan), and to innovate in their courses. There is no reason to think that adjuncts are marginalized in the same ways as they are in other colleges. Overall, the increase in the number of adjuncts may seem inexorable, particularly in a period of dwindling funding, but there are ways to make sure that this does not negatively affect the instructional program.

Based on our observations and interviews, the problems associated with high numbers of adjunct instructors are more serious than most observers of basic skills programs have acknowledged. A trifecta of institutional conditions—the tendency to be handed a syllabus and textbook from full-time instructors; the lack of time for instructional improvement; and adjuncts' isolation from colleagues and from professional development efforts—all reinforce the tendency for part-timers to use conventional remedial approaches, and to be immune from efforts to improve instruction. Improvements in developmental instruction will be hard to achieve until colleges confront the dilemmas (and possibilities) posed by large numbers of adjuncts.

Institutional Research and Limited Capacity

During the past decade, the idea of data-driven reform has become increasingly popular, in both community colleges and K-12 education. At the national level, the Lumina Foundation has spent millions of dollars working with 26 initial colleges, improving their capacities to analyze data and then to use the results to improve college policy. Although the initial results of this experiment are distinctly mixed, with no changes in student outcomes and most improvement efforts being relatively small (Rutschow et al., 2011), no one doubts that more data can be useful. For basic skills in particular, better data can identify where in the trajectory of basic skills courses students are dropping out, which is an important way to identify those parts of the system that need strengthening.

To be sure, several of the colleges we examined have used data in precisely these ways. As mentioned in chapter 6, Chaffey College had a strong data analysis capacity from the beginning of its reforms in the late 1990s. This was useful first in clarifying to faculty the extent of the "crisis" in basic skills, and then in more closely analyzing where students were having trouble completing the trajectory of courses, thereby identifying points where student services might be useful. The college has also examined which students use student services and which ones do not in order to target information about services more precisely; it has identified the courses in which pass rates are the lowest, and focused supplemental instruction on these particular courses. Faculty members have access to the college's longitudinal data system through an easily used program so they can produce their own analyses.

In two of the 13 colleges we visited, institutional research offices were comparably strong. For example, Chisholm College carries out analyses of passing rates to see where tutoring or supplemental instruction might be needed. This college has also used its data system to encourage instructor research efforts. A second college has pioneered the use of data clarifying the noncompletion rates associated with long series of courses, leading to ideas of acceleration; that is, shortening the period of time in basic skills to reduce the likelihood of dropping out. Both have developed longitudinal data systems, in which students can be tracked over time as they take different courses. Both have relatively well-staffed institutional research offices, which are regularly consulted on issues of improvement. In such institutions, data become one of the central mechanisms for participating in rational problem solving. Reforms are proposed only after problems are identified and their causes are examined based on longitudinal information.

However, in the other 11 colleges we examined, data analysis was either weak, or in three colleges, missing completely because of the lack of an office of institutional research.[4] Two colleges were part of a district where all the institutional researchers were fired by a chancellor described as a "dictator who expects people to heed his word." Another college had a prominent institutional researcher who moved away and was never replaced; one dean there acknowledged "that [data] is something we as deans don't do a good job of. When we meet, we don't go through the data." In yet another case, the office of institutional research had sufficient resources, but they were largely devoted to conventional reports for the college, rather than for diagnostic analyses that might lead to change.

One difference among colleges is the perspective of the institutional research office. In many colleges, institutional researchers are relatively passive, responding to requests for research but not searching out opportunities to pose questions or address troublesome issues. Institutional research is commonly used for conventional reports to funders and for public relations; data on student enrollment is typically used for enrollment management, to make sure that course sections are full, rather than for improvement. In contrast, in the two colleges with the best developed research capacity, institutional researchers participate in defining researchable questions. The institutional researcher at Chisholm commented that she was on a large number of committees because "other programs I'm evaluating, I join their committees just so that I am more involved with them and understand what they're doing. Rather than being the outsider receiving the information, I try to be inside." Furthermore, this IR office is clearly focused on improvement; as the director noted,

> We've tried to get away from "Ooh, it would be nice to know" items. We required them [faculty] to submit an action plan once they got the data back.... We will not work on another request from that office or that department until they've submitted the action plan.

In addition, "They have to submit a research request form that identifies how it connects with our basic skills plan." In this college, data analysis is always linked to action plans, and action plans are linked to the college's overall basic skills plans. This IR office carries out a large number of studies tracking student success, "so we're very much focused on improving the success rates of students and getting them through the pipeline faster, and having the skills." One way to summarize the different attitude of this institutional research office—and of others in colleges with active research programs—is that they look at data analysis as tools for *evaluation and improvement*, rather than simply for institutional requirements.

Finally, we suspect (though we can't prove it) that basic skills research is a relatively low priority for most colleges. One reason for our suspicion is that most colleges were unable to give us even rudimentary data on their basic skills programs, because their institutional research offices were so understaffed. In one college, a researcher hired with state money to do research specifically on basic skills noted, "[In most colleges], institutional research is so busy doing other things and they don't have a researcher for their basic skills program. So, they're like, 'Ah, we don't know what to do.'" In the absence of a position earmarked for basic skills research, projects related to developmental education have to get in line with other research projects, some of which are mandated by the state and some of which are necessary for reports to local constituents. This can work both ways: in Chisholm College, with its active approach to basic skills, the institutional researcher claimed, "Anytime their requests come my way, it really gets bumped up [in the queue of research]." But in the battle over priorities for research in most colleges, we suspect that developmental education often loses out to other subjects that are institutionally more important.

As is typical in education, the capacity for data analysis and data-driven reform varies substantially among colleges. A small number of colleges have highly competent research offices, with sufficient resources to conduct evaluative research; their attitudes toward what they do, and their embrace of evaluation and improvement, are markedly different from other IR departments. But many colleges have very little research capacity: they turn out only routine reports, they have very little evaluative capacity, and they seem to put basic skills at the bottom of their priorities. In these colleges, our questions about basic skills were often met with a simple declaration: "We don't know." And another (smaller) number of colleges have no research capacity since they don't have any institutional researchers at all. Under these conditions, the promise that data might contribute to reform is simply empty.

The Community College as a Laissez-Faire Institution

One of the dominant traits of community colleges is that they are laissez-faire institutions where most members of the institution, but especially faculty and students, are allowed to act as they wish, rather than in accordance with institutional norms and expectations. We saw laissez-faire practices dominating basic skills in community colleges in many ways.

On the student side, initial assessments are not uniformly enforced, since many students can escape the initial assessment entirely (see chapter 7). Also, in many cases, prerequisites are not enforced, and students can enroll in courses for which they lack basic skills. This, in turn, puts instructors in a difficult position, which is not of their own making, where they either flunk students without such skills or engage in "hidden remediation."

Usually, no effective mechanism exists to lead students to plan for their college careers; contact with counselors is minimal. Except in the few colleges with effective early warning systems, nothing forces students who have fallen behind to meet with counselors or other advisors. In contrast, a director of an Extended Opportunity Programs and Services program (EOPS), for low income students, noted that she was able to require that such students see her three times per semester to check on their progress, so that "EOPS is more focused and intense."

In addition, student support services are almost always voluntary (illustrated in chapter 5), with the result that the students who most need them do not receive them, in contrast to an approach like that at Chaffey College where courses usually require some participation in support services. So, most students are able to drift through the curriculum without any plans for making progress or any requirement to check in with counselors or student support personnel.

On the faculty side, the notion of academic freedom pervades colleges, and is usually interpreted as the freedom to teach what and how an individual prefers. As one faculty member defined academic freedom, "Every faculty member has academic freedom; they're really allowed to teach as they see fit or not." In other words, the practice where some faculty never teach basic skills courses is the direct result of academic freedom and a laissez-faire policy, except where departments have come together and worked out an agreement that, for example, all faculty teach basic skills classes in rotation. By and large, faculty teach their courses in isolation from one another, which is one of the factors that makes the articulation of any sequence of basic skills courses more difficult. As one faculty member lamented,

> I think way back when, before I even came there, there was more departmental time, more shared norming sessions, and more curricular discussions and that sort of thing—more sense of us as a department as opposed to us just teaching courses.

This complaint illustrates the difference between a department with expectations of how its members behave and a laissez-faire department "with us just teaching courses." The idea of professional development as a series of flex days, where individual faculty can choose from a variety of offerings and "everything's voluntary," is also consistent with a laissez-faire college. The alternative occurs in departments that have organized themselves with professional development activities that follow specific instructional objectives: all members of the department follow a similar set of professional development activities that are related to instructional improvement (see chapter 4 on innovations).

The difficulty that colleges have had in aligning developmental courses in a sequence is also testimony to the domination of the laissez-faire college. When instructors teach in isolation from one another—when it's "us just teaching courses," rather than a coherent department—it becomes difficult to make sure that any one course prepares students well for the next course (demonstrated in chapter 7 on assessment and articulation). Articulation normally requires discussions about course content and then joint decisions about what is to be taught in various sequential courses, something that does not happen in the laissez-faire college.

"Programmitis," where any discretionary funds are spent in ways that satisfy individual faculty desires for small-scale experimentation, rather than establishing larger priorities for the college as a whole, is also part of the laissez-faire college. The weak state of data analysis and institutional research in many colleges is also consistent with laissez-faire policies; without data, it is impossible to identify problems that might lead to solutions that could restrict student or faculty prerogatives. In programmitis and other practices advocated by upper-level administrators we can even see a conception of leadership that is consistent with laissez-faire principles. As one president of a college stated, her goal was "empowering people who are creative by recognizing their activities. If I hear that Kate or Jessica gains some notoriety, I put it in an e-mail to the community." That is, she assumes that faculty will respond to this kind of incentive, rather than structuring the college and its culture so that faculty work together (not individually and idiosyncratically) on developing new practices. This conception of leadership avoids the need to create college-wide priorities and expectations of faculty, focusing instead on fostering innovations that are relatively small in scale and, like the idiosyncratic innovations I examined in chapter 4, limited in the number of students they reach.

In contrast, when faculty and administrators talk about the practices they would like to see in place of laissez-faire policies, they invariably mention stronger requirements and expectations of faculty, coordination and centralization rather than decentralization of services, and the vision and culture of the college as a whole, all of which are ways of moving away from laissez-faire practices. In one college, the president acknowledged that the centralization and coordination of initiatives was a major challenge. He attributed this to an organizational structure bound by personalities, with many faculty "set in their ways" who then "rule the day," and he acknowledged that it was difficult to promote change when there were so many "built-in trenches." Interestingly, he did not see himself as having the power to change these elements of the laissez-faire college; he seemed resigned to this as the way it was at his college and every other. In another college, a common refrain from deans and department chairs was they didn't think they could "push it," or risk the support of faculty by pressing too hard for innovations. The dean of mathematics resolved this problem by developing a voluntary program using adjuncts, but leaving the core faculty of the college alone. Similarly, from the faculty side, a biology instructor lamented, "One of the questions I often have here is: What are the priorities of the college as a whole? I'm honestly not sure." She had a vision of a college where every faculty member reinforces certain basic skills, like writing; in effect, she was calling for an institution where agreements and priorities can be hammered out and then followed by individual faculty members—a far cry from the laissez-faire college.

In many colleges, the recommendations of basic skills committees and coordinators included a more "centralized" system, which referred to different things in different colleges. In one college, it meant all students seeing counselors, who then followed up more actively with students ("intrusive counseling"). This included more coordination of courses (like integrating reading and writing) and the presence of counselors in classrooms, who started looking more carefully at curricula and their alignment, reporting everything to the institutional research office, and getting back reports on progress and problems ("analyzing the data"). These strategies create clear expectations of students, instructors, and staff like counselors and institutional researchers. In another college, the dean of student development declared, "The primary thing I'm looking at is more coordinated effort between language arts, library, and instructional resources, and trying to get them to work more collaboratively." Her vision was focused on changes in instruction, and trying to make sure that instructional resources (especially tutoring), basic skills in writing, and reading were being done more collaboratively. However, when we asked about her strategy for doing this, she grumbled, "Don't ask me today! Right now, we're getting to the point where we're talking and trying to identify some of the issues. That's the first thing." Her response indicated frustration with even getting discussions going about priorities and collaboration, never mind coming up with solutions to laissez-faire practices.

Alternatives to laissez-faire treatment of students include well-enforced requirements that students take initial assessments, meet with counselors, and develop educational plans that they either adhere to or change in thoughtful ways. Such practices have recently been recommended by California's Community College Student Success Task Force, which (in many ways) envisions a much more definitive set of requirements that students must meet in order to stay in good standing.[5] Similarly, a greater centralization and coordination of student services is one of the impulses behind a different approach to student support; for example, by a Learning Center or a series of Student Success Centers so that the student services follow some basic principles.. As quoted in previous chapters, "You want to give the Learning Center its due so you don't have people all over the place."

An alternative to the laissez-faire college would also forego programmitis in favor of establishing a few larger priorities for innovation, which is precisely what many of the basic skills committees and coordinators have tried to do with California's Basic Skills Initiative. This alternative is not necessarily undemocratic (unless senior administrators make decisions without faculty and staff input), and it still provides opportunities for many faculty members and administrators to weigh in on the priorities of a college. It's simply that, once overarching priorities are established, they are used to decide what specific activities should be supported, rather than leaving these to the preferences of individual faculty members.

The alternatives to laissez-faire colleges have been articulated relatively clearly in K-12 education. One idea is that organizations should demonstrate *internal accountability* where faculty, leaders, and students all face norms and expectations for the ways they behave toward one another and toward instructional responsibilities (Carnoy, Elmore, & Siskin, 2003). Internal accountability turns out to be a prerequisite for an organization to respond to *external* accountability; for example, state and federal accountability requirements. Internal accountability is also necessary to change instructional approaches; otherwise, only a few individual faculty members will change their instruction. As one developmental math instructor said,

> A lot of things I would normally use in high school—maybe like worksheets as guided discovery or having discussions and they [students] report back—I can't really use that. Yes, those are good practices, yes they are, but I can't do it in classes with these types of demographics unless it's some sort of systematic effort where we [the department] actually plan out. So, we have *all* got to use group techniques ... and then, when they [students] go to the next class, they continue to do that with the people around them.

In other words, if students are uniformly taught to use group discussions (or any other instructional approach) in all their math classes with "some sort of systematic effort," then they become used to them and all instructors can draw on such approaches. But individual instructors trying to use them independently will find that they "can't really use that" because students will not understand such instructional approaches. Therefore, in the absence of some coherent and collective approach to instructional change, the default remains remedial pedagogy.

Internal accountability also includes the notion that students (as well as faculty and leaders) have obligations to the organization. The notion that assessments, prerequisites, and educational plans should all be mandatory rather than voluntary is an implicit argument that students need to behave in certain ways, in their own interests, and over the long run. Similarly, the common complaint that many basic skills students are "not ready to be college students" is a statement that students need to behave in certain ways in order to move through college expeditiously. When this complaint is combined with college efforts to prepare students to be "college students," for example, through Student Success courses and explicit orientation programs, it recognizes parallel obligations on the part of both students and the college in supporting college readiness. Thus, internal accountability imposes clear expectations on students, faculty, leaders, and colleges as a whole about how they behave.

In addition to internal alignment, others in K-12 education have articulated the idea of a professional learning community; that is, a community of instructors where, through discussion and sharing student work, a department or grade-level group comes to common understandings about instructional approaches (DuFour & Eaker, 1998). A professional learning community is the antithesis of isolated instructors following their own proclivities about instruction—the opposite of a laissez-faire department. The analogue in community colleges includes those departments I described in chapter 4 on innovations, where a department has worked over long periods of time to develop common understandings of students, their needs, and instructional approaches that can best serve them. Professional learning communities also include Faculty Inquiry Groups (FIGs) with similar goals. The discovery that professional learning communities have generally developed a common pedagogical approach is also a recognition that internal alignment is necessary before there can be widespread change in instructional approaches.

So, the alternatives to laissez-faire colleges are not particularly mysterious: these ideas emerge whenever faculty and administrators talk about centralization, coordination, alignment, more coherent departments, or professional learning communities in place of "us just teaching courses." But the shift away from a laissez-faire college is not something that can take place with one or two instructors deciding to change their practice. By definition, it requires institutional consensus and decisions, a vision of what a different type of community college might look like, a different kind of leadership, and faculty who are willing to accept a loss of individual freedom ("academic freedom") in the interests of a stronger institutional approach to instruction. If these conditions cannot be developed—if indeed, as one dean lamented, "It has been a challenge to get everybody to buy in and everybody to get involved"—then the fallback position is the laissez-faire college.

Conclusions and Implications

The seven institutional issues examined in chapters 7 through 9 are quite varied. They include basic institutional practices that affect all educational institutions, the course as the unit of instruction, the dilemmas of funding, and resource issues. They affect also those issues that are particular to community colleges, like the importance of adjunct faculty in teaching basic skills, the influence of the Basic Skills Initiative, and the very size of the basic skills enterprise. Nevertheless, these issues have a number of elements in common.

First, because these seven practices all describe institutional patterns it is clear that individual faculty (or even groups of faculty such as departments) cannot make much headway in resolving the dilemmas that these approaches create. There are exceptions; for example, an individual department can create forms of professional development for its own members. But for most of these patterns, change requires the institution as a whole to come to a decision about innovation and make uniform changes that affect all courses, instructors, and administrators. This requirement for institutional action runs contrary to the fact that many changes and improvements in basic skills are the work of individuals (as reviewed in chapter 4 on innovations). But that's precisely what it means to identify institutional patterns that affect all faculty and all courses: reform and innovation require collective rather than individual action.

Second, these institutional patterns and constraints lead to a substantial, even overwhelming agenda for change and reform. I won't list everything here, since every section of this chapter contains a number of explicit recommendations for reform. There is the conceptually simple change that provides more professional development focused on instruction, for example, or investing more in data analysis capacity; and there is the more complex change, like thinking about alternatives to the course as the basic unit of instruction. Even apparently simple changes require different ways of thinking about community colleges; for example, enhancing the ability to engage in data-driven reform requires both an enhancement of capacity (i.e., the number of institutional researchers) and a shift to thinking about institutional research as a form of assessment and evaluation rather than just a way to report the facts. Reducing the numbers and the isolation of adjunct faculty would require not only the provision of many more full-time faculty positions, but also treating the remaining adjuncts in more collegial and inclusive ways. So, the reform agenda outlined by these institutional patterns requires both changes in institutional practice and changes in the ways of thinking about elements of the community college.

Fourth, some innovations implied in this chapter obviously cost substantial sums of money. Addressing the chronic underfunding of basic skills, enhancing the data capacity in colleges that lack it, and replacing adjuncts with full-time faculty—or paying for adjunct faculty to participate fully in colleges—cost money in obvious ways, and in this sense, the common insistence on the centrality of funding (the Money Myth) is correct. In a period like the present, when virtually all states are suffering from decreased revenues, investing in these particular reforms may be impossible, and may need to wait until fiscal conditions improve. However, many other reforms require using existing resources in different ways, and can therefore be undertaken without expanded funding. These include changing the nature of professional development so that it is more collective, in place of flex days and other forms of PD that bring external experts for Friday afternoon lectures; taking a more flexible approach to courses; moving away from programmitis and thinking more collectively about how to use external funds. Some elements of reforming the laissez-faire college, like making certain practices compulsory, could be done with existing resources. So, along with the Money Myth, it's incorrect to think that all institutional reforms require waiting for new funding. In reality, many solutions could be undertaken within existing budget constraints.

Fourth, the reforms implicit in these institutional patterns, some more than others, challenge basic assumptions of the community college. Trying to think about alternatives to the course as the basic unit of instruction might, for example, lead to an educational institution structured quite differently from most. Taking professional development seriously runs counter to the assumption in all of postsecondary education that content knowledge is sufficient for teaching. Pushed to its logical extreme, it implies that preservice preparation might be a prerequisite for teaching, especially in subjects like developmental education where strong teaching is so difficult. Notions of data-driven reform, particularly where data are extensively used to monitor student success and progress, are quite different from assumptions that merely providing courses is sufficient for student success. Overturning the tendency in some colleges to engage in programmitis requires thinking about colleges in different ways, as collectives with institutional interests rather than as institutions that serve the predilections of individual faculty and departments. This is, of course, what it means to challenge institutional patterns and practices, but it implies that the prerequisites for reform are all the more difficult.

Finally, challenging the assumptions and practices of the laissez-faire college is another substantial reform that requires rethinking what an educational institution should be. The alternative, in which all participants have obligations to the institution, implies different roles for faculty, for students, and for leaders and administrators. In the alternative approach, faculty have obligations to the institution, rather than just to teaching their individual courses. These obligations, in turn, require participation in collective decisions; for example, about approaches to instruction, about the appropriate role of remedial pedagogy and the alternatives, about the prerogatives of full-time faculty relative to adjuncts that might serve students better in terms of their success. Students have obligations to the institution as well, such as becoming "ready to be college students," with the patterns of behavior and the habits of mind that are part of being in college. This would include such issues as participation in mandatory practices that are demonstrably in their own interests, planfulness, readiness to engage in student-centered teaching, and attention to the requirements of higher order academic work. And administrators should think differently about their positions, too, and act less in top-down and hierarchical ways and more in the collaborative patterns associated with distributed leadership and innovating from the middle, with administrators and faculty supporting reforms together.

These conclusions may seem a long way from the basic skills classroom. But I stress once again that what happens in classrooms cannot be understood independently of what happens in the institutions in which they are embedded. More importantly, what happens in classrooms cannot be changed for the majority of students without the reforms outlined in chapters 7 through 9 because these are institutional reforms that cannot be achieved by individual faculty members working alone.

10

RESOLVING THE BASIC SKILLS DILEMMA

Conclusions and Recommendations

I began this book by clarifying the current "crisis" in basic skills instruction within community colleges. One of its sources, the large number of students who come to community colleges without sufficient preparation for college-level work, is not the fault of the colleges, although they can take various steps in their assessments and in cooperation with high schools to moderate the numbers of these students. The second source, which is more under colleges' control, is that so few students entering developmental courses ever manage to complete a sequence of courses and move into college-level work. Thus, addressing the basic skills dilemma requires paying attention to two different problems, with different kinds of solutions.

Throughout this book, I have noted the issues that are systemic features of the entire system of formal schooling in this country, from at least kindergarten through the fourth year of college, or K-16. Following the analysis of dynamic inequality (Grubb, 2009, ch. 6), individuals start schooling at kindergarten with initial differences in cognitive abilities *and* school readiness; that is, the understandings and values that either support or detract from academic performance. Then, these initial differences become more pronounced the longer that individuals stay in school; they become so great that some kind of remedial or developmental education is necessary, at least by ninth grade if not at the beginning of middle school. In this country, always a nation of immigrants, a constant stream of immigrants at every level of the schooling system further increases the need for instruction in English as a second language (ESL). While there are reasons to think that the size of developmental education is especially large in community colleges, my central point is that our entire *system* of education suffers from a tendency to create greater needs for remediation over time—even if these needs are sometimes not recognized, and therefore continue to multiply.[1] A real solution to the "crisis" in community colleges would therefore require a systemic reform of different levels of our educational system, not simply changes in community colleges.

At the same time, there is a great deal that community colleges could do on their own, particularly in addressing the second element of the dilemma, namely, the tendency of basic skills students to get "stuck behind the wall of remediation," unable to progress out of developmental courses and into college-level work. In this chapter, I bring together the analyses of earlier chapters and present a series of recommendations that could guide the development of a systemic set of reforms, all of which are illuminated by the experiences of the many community colleges we observed. Unfortunately, this generates a large (even overwhelming) number of recommendations, each of which could merit a great deal of elaboration and specificity. But I tend to view this plethora of recommendations positively, since it indicates how many paths to improvement there are. Ideally, the result would be a system in which many more students can complete a trajectory of basic skills and move on to college-level coursework.

Improving Basic Skills Instruction and Pedagogy (Chapter 3)

A key finding in the community colleges we observed was the domination of remedial pedagogy: drill and practice on small subskills, in decontextualized courses devoid of any connection to further study, more advanced coursework, or the world outside the classroom. Unfortunately, remedial pedagogy violates most of the precepts for powerful teaching, including the conditions for motivation and engagement. We observed the lack of engagement in students' responses to remedial pedagogies—like coming late to class and leaving early, texting throughout, and otherwise not paying attention. Therefore, the ubiquitous claim that students are "not ready to be college students" is partly the fault of instructors, since such behavior is much less prominent in classes dominated by conceptual and student-centered pedagogical approaches.

Furthermore, remedial pedagogy shows up elsewhere in developmental education, in textbooks, in computer-based materials, in tutoring, and in other student services. In many ways, it is the default pedagogy in basic skills instruction that emerges unless there is substantial support for an alternative.

Recommendation 1: *Educational institutions should recognize and when possible avoid the methods of remedial pedagogy.* This is not a statement that drill and practice are never necessary (since they obviously are), but that they should be subordinated to more conceptual and contextualized approaches to math, English, and second-language instruction. In community colleges, for example, short workshops and modules can be used for specific subskills, while courses can cover material in more constructivist and student-centered ways so that developmental students are taught both specific skills and the higher level competencies required in future coursework. This is a "both-and" solution rather than an "either-or" approach. Even though they are still rare, the mechanisms of contextualizing instruction have been developed in community colleges, including learning communities and linked courses.

Recommendation 2: *Colleges and schools should understand the pedagogy of the textbooks and computer-based programs they plan to use.* In some cases, this would allow colleges to avoid using programs that embrace remedial pedagogy; in other cases, like short specific skills modules, computer-based programs might be perfectly appropriate for drill and practice. But educational institutions should be wary of claims about "proven practices" since so many computer-based programs appear to follow the patterns of remedial pedagogy.

Recommendation 3: *When possible, institutions should avoid the stigma usually associated with developmental education.* This means being careful about language used to describe the roles of basic skills instruction, and as much as possible viewing such coursework as part of the normal trajectory of all students ("all education is developmental"). Less stigmatizing and more constructivist approaches appear to avoid the problem of identity threat (Steele, 2010), which has been shown to be powerful in reducing the motivation of African American, Latino, other racial minority, and female students.

Innovation (Chapters 4 and 6)

We saw an enormous amount of innovation in the colleges we observed. Unfortunately, a great deal of that was due to the efforts of individual instructors, who were essentially acting alone. We therefore tried to find instances where greater numbers of faculty and administrators participated. Among the most promising examples occurred when departments organized themselves to develop new approaches, write better curriculum materials, hire new faculty, and provide professional development. Other encouraging approaches borrowed from K-12 innovations, including Reading Apprenticeship and the writing process of the National Writing Project.

The most thorough innovations appear to emanate from the middle; that is, from senior faculty and midlevel administrators working together to sustain change. In contrast, innovations from the bottom and the top are usually short-lived, as are innovations developed wholly with outside funding.

Recommendation 4: *Community colleges should recognize that innovation should be more widespread than what individual faculty can accomplish.* This, in turn, means that widespread reform—including instructional reform (Recommendation 1)—requires institutional initiative and support, not just the efforts of isolated faculty.

Recommendation 5: *Centers for teaching and learning serving faculty are some of the simplest and most powerful ways to improve the quality of instruction*, particularly since such centers can address many different dimensions of instruction and innovation.

Recommendation 6: *Innovations in basic skills instruction can borrow from other levels of the education system*, just as colleges have borrowed the methods of Reading Apprenticeship and the writing process of the National Writing Project. Of course, such practices require adjustment to fit the appropriate level of the system.

Student Services (Chapters 5 and 6)

Student services encompass a wide variety of specific services. Some provide direct support for coursework; others (like student success courses) help students learn "how to be college students"; and still others (like counseling and guidance) provide direction in planning programs of study. On closer analysis, however, many services fall into the category of "tutoring"—helping students get the right answers to problem sets and writing assignments while following the methods of remedial pedagogy. Many are quite independent of coursework, and thus create a divide between instruction and student services. Finally, the students who most need supplementary services often do not receive them, undermining the role of services in enhancing academic performance.

Recommendation 7: *Student service programs should not let all services follow remedial pedagogy.* Student service programs encompass a portfolio of options besides tutoring and individual help, including supplemental instruction and specific workshops, each with its own purpose and pedagogy. Some of these services can provide drill and practice on specific skills, but others should reinforce the more conceptual material of courses.

Recommendation 8: *Student services, as a complement to conventional coursework, should be mandatory and linked tightly to coursework.* Mandatory participation avoids the problem of such services being seen as necessary only for weak students, and addresses the issue of students most in need not receiving such services.

Recommendation 9: *Guidance and counseling need to be strengthened at many community colleges.* Strengthening counseling involves not only increasing the ratios of counselors to students, but also focusing on different issues—such as student success and student readiness for the next level of schooling—in addition to the procedures related to academic progress.

Recommendation 10: *Student services should include some capacity to identify learning disabilities and mental health problems*, since these are issues affecting the classroom that instructors are not prepared to address on their own.

Student Issues (Chapter 2)

The heterogeneity of community college students is well known, encompassing transfer students, occupational students, older students with varied backgrounds, avocational students, and "experimenters" seeking to learn whether college is right for them. But basic skills classrooms have additional dimensions of student variation. Some learners are "brush-up" students who need only a program of review in order to be college-ready. Others have been misclassified by inappropriate assessments. Still others have learning disabilities or mental health problems that make learning difficult. These students with extremely varied instructional needs are now commingled in the same classes.

When faculty talk about students, they are highly sympathetic, acknowledging the students' commitment as well as the busy conditions of their lives. But faculty also view many of them as "not ready to be college students." Such language is often a way of dismissing those students, although most colleges have developed workshops, first-year experience programs, and student success courses among other methods to teach them "how to be college students."

Recommendation 11: *Since students are a crucial part of the triangle of instruction, the faculty claims that many students "are not ready to be college students" must be taken seriously.* This implies that students (as well as the colleges) bear some of the responsibility for becoming "college students"; for example, by taking the student success courses devised by the colleges to help them in this regard.

Recommendation 12: *Complaints that some students "are not ready to be college students" should never be used to abandon efforts to help such students.* Rather, they should lead to alternatives that would help make such students "college-ready"; for example, through summer bridge programs, matriculation activities, first-year experience programs, and student success courses. These approaches emphasize the noncognitive aspects of basic skills acquisition.

Recommendation 13: *Colleges should take steps to eliminate certain students from basic skills classrooms.* This is especially important regarding brush-up students and those who are misclassified, and it can be done by providing bridge programs or practice before assessments, and by allowing students to challenge their placements. In addition, the heterogeneity of students, which is one of the unique aspects of community colleges, may be too much for instructors in basic skills courses to handle. Accordingly, developmental education programs need to provide additional diagnostic and support mechanisms for students with learning disabilities or mental health problems.

The institutions in which classrooms are embedded also influence what happens inside the classroom. The institutional setting of colleges constrains as well as facilitates the provision of basic skills, and it is necessary to recognize these constraints to expand the prospects for change and reform. Assessment and alignment are two of these institutional influences, reflecting the activities of many participants rather than just individual faculty. Funding and resources (chapter 8) and the other factors considered in chapter 9 represent other such institutional influences.

Assessment and Alignment (Chapter 7)

Developmental education is really a dynamic process that starts in high school with college readiness, proceeding to assessments that may direct students into basic skills classes, and then leads students through a sequence of courses into college-level classes. Each piece of this trajectory may be well or poorly aligned with adjacent pieces. Misalignment means that students are either under- or overqualified for the next stage in the sequence, each of which brings its own dangers. But the mechanisms that might guarantee alignment are not generally in place, which results in several different kinds of misalignment: of assessments with developmental courses, horizontal misalignment of courses at the same level, and vertical misalignment of adjacent courses in a sequence.

Recommendation 14: *The alignment of adjacent levels of schooling requires much more attention than it has been given (e.g., middle school with high school, high school with college).* This could involve alignment of curriculum (truly a system issue); early warning systems (like the Early Assessment Program of the California State University system) to detect which students are likely to be unready for the next stage of their schooling; summer bridge programs; and matriculation programs for students just entering community colleges. These activities are all part of assuring college readiness and are other ways of preventing misplacement of students in basic skills (see Recommendation 13).

Recommendation 15: *Assessments that direct students toward basic skills courses must be more carefully constructed.* In particular, they must be aligned with the sequence of developmental courses, up to and including beginning college-level courses. They should involve multiple measures, including grades and performance at earlier levels of schooling (as well as test scores). There must be some provision for test preparation for those assessment processes that include conventional tests. The tests themselves should be diagnostic rather than merely being placement tests, and there should be mechanisms for retesting or testing out of any developmental sequence. The goal of these revised assessment procedures is to minimize inappropriate placements, both false positives—students assessed into basic skills courses who don't need them—and false negatives, or students who do need some form of basic skills instruction but escape being placed in the appropriate developmental course or module.

Recommendation 16: *Courses in any developmental sequence, or in any sequence like a high school program, should be vertically and horizontally aligned.* Both forms of alignment may require common exams for all course sections, end-of-course exams, and mastery learning methods that are carefully constructed to avoid the pedagogical and assessment problems typical of mastery learning. This recommendation might (by itself) end the process of passing along students who are not ready for the next level of schooling—something that generates the high numbers of students requiring remediation at every level.

Funding and Resources (Chapter 8)

The relationship among funding, educational resources, and outcomes is one of the most difficult in all of education. On the one hand, the conventional wisdom, the Money Myth, stresses that more money is necessary for reform, and some innovations certainly require additional funding. On the other hand, many solutions cost very little (if anything). Moreover, the money that is spent is often wasted, particularly in funding small programs that don't survive ("programmitis"). So, colleges and policy makers need a more fluid conception of money and outcomes, one that recognizes that spending does not always lead to effective resources, and that the effectiveness of resources must always be questioned (especially if they cost a great deal).

Recommendation 17: *Educational institutions should strive to engage in activities that can effect change without requiring money to do so.* There is certainly no substitute for adequate funding of developmental programs, and many recommendations in this chapter require additional funding, though quite a few do not. Colleges could, for example, eliminate waste by carrying out "waste audits." They should also avoid investing in small, idiosyncratic programs that cannot reach many students; instead, colleges should think about how small programs might be incorporated into larger sustainable reforms. Finally, colleges should recognize cases where improvements do not cost additional funds but rather involve redistributing funds from unproductive uses to more effective practices.

Other Institutional Influences (Chapter 9)

Recommendation 18: *Educational institutions need not think of the course as the only (or even the dominant) unit of basic skills instruction.* Instead, courses, workshops, modules, and independent learning can be used flexibly to meet different kinds of basic skills needs. Some of these formats are smaller and less intense than conventional courses; others combine several courses; for example, learning communities and linked courses. Under some conditions, a series of modules might even serve in place of courses, though it would be necessary not to fall back into the trap of remedial pedagogy. Some of these modules and workshops could potentially be devoted to drill and practice, while others could be concerned with more conceptual understanding.

Recommendation 19: *All individuals teaching in developmental education should be well prepared in instructional methods through preservice programs and subsequent professional development.* Adhering to this recommendation would strengthen instruction in basic skills, rather than assuming that English teachers or math teachers are automatically skilled at teaching developmental subjects. Similarly, educational institutions should not assign the most marginal instructors—part-time or adjunct instructors in community colleges, or new teachers in high schools with the least amount of time to improve instruction—to developmental teaching. This is a common practice that tends to assign the least experienced teachers to the most needy students. This recommendation applies as well to instructors in student services teaching workshops, modules, and tutorials.

Recommendation 20: *Colleges should work assiduously both to reduce the numbers of adjunct instructors and to incorporate such instructors into the college.* Adjunct instructors now teach the majority of basic skills courses, and they tend to be isolated from the rest of the institution as well as from professional development opportunities. Although reducing the number of adjuncts is an admittedly costly reform, professional development programs aimed at adjuncts are comparatively less expensive.

Recommendation 21: *Data, especially longitudinal data, should be used to help all educational institutions discover where students are having the most difficulty in developmental programs.* Strengthening the use of data typically requires both enhancing the capacity for data analysis and fostering a culture of inquiry and evaluation around basic skills education.

Final Thoughts

While these recommendations apply to developmental education in community colleges, most are just as appropriate for 4-year colleges, and can also be adapted to meet the needs of middle schools and high schools. If they could all be implemented at different levels of the K-16 education system, then the need for remediation in the first place would be reduced, and developmental programs would be more effective than is currently the case. But in order to develop an educational *system* without substantial need for remediation, it is necessary to pay attention to developmental education at multiple levels of the existing system.

These recommendations, if implemented, would virtually eliminate one problem that now all afflicts basic skills instruction—the fact of being a second-chance form of schooling, with all the stigma, marginalization, and inferior funding that affect every second-chance program. As I argued in chapter 1, second-chance programs reflect the inclusiveness and potential equity of public schooling, but are all too often relegated to the margins of educational enterprises. If educators and policy makers are serious about the inclusive promise of public schooling—a promise that dates from the mid-19th century—then they should be equally serious about these recommendations for developmental education.

The beneficiaries of a more coherent approach to basic skills would be not only the students—who would be less likely to be "stuck behind the wall of remediation"—but also the institutions of education. With greater success in reducing the remedial problem, community colleges in particular could cease to be "remedial campuses." The revolving door of basic skills instruction could be turned into a pathway to college-level coursework. No institution wants to be viewed primarily as a place for remedial education, but community colleges in particular have been forced into this role by the effects of other levels of schooling; that is, the ways high schools and 4-year colleges work. So, systemic attention to improvements related to developmental education might restore community colleges to their original purpose—as pathways into and through postsecondary education for a large group of students.

In another way, the recommendations in this chapter fulfill the promises made in the beginning of this book. The triangle of instruction presented in chapter 1 clarifies that *instructors* and *students*, interacting with the *content* of classes, modules, and services set within *institutions* with their own pervasive influences, all affect the success or failure of any educational enterprise. In other words, numerous factors influence the success and failure of basic skills instruction. It is not surprising, therefore, that a final distillation of this study should incorporate as many as 21 recommendations. The classroom is a complex place, with much more going on than the simple interaction of teacher and student—and even that interaction itself is far from simple, as the analysis of instructional approaches in chapters 3 and 4 illustrated. Therefore, no single recommendation or practice can substantially improve basic skills education since its practices have so many causes.

In the end, the educational institutions we build as a nation reflect the priorities we have, particularly for publicly supported education. If we want schooling to serve simply as a filter, identifying the students whose prior preparation has been the strongest and whose family and community influences are the most consistent with academic success, then we can develop—indeed, we have developed—a system that acts as a series of gates or barriers to success for those who are least prepared. But if we want our institutions to be truly developmental at every stage and level, then we need a system that takes improvement in basic skills education as seriously as any other activity. Such a system would produce and support institutions worthy of being considered truly educational.

APPENDIX

The Methodology of the Study

To understand what happens in basic skills instruction, or indeed to understand any educational setting, it is necessary to examine all elements in the triangle of instruction. To do this, we initially carried out case studies of 13 colleges in California, where we could interview administrators and instructors to understand the institutional setting, observe classrooms to understand the nature of instruction, and interview classroom instructors to understand their perspectives on their own teaching, on the institutions they taught in, and on their students. In these case studies we were not able initially to interview students systematically, though we talked with them informally whenever we could.

The 13 colleges were chosen in different ways. We first selected two colleges with quite different reputations that were well-known to the researchers, as a pilot test of the methodology we developed.

We then attempted to identify three high-quality developmental programs and three low-quality programs, based on the data that Peter Bahr developed for California (e.g., Bahr, 2010). However, this method for choosing colleges, selecting colleges with positive and negative outliers for both math and reading scores, proved to work poorly. Many of the colleges identified as particularly successful were middle-class suburban colleges; other colleges had idiosyncratic conditions that accounted for their success. The six colleges chosen in this way provided a good mix of urban and suburban colleges, but we do not consider them a priori either high- or low-quality. One implication of the failure of this method is that rewarding colleges based on raw data on success rates in remediation probably fails to identify especially high-quality programs, because there are too many other variables associated with student background and preparation levels that cannot be considered with such crude methods.

We identified a third group of six colleges by exploiting the variety in rural colleges in both Northern and Southern California. One of these did not want to participate in the study so we were left with a sample of 13 colleges. Later, in 2011, we conducted a visit to a 14th college (Chaffey College) that kept coming up as particularly innovative. With the exception of Chaffey, which gave us permission to use its name, all colleges and all interviewees are anonymous.

At each college we interviewed the deans of instruction and student services, the department chairs in math, reading, writing, and ESL, the institutional researcher, the basic skills coordinator or the chair of the basic skills committee, the head of EOPS, and any other administrators identified as important in basic skills. At the outset, we did not interview the heads of Disabled Students Program and Services (DSPS) because we did not appreciate the potential magnitude of learning disabilities. Once we had observed a number of classrooms, the presence of both learning disabilities and mental health problems became obvious (see chapter 2). At that point, we interviewed three heads of DSPS. We asked administrators about the magnitude of developmental education at their colleges, college approaches and innovations, priorities of their colleges, what the college did in response to California's Basic Skills Initiative, and their perceptions about how well different dimensions of basic skills were working, instruction, assessment, articulation among courses, student services, and professional development.

We requested each college to provide us with lists of basic skills instructors in math, reading, writing, and ESL; we then contacted these individuals to observe between 3 and 6 hours of class, plus a 1-hour interview for each instructor. We hoped to observe and interview about 16 instructors in each college, four in each of the four subject areas. Unfortunately, the success of this element of the project varied considerably. Some colleges provided names and helped in setting up interviews. Others seemed not to understand that we truly wanted to observe classes, and scheduled many interviews with administrators but few classroom observations, despite our repeated efforts. In the end, we observed 144 classes in the initial 13 colleges, and we conducted interviews of 246 individuals, all during 2009–2010.

We then devoted 2010-2011 to examining innovations and promising practices in our original 13 colleges and in other colleges where we had learned about interesting developments. We revisited two of the original 13 colleges to examine more deeply some of their practices, especially departments that had developed their own coherent approaches (analyzed in chapter 4). We observed and interviewed a group of teachers in five colleges that were using Reading Apprenticeship, interviewed and observed four instructors using the techniques of the National Writing Project, and visited one additional college to observe its math classes. We also visited Chaffey College to report on its well-known student services (see chapter 6). In this phase of the research, we visited an additional seven colleges, observed an additional 25 classrooms, and carried out 77 interviews. This material on innovations is principally reported in chapter 4, though it appears in other chapters as well.

Altogether, we observed 169 classes and we interviewed 325 instructors and administrators in about 20 colleges. In many ways, this research followed the pattern of *Honored But Invisible* (Grubb & Associates, 1999), my earlier book that examined community college teaching in a variety of subjects. Those subjects included not only basic skills but also academic or transfer courses, occupational or CTE courses, literacy practices in a variety of subjects, and various innovations. The underlying methodology in both studies relied on classroom observations as the only way to understand the nature of instruction, followed by interviews with both instructors and administrators, to understand the institutional setting of the college and its influences on instruction.

NOTES

Chapter 1

1   See the analysis by Harvey and Houseman (2004) of a discourse of crisis in many reports about education, contrasted with a discourse of possibility that leads to more student-centered and community-centered approaches.

2   In California, the rate at which students assess into basic skills courses in the state universities hovers around 50%, lower than in most community colleges but still high by any standard.

3   Building American skills by strengthening community colleges. Retrieved from www. whitehouse.gov/communitycollege

4   Based on National Assessment of Educational Progress (NAEP) data, California eighth graders ranked 44th among all states (tied with seven other states and ahead of only one state) in English; in math, California was 43rd (tied with five other states and higher than only two others; see nces.ed.gov/nationsreportcard/states. California did not participate in the 12th grade NAEP. The sorry state of California's K-12 system, the result of three decades of education disinvestment since Prop 13 passed in 1978, is partly responsible for patterns in both K-12 and community colleges.

5   Figures are calculated from the Chancellor's Office Datamart. Retrieved from misweb.cccco. edu/mis/onlinestat/ret_sucs.cfm

6   On education gaps, see Timar and Maxwell-Jolly (2011). On growing inequality over grades, see the analysis of dynamic inequality in Grubb (2009, ch. 6–7).

7   The literature on peer effects largely comes from K-12 research, and it shows that peers influence students in various ways. For example, students whose peers intend to go to college are themselves more likely to matriculate; conversely, students whose peers are unlikely to go to college are less likely to progress through high school and enter any type of college; see Grubb (2009, ch. 2).

8   See, for example, the transition to college program Making Waves, apparently costing an additional $12,000 to $13,000 per student per year (Grubb, 2008); the job training program New Chance, with few positive outcomes despite an extensive array of supports (Quint, Polit, Bos, & Cave, 1994); the residential Job Corps program; and the much-touted Perry Pre-school program, a very high-quality early childhood program.

9   Lurking under this statement is a contention about research methods. Several recent reviews have examined supposedly "rigorous" research, by which the authors mean random assignment experiments and results using sophisticated statistical methods. But postsecondary

data are usually quite limited, particularly with regard to the family background and K-12 experiences of students, so quasi-experimental statistical analysis is usually poorly specified. Random assignment methods—quite apart from being expensive, sometimes unethical, and usually unable to explain why a program works or doesn't—are best suited to evaluating the small-scale, self-contained programs we critique (in chapter 8) as "programmitis." Qualitative research can be rigorous, too, and it is often better than other methods at indicating why an initiative succeeds or fails.

10 On how administrators misunderstand teaching, see Grubb and Associates (1999, pp. 301–310).

11 One problem is what instructors in college-level courses do when confronted with large numbers of students lacking basic skills. As documented in Grubb and Associates (1999, ch. 6), one approach is to turn the courses into "hidden remediation," or dumbing down the course; another is to ignore the extent of basic skills needed, leaving some students behind; and a third is to change pedagogical strategies. This study did not examine nonbasic skills courses in this research, so when I turn to this situation in chapter 7 on the trajectory of basic skills, I will rely on this earlier research.

12 Here, we made an error: When we began this research, we did not appreciate how many students in basic education might have learning disabilities. This became apparent only after we had completed an initial round of observations and interviews without interviewing heads of DSPS. We ended up interviewing three heads of DSPS in our 13 initial colleges.

13 For corroboration, see the publications on basic skills instruction by the Community College Research Center, Columbia University, and MDRC, including several reviews of the literature published by both organizations.

14 Barr and Tagg (1995) used the term *teaching* to refer to teacher-centered, behaviorist instruction, and *learning* to refer to student-centered and constructivist methods; there then followed a great deal of talk about creating "teaching colleges" without clarifying how to do this. The problem with the Barr and Tagg formulation is that "teaching" and "learning" have conventional meanings; instructors in constructivist classrooms are still teaching, and students in behaviorist classrooms are still learning (one hopes).

15 See Grubb (2009, ch. 2) or Grubb (2008); Elliott (1998); Goldhaber and Brewer (1997); Knapp and Associates (1995); and Newmann et al. (2001); Raudenbusch, Fotiu, and Cheong (1998).

16 See especially Cox (2009) for her description of students who believe that learning means information transfer and mastery of subskills, while instructors are looking for more conceptual and analytic abilities.

17 The structural reason that most community students have probably been taught with routine methods is the strong tendency within K-12 education to reserve more conceptual teaching for upper-track and high-performing students, with more skills-oriented teaching for the low tracks and low performing students; see, for example, Powell, Farrar, and Cohen (1985).

18 See Grubb and Associates (1999, pp. 106–119), on the various meanings of "hands-on"—basically, everything that isn't a direct lecture.

19 See the review of innovative practices in Grubb and Associates (1999, Ch. 7), presenting both positive and negative examples of supposed innovation.

20 An enormous amount has been written on the idea of contextualization, though there seems to be much less of it in practice. See Perin (2011) for a review, as well as Center for Student Success, RP Group, and Academic Senate for California Community Colleges (2009).

21 On several dimensions of quality with supporting evidence, see Lesgold and Welch-Ross (2012, pp. 109-112).

22 According to data in Perry, Bahr, Rosin, and Woodward (2010), 52% of students in remedial writing were only one level below the college level, though only 23% of those in the remedial math sequence were one level below.

Chapter 2

1 However, a very small number of students may have avoided large chunks of their school-ing. One student told us a story of being called stupid in fourth grade, at which point she left school until she managed to enroll in the community college.
2 Instructors in adult education usually prepare students to pass the GED exam, but because this exam tests a series of subskills, it readily leads to remedial pedagogy.
3 See California Tomorrow (2002); Gittell and Steffey (2000); Matus-Grossman and Gooden (2002); and Woodlief, Thomas, and Orozco (2003, especially ch. 3).
4 On experimenters, see Manski (1989) and Grubb and Associates (1999, pp. 4–5).
5 The instructor replicated almost precisely the analysis of Melvin Kohn's *Class and Confor-mity* (1969). This now little-read book confirmed with a great deal of data from the United States and Italy how middle-class parents tend to rear their children to be independent and self-motivated. In contrast, working-class parents are more likely to rear their children to conform to and obey the rules (just as working-class jobs require). This finding replicates the divisions between students with initiative and independence versus those that passively responded to the rules and requirements of the class, but no more than that.
6 This particular observer has spent her career teaching basic skills, so her perception of stu-dents "squashed down by school" is the result of extensive experience.
7 In this case, "we" refers to Tom deWit and Sean McFarland of Chabot College. They and their students filmed these videos in five community colleges as part of classes in which students videotaped other students. Kate Frankel and Norton Grubb developed the ques-tions that were posed to basic skills students, and they also reviewed the footage to distill the conclusions for this section of the book. The videos themselves are confidential (to protect the identities of the students).
8 On classes that "collapse" in this way, see Grubb and Associates (1999, ch. 10).

Chapter 3

1 On microaggressions, see Solórzano (2001).
2 See especially the discussion of distressed and collapsed classes in Grubb and Associates (1999, pp. 218–229). For that work, we kept a list of Really Bad Teachers (RBTs)—almost uni-formly poor instructors who belittled their students.
3 Basic skills students often lack number sense—the intuitive understanding of what numbers mean, their magnitudes, relationships to one another, and how they are affected by various operations. In watching them transform decimals into fractions, many don't understand place value, that is, the meaning of 4 and 7 in the number 10.457. Document literacy is the ability to extract meaning from the documents (including numbers) in daily life such as graphs and pie charts, thermometers and other measuring devices, and maps and other geometric depic-tions; the International Adult Literacy Survey has found enormous variation in document literacy.
4 This example is described in Grubb and Associates (1999, pp. 272–273). We came across only one math course contextualized with CTE applications in our 13 colleges, and our working hypothesis is that this practice has dwindled since the 1990s.
5 In the 1990s, Grubb and his colleagues documented many examples of integrating academic and occupational education in community colleges, including basic skills or applied math courses contextualized by specific occupational areas or related areas; see Badway and Grubb (1997). Similarly, Grubb and Associates (1999) found a number of contextualized basic skills courses.
6 See the section on "Basic Principles" in American Mathematical Association of Two-Year Colleges (AMATYC; 2009).
7 On the nonstandard forms of academic skills found in occupational classes, see Grubb and

Associates (1999, ch. 4) on teaching in occupational classes, or Achtenhagen and Grubb (1999).

8   See Grubb and Associates (1999, pp. 272–273) for this particular example, as well as several others, of integrating basic skills with CTE.

9   On the general decline in reading in the American population, including among people with baccalaureate degrees, see the report of the National Endowment for the Arts (2007), *To Read or Not to Read: A Question of National Consequence*.

10 Again, see Deshler, Palincsar, Biancaros, and Nair (2007, especially pp. 21–36). The introductory chapters are excellent guides to the questions of what reading is and how it can be taught. The volume focuses on adolescent readers, presumably in high schools and middle schools, but everything in the book is applicable to young adults in community colleges as well. For a recent book about adult literacy, where adults are defined as those 16 and over not in high school, see Lesgold and Welch-Ross (2012).

11 See Genesee, Lindholm-Leary, Saunders, and Christian (2006, ch. 6), as well as August and Shanahan (2006); García (2005, especially ch. 3); Minami and Ovando (2004); and Thomas and Collier (1995).

12 But see Hodara (2011, pp. 20–22), where she explicitly contrasts drill and practice software derived from Skinner's behaviorist approaches with more balanced pedagogies when computer-based programs may incorporate conceptual understanding, as well as procedural skills.

13 Most often, this "research" provides some examples of a few classes that have participated in the program contrasted with other classes without the program—but the composition of the two comparison groups is unknown, the nature of the alternative is unclear, and the impacts of particularly motivated instructors and students (i.e., selection effects) are uninvestigated. In the language of evaluation, most of the threats to the validity of these research findings have been ignored.

14 This is not universally true, of course. One text, Bittinger (2002), presents the usual topics from whole numbers to solving simple equations. However, it also incorporates a large number of word problems about various topics—the size of a field hockey field, the Leaning Tower of Pisa, batting averages—that illustrate the many ways math is used in daily life, and could also provide students with number sense. But the instructor chose not to use any of these examples, thereby creating a wholly decontextualized class.

Chapter 4

1   See Shaughnessy (1977) and her insistence that "bad writing" can be diagnosed as having a certain pattern and consistency that must be diagnosed and then corrected to produce proficient writers.

2   For other evidence on the dominance of trial and error, see Grubb et al. (1999, pp. 44–49).

3   We visited one college, in addition to our original 13, specifically to see its math department.

4   The department has taken a mastery approach in which students are reportedly not flunked based on their results on these quizzes, but may be required to do some makeup work to achieve mastery before moving on. Mastery learning methods are commonly responsible for creating tests oriented toward narrow questions and remedial drill, so the use of mastery learning in a more constructivist department is noteworthy. The issues of mastery learning will be taken up in the final chapter.

5   This section benefits from work in progress by Gabriner (2011), which provides much more detail about what this process looks like and what its implications are for leadership development.

6   This kind of innovation in community colleges is similar to conceptions of distributed leadership and the centrality of teacher-leaders in K-12 education; see Spillane (2006) on distributed leadership, and Grubb and Tredway (2010) for an analysis of what teacher-leaders need to understand about their schools.

7   For some descriptions of Learning Communities, see Grubb and Associates (1999); Price and Lee (2005); Matthews (1994); Smith (1991); Tinto, Russell, and Kadel (1994); and the extensive work of the Washington State Center for Improving the Quality of Undergraduate Education at Evergreen State College in Washington (www.evergreen.edu/washcenter/home.asp). For further evaluations, see Tinto and Goodsell-Love (1995); Tinto, Goodsell-Love, and Russo (1994); and Tinto, Russo, and Goodsell-Love (n.d.). For more recent random assignment evaluations, see Visher, Teres, with Richman (2011); Weiss et al. (2010); Weissman et al. (2011); and Scrivener et al. (2008) for some of the most positive results (the effects tend to be modest and confined to the semester of the learning community, however). Given our finding in this chapter of how long it takes innovations to fully develop, we suspect that the methodology of MDRC's evaluations—where learning communities are evaluated soon after they are created—yields serious underestimates of the outcomes if these innovations could be brought to maturity.

8   For example, colleges in Washington and Oregon benefit from the proximity of the Washington State Center, and Washington's I-Best program supports learning communities with CTE courses.

9   On evidence for California, see Wisely (2011), as well as oral communication by Mary Visher from MDRC, based on the extensive work of MDRC evaluating learning communities across the country.

10 We can reasonably surmise that the colleges responding included a disproportionate number of those with contextualized courses and learning communities, and that those not responding did not have any contextualized courses. Even if this is not taken into account, and the proportion of contextualized courses is assumed to be consistent across the 112 community colleges in California, an estimate of 35 contextualized courses for a system that serves more than 2.9 million community college students every year is a particularly small drop in a very large bucket.

11 We also benefitted from evaluations of RA by members of the Research and Planning Group; see Mery and Schiorring (2009-2010; 2010).

12 One of the clever elements in the 2-hour workshop is an application of RA methods to a cartoon, clarifying that a "text" need not be a conventional written text. Thus, RA would be useful in reading charts, tables, and maps (a facility sometimes called document literacy), as well as the complex visual representations used in occupational classes. However, virtually all of the uses of RA we observed involved conventional written texts.

13 SPQ3R is a reading strategy of surveying the text; predicting what it is likely to be about; generating questions to ask; reading the text, reciting or writing what the reader has learned, and finally, reviewing the text, predictions and questions, and the information gained from the text. The technique seems designed principally for reading for information transfer, fostering less interpretation than the methods of RA.

14 This summary of the evaluations skips over many technical details. For the ninth grade evaluation, see Kemple et al. (2008); for the 10th grade results, see Somers et al. (2010). The Enhanced Reading Opportunities Study evaluated one program in addition to RA—Xtreme Reading from the University of Kansas. The two programs did not differ in their effects, but we have not heard of any efforts to use Xtreme Reading in community colleges.

15 Unfortunately, federal funding for the NWP was eliminated by a short-sighted Congress during the funding crises of 2011. We seem to be having two disjointed conversations in this country—the need for higher levels of skills so that we can be internationally competitive, at the same time that national and state governments are cutting funding for all levels of education, as well as for projects like the NWP that could enhance the quality of student work.

16 For a California FIN focused on basic skills issues, see http://facultyinquiry.net

17 We thank Rose Asera, the director of SPECC, for encouraging us to pursue the SPECC directors, and for providing their contact information. The publications of SPECC can be found on the website of the Carnegie Foundation, www.carnegiefoundation.org/publications_archive.

18 For more on the isolation of faculty, see Grubb and Associates (1999, pp. 49–56).

19 Acceleration has become popular in California partly because of an evaluation of the program at Chabot College by Hern and Snell (2010) that shows much greater success in passing accelerated courses than equivalent nonaccelerated sequences. However, a large (but unknown) fraction of students in the accelerated courses were also enrolled in a learning community for African American students, DERAJA, so the positive effects might be due either to acceleration or to DERAJA—no one knows for sure.

Chapter 5

1 Colleges intended to spend up to 37% of their 2010-2011 Basic Skills Initiative funding on supplemental instruction, tutoring, and professional development, providing substantial funding in many cases for tutor training. Data come from Mark Wade Lieu, Chancellor's Office, California Community Colleges.

2 See Cox (2009) on the ways that students economize on time spent if they think that a task is not directly related to their grade or credit.

3 For a similar argument, see Karp, O'Gara, and Hughes (2008).

4 Some of this is a data problem: Most colleges do not collect good data on which students use student services. However, Chaffey has a check-in system where students use their student ID cards every time they use any service—so there are quite precise statistics on who uses student services and how often.

5 This quote comes from a study of counselors in 16 colleges across the country; see Grubb (2006, p. 211; see also pp. 206, 210–211 on intrusive counseling). It's noteworthy that the same language emerged in two different studies.

6 In figures from the Chancellor's Office provided by Mark Wade Lieu, colleges intended to spend 51.7% of their 2010-2011 BSI funding on advisement, counseling, supplemental instruction, and tutoring, while spending only about half that (27.7%) on categories related to instructional change.

7 See Grubb (2006) for another analysis of guidance and counseling, based on a national sample of 16 colleges.

8 For the complexity of decision making even in the conventional model of maximizing expected present value, see Grubb (2002). A recently established branch of economics called behavioral economics has confirmed that decision makers make "irrational" decisions in consistent ways; see, for example, Jabbar (2012) for an introduction to behavioral economics and its applications to education.

9 See Grubb (2006) for these various exemplars of guidance and counseling.

10 On experimenters, see Grubb and Associates (1999, pp. 4–7); see also Manski (1989).

11 Grubb and Associates (1999, p. 328). This instructor was talking about how faculty development is peripheral and vulnerable to funding cutbacks, but the logic is precisely the same for student services.

Chapter 6

1 To remind the reader, in our research, we have used pseudonyms so that colleges we examined might remain anonymous. However, so much of the Chaffey story is well known that anonymity would have been virtually impossible. We therefore received permission from the President of the College, Dr. Henry Shannon, to identify the college and some of its administrators in this chapter.

2 This chapter was written by Robert Gabriner and Norton Grubb.

3 The Abilene paradox was introduced by management expert Jerry B. Harvey in his article, "The Abilene Paradox: The Management of Agreement." The name of the phenomenon

comes from an anecdote in which a family collectively decided to take a long, hot drive to Abilene even though none of them individually wanted to do so.

4 The EAP was devised by the California State University system to alert high school juniors to possible deficiencies in math and reading. CSU has also developed remedial courses that high school seniors can take, with the hope that they can avoid the need for developmental coursework at the postsecondary level.

5 The CRLA model is one that professionalizes tutoring by providing training and then a credentialing system; see www.crla.net/ittpc/index.htm.

6 The "Poppy Copy" is the informal name for Basic Skills as the Foundation for Success in the California Community Colleges (2007, 2010).

Chapter 7

1 For prior work on the assessment process, see Safran and Visher (2010); for student perspectives, see Venezia, Bracco, and Nodine (2010).

2 In theory, these scores should be one of multiple measures used in placing students, but in practice, colleges either do not use multiple measures or fail to use them in coherent and consistent ways.

3 See Bettinger and Long (2009); Losak and Morris (1985); Morris (1994)..

4 On the concept of internal alignment, see Carnoy, Elmore, and Siskin (2003).

5 Cal-PASS is a nonprofit organization dedicated to establishing alliances among the various education institutions in California. Theoretically, it could help smooth the transition from high school to college, though we have been unable to find out much about the accomplishments of this group.

6 See the National Research Council (2011), Summary, Conclusion 2.

Chapter 8

1 California Postsecondary Education Commission, Fiscal Profiles, Displays 17–19, Retrieved from www.cpec.ca.gov/completereports/2010reports/FiscalProfiles2010.asp.

2 This issue is similar to that in K-12 education, where it has been difficult to show that smaller classes make much difference to outcomes—partly because if teachers continue to lecture, it doesn't matter whether a class is large or small.

3 In addition to the example of Chaffey College examined in chapter 6, see Grubb and Associates (1999, pp. 311–317) for information on the possibilities for such centers.

4 For some corroboration of this pattern, see the evaluation of Achieving the Dream, in which a majority of the strategies adopted to improve student achievement were small in scale. See Rutschow et al. (2011, Overview, p. iii).

5 A different faculty member at the same college was skeptical that Quest for Success would work: "I just don't think it's going to fly that well with the college—they need to feel that they own it, you know?" In this case, a small advisory committee had come up with Quest for Success, rather than the faculty as a whole.

6 See, for example, Tool 3-A, "Identifying Sources of Waste in Schools," in Grubb and Tredway (2009, Ch. 3).

7 The federal government supports some community college innovations through the Fund for the Improvement of Postsecondary Education (FIPSE), but most of its funding to community colleges comes through grants and loans to students and through Perkins funds for occupational education. However, the federal government does fund other kinds of basic skills through the Adult Education Act, the Workforce Investment Act, in welfare-to-work programs, and in miscellaneous other ways through funding to community-based organizations that provide basic skills instruction. For one (now outdated) effort to look at all the different sources of basic skills funding, see Grubb and Kalman (1996).

8 The BSI funds were earmarked for developmental education but not for any specific kind of use. In other states, funding has been more specifically earmarked; for example, in Washington, new funds were restricted to funding for the I-BEST program, a learning community joining basic skills with CTE.

9 Substitution is usually difficult to detect; these two cases are unusual in that the evidence for substitution was clear.

10 These figures come from an e-mail communication on October 11, 2011 with Mark Wade Lieu, Director of Basic Skills, Chancellor's Office, California Community Colleges.

Chapter 9

1 For more evidence on flex days, see Grubb and Associates (1999, pp. 296–300).

2 One report noted that 56.5% of California basic skills courses in 2000 were taught by part-timers. This is precisely the same number (56%) reported by Lutzer et al. (2007) in their analysis of part-time teaching in precollegiate math courses in Fall 2005. However, these numbers seem low compared to some of the figures we heard at our sample of 13 colleges. See "The State of Basic Skills Instruction in California Community Colleges," Basic Skills Ad Hoc Committee of the Academic Senate, adopted April 2000; retrieved from losmedanos. edu/deved/AcademicSenateBasicSkills.pdf.

3 See Grubb and Associates (1999, pp. 331–332 and note 10).

4 Early on in this research, we had hoped to find enough data to carry out evaluations of basic skills programs at different colleges. However, these plans were abandoned when we found how rare it was to find real data capabilities at these colleges.

5 See the Final Report of the Task Force on Student Success, Sacramento, CA: Chancellor's Office, California Community Colleges, December, 2011.

Chapter 10

1 I could extend this analysis to the system of education and training, since many programs outside formal schooling end up supporting basic skills education; for example, short-term job training programs funded by the Workforce Investment Act, adult education programs, welfare-to-work programs, and many programs run by community-based organizations. For one now-outdated analysis of all these forms of basic skills education, see Grubb and Kalman (1991). However, for simplicity, the focus here is confined to the K–16 system.

REFERENCES

Achtenhagen, F., & Grubb, W. N. (1999). Vocational and occupational education: Pedagogical complexity, institutional indifference. In V. Richardson (Ed.), *Handbook of research on teaching* (4th ed, pp. 176–206). Washington, DC: American Educational Research Association.

American Mathematical Association of Two-Year Colleges (AMATYC). (2006). *Beyond crossroads: Implementing mathematics standards in the first two years of college*. Memphis: Southwest Tennessee Community College.

American Mathematical Association of Two-Year Colleges (AMATYC). (2009). *Crossroads in mathematics standards for introductory college mathematics before calculus*. www.amatyc.org/Crossroads/CROSSROADS/V1/index.htm

Asera, R. (2011). Innovation at scale: How Virginia community colleges are collaborating to improve developmental education and increase dtudent success. Retrieved from Achieving the Dream, http://www.achievingthedream.org/sites/default/files/resources/ATD_InnovationAtScale_101411.pdf

Attewell, P., Lavin, D., Domina, T., & Levey, T. (2006). New evidence on remediation. *Journal of Higher Education, 77*(5), 886–924.

August, D., & Shanahan, T. (Eds.). (2006). *Developing literacy in second language learners: Report of the National Literacy Panel on Language Minority Children and Youth*. New York: Erlbaum.

Badway, N., & Grubb, W. N. (1997, October). *A sourcebook for reshaping the community college: Curriculum integration and the multiple domains of career preparation* (Vols. 1 & 2). Berkeley, CA: National Center for Research in Vocational Education.

Bahr, P. R. (2010). Preparing the under-prepared: An analysis of racial disparities in postsecondary mathematics remediation. *Journal of Higher Education, 81*(2), 209–237.

Bahr, P. R. (2011). Basic skills in California's community colleges: Evidence from staff and self-referrals. *Educational Evaluation and Policy Analysis*. forthcoming.

Bailey, T. (2009). Challenge and opportunity: Rethinking the role and function of developmental education in community colleges. *New Directions for Community Colleges, 145*, 11–30.

Barr, B. R., & Tagg, J. (1995, November/December). From teaching to learning: A new paradigm for undergraduate education. *Change,* 13–25.

Basic Skills as the Foundation for Success in the California Community Colleges. (2007). Berkeley, CA: Research and Planning Group of the California Community Colleges.

Berliner, D. (2009, March). *Poverty and potential: Out-of-school factors and school success*. Boulder CO: Public Interest Center, & Tempe AZ: Educational Policy Research Unit. Retrieved from http://epicpolicy.org/publication/poverty-and-potential

Bettinger, E., & Long, B. (2009). Addressing the needs of under-prepared students in higher education: Does college remediation work? *Journal of Human Resources, 44*(3) 736–771.

Bittinger, M. (2002). *Basic mathematics.* Reading MA: Addison Wesley.

Bransford, J. D., Brown, A. L., & Cocking, R. R. (1999). *How people learn: Brain, mind, experience, and school.* Washington, DC: National Academy Press.

Bryk, A. (2010). Organizing schools for improvement. *Phi Delta Kappan, 91*(7), 23–30.

Bryk, A., Sebring, P., Allensworth, E., Leppuscu, S., & Easton, J. (2010). *Organizing schools for improvement: Lessons from Chicago.* Chicago, IL: University of Chicago Press.

Burns, M. S., Griffin, P., & Snow, C. E. (Eds.). (1999). *Starting out right: A guide to promoting children's reading success.* Washington, DC: National Academy Press.

California Tomorrow. (2002). *A new look at California community colleges: Keeping the promise alive for students of color and immigrants.* Unpublished report. Oakland: California Tomorrow.

Carnoy, M., Elmore, R., & Siskin, L. (Eds.). (2003). *The new accountability: High schools and high-stakes testing.* New York: Routledge.

Center for Student Success. (2005). *Environmental scan: A summary of key issues facing California community colleges pertinent to the strategic planning process.* Berkeley, CA: Research and Planning Group for California Community Colleges.

Center for Student Success, RP Group, and Academic Senate for California Community Colleges. (2009). *Contextualized teaching and learning.* Berkeley, CA: Academic Senate.

Cho, S. W. & Karp, M. (2012). *Student success courses and educational outcomes in Virginia community colleges. Working Paper No 40,* Community College Research Center, Columbia University.

Cohen, A., & Brawer, F. (2008). *The American community college* (5th ed.). San Francisco, CA: Jossey-Bass.

Conley, D. (2007). *Toward a more comprehensive conception of college readiness.* Eugene, OR: Educational Policy Improvement Center.

Cotton, K. (1990). *Educational time factors* (School Improvement Research Series #8, Northwest Regional Educational Laboratory). Retrieved from www.nwrel.org/scpd/sirs/4/cu8.html

Cox, R. (2009). *The college fear factor: How students and professors misunderstand one another.* Cambridge, MA: Harvard University Press.

Cuban, L. (1990). Reforming again, again, and again. *Educational Researcher, 19*(1), 3–13.

Deshler, D., Palincsar, A., Biancarosa, G., & Nair, M. (2007). *Informed choices for struggling adolescents: A research-based guide to instructional programs and practices.* Newark, NJ: International Reading Association.

Dewey, J. (1938). *Experience and education.* New York: Collier Books.

Donovan, M. S., & Bransford, J. (Eds.). (2005). *How children learn.* Washington, DC: National Academies Press.

Duckworth, A., Peterson, C., Matthews, M., & Kelly, D. (2007). Grit, perseverance, and passion for long-term goals. *Journal of Personality and Social Psychology, 92*(6), 1087–1101.

DuFour R., & Eaker, R. (1998). *Professional learning communities at work: Best practices for enhancing student achievement.* Bloomington IN: National Education Services.

Elliott, M. (1998). School finance and opportunity to learn: Does money well-spent enhance students' achievement? *Sociology of Education, 71*(3), 223–245.

Gabriner, R. (2011). *Chapter for RP Program for leadership development.* Unpublished paper. California State University at San Francisco.

García, G. (2005). *Teaching and learning in two languages: Bilingualism and schooling in the United States.* New York: Teachers College Press.

Genesee, F., Lindholm-Leary, K., Saunders, W., & Christian, D. (2006). *Educating English language learners: A synthesis of research evidence.* New York: Cambridge University Press.

Gittell, M., & Steffey, T. (2000). *Community colleges addressing students' needs: A case study of LaGuardia Community College.* New York: Howard Samuels State Management and Policy Center, City University of New York.

Goldhaber, D. D., & Brewer, D. J. (1997). Why don't schools and teachers seem to matter? Assessing the impact of observables on educational productivity. *Journal of Human Resources, 32*(3), 505–523.

Grubb, W. N. (2002). *Who I am: The inadequacy of career information in the information age*. Brussels, Belgium: European Commission; Paris: Organization for Economic Co-operation and Development.

Grubb, W. N. (2006). "Like, what do I do now?" The dilemmas of guidance counseling. In T. Bailey & V. Morest (Eds.), *Defending the community college equity agenda* (pp. 195–222). Baltimore, MD: Johns Hopkins Press.

Grubb, W. N. (2008). Dreams and Leaks, Reforms, and Band-aids: The Transition from High School to Postsecondary Education. In *The conditions of education in California 2008* (pp. 89–102). Stanford CA: Policy Analysis for California Education.

Grubb, W. N. (2009). *The money myth: School resources, outcomes, and equity*. New York: Russell Sage Foundation.

Grubb, W. N., & Anyon, Y. (2012). *A trio of changes to enhance student capacities: Integrating school reforms and support services*. Unpublished paper under submission to *Teachers College Record*.

Grubb, W. N., & Associates (1999). *Honored but invisible: An inside look at teaching in community colleges*. New York: Routledge.

Grubb, W. N., & Kalman, J. (1994). Relearning to earn: The role of remediation in vocational education and job training. *American Journal of Education, 103*(1), 54–93.

Grubb, W. N., & Lazerson, M. (2004). *The education gospel: The economic power of schooling*. Cambridge, MA: Harvard University Press.

Grubb, W. N. & Tredway, L. (2010). *Leading from the inside out: Expanded roles for teachers in equitable schools*. Boulder, CO: Paradigm.

Hargis, C. (2006). Setting standards: An exercise in futility? *Phi Delta Kappan, 87*(5), 393–395.

Hattie, J. (2009). *Visible Learning: A synthesis of over 800 meta-analyses relating to achievement*. London: Routledge.

Harvey, J. (1974). The Abilene paradox: The management of agreement. *Organizational Dynamics*, 3, 63–80.

Harvey, J., & Housman, N. (2004). *Crisis or possibility: Conversations about the American high school*. Washington, DC: National High School Alliance.

Hern, K., & Snell, M. (2010). Exponential attrition and the promise of acceleration in developmental English and math. Research and Planning Group of the California Community Colleges. Retrieved from http://www.rpgroup.org/rpsearch/results/taxonomy%3A17.

Hochschild, J., & Scovronek, N. (2003). *The American dream and the public schools*. New York: Oxford University Press.

Hodara, M. (2011). *Reforming mathematics classroom pedagogy: Evidence-based findings and recommendations for the developmental classroom* (Working Paper No. 27). New York: Community College Research Center, Teachers College, Columbia University.

Hughes, K., & Scott-Clayton, J. (2010). *Assessing developmental assessment in community colleges: A review of the literature* (Working Paper). New York: Community College Research Center, Teachers College, Columbia University.

Jabbar, H. (2012). The behavioral economics of education: New directions for research. *Review of Education Research, 40*(9), 446–453.

Karp, M., O'Gara, L., & Hughes, K. (2008). *Do support services at community colleges encourage success or reproduce disadvantage?* (CCRC Working Paper). Community College Research Center, Teachers College, New York.

Kemple, J., Corrin, W., Nelson, E., Salinger, T., Herrmann, S., & Drummond, K (2008). *The enhanced reading opportunities study: Early impacts and implementation findings*. New York: MDRC.

Kilpatrick J., Swafford, J., & Findell, B. (Eds.). (2001). *Adding it up: Helping children learn mathematics*. Washington, DC: National Academy Press.

Knapp, M. & Associates. (1995). *Teaching for meaning in high-poverty classrooms*. New York: Teachers College Press.

Kohn, M. (1969). *Class and Conformity: A Study in Values*. Chicago: University of Chicago Press.

Labaree, D. (2010). *Someone has to fail: The zero-sum game of public schooling*. Cambridge, MA: Harvard University Press.

Lampert, M. (1991). *Teaching problems and the problems of teaching.* New Haven, CT: Yale University Press.

Lemons, R., Luschel, T., & Siskin, L. (2003). Leadership and the demands for standards-based accountability. In M. Carnoy, R. Elmore, & L. Siskin (Eds.), *The new accountability: High schools and high-stakes testing* (pp. 99–128). New York: Routledge.

Lesgold, A., & Welch-Ross, M. (Eds.). (2012). *Improving adult literacy instruction: Options for practice and research.* Committee on Learning Sciences, Foundations and Applications to Adolescent and Adult Literacy, National Research Council. Washington, DC: National Academies Press.

Little, J. W. (2006). *Professional development and professional community in the learner-centered school.* Washington, DC: National Education Association.

Losak, J., & Morris, C. (1985). *Comparing treatment effects for students who successfully complete college preparatory work* (Research Report No. 85–45). Miami, FL: Miami-Dade Community College, Office of Institutional Research.

Lutzer, D. J., Maxwell, J. W., & Rodi, S. B. (2002). *Statistical analysis of undergraduate programs in the United States.* Retrieved from http://www.ams.org/profession/data/cmbs-survey/cbms-survey-whole.pdf

Manski, C. (1989). Schooling as experimentation: A reappraisal of the college dropout phenomenon. *Economics of Education Review, 8*(4), 305–312.

Matthews, R. S. (1994). Enriching teaching and learning through learning communities. In T. O'Banion & Associates (Eds.), *Teaching and learning in the community college* (pp. 179–200). Washington, DC: American Association of Community Colleges.

Matus-Grossman, L., & Gooden, S. (2002, July). *Opening doors: Students' perspectives on juggling work, family, and college.* New York: MDRC.

Mery, P., & Schiorring, E. (2010). *Reading apprenticeship: RA incorporation in community colleges findings and highlights 2008–2010* (External Evaluation Report No. 6). Berkeley, CA: Research and Planning Group for California Community Colleges.

Mery, P., & Schiorring, E. (2009-10). *How reading apprenticeship improves disciplinary learning in secondary and college classrooms.* Berkeley, CA: Research and Planning Group for California Community Colleges.

Minami, M., & Ovando, C. J. (2004). Language issues in multicultural contexts. In J. Banks & C. M. Banks (Eds.), *Handbook of research on multicultural education* (2nd ed., pp. 567–588). San Francisco, CA: Jossey-Bass.

Morris, C. (1994). *Success of students who needed and completed college preparatory instruction* (Research Report No. 94-19R). Miami, FL: Institutional Research, Miami-Dade Community College.

National Center for Public Policy in Higher Education and Southern Regional Education Board. (2010). *Beyond the rhetoric: Improving college readiness through coherent state policy.* Washington, DC: Author.

National Endowment for the Arts. (2007). *To read or not to read: A question of national consequence.* Washington, DC: Author.

National Research Council. (2011). *Incentives and test-based accountability in public education.* Washington, DC: National Academies Press.

National Research Council, Committee on Increasing High School Students' Engagement and Motivation to Learn. (2004). *Engaging schools: Fostering high school students' motivation to learn.* Washington, DC: National Academy Press.

Newmann, F., Bryk, A., & Nagoaka, J. (2001). *Authentic intellectual work and standardized tests: Conflict or coexistence?* Chicago, IL: Consortium on Chicago School Research at the University of Chicago.

Newmann, F. M., Smith, B. A., Allensworth, E., & Bryk, A. S. (2001). Instructional program coherence: What it is and why it should guide school improvement policy. *Educational Evaluation and Policy Analysis, 23*(4), 297–321.

PACE (2012). *California's Early Assessment Program: Its Effectiveness and the Obstacles to Successful Program Implementation.* Stanford, CA: Policy Analysis for California Education.

Perin, D. (2011). *Facilitating student learning through contextualization* (Working Paper No. 29, Assessment of Evidence Series). New York: Community College Research Center, Teachers College, Columbia University.

Perry, M., Bahr, P. R., Rosin, M., & Woodward, K. (2010). *Course-taking patterns, policies, and practices in developmental education in the California community colleges.* Mountain View, CA: EdSource.

Phillips, M., Crouse, J., & Ralph, J. (1998). Does the Black-White test score gap widen after children enter school? In C. Jencks & M. Phillips (Eds.), *The Black-White test score gap* (pp. 229–272). Washington, DC: Brookings Institution.

Powell, A. G., Farrar, E., & Cohen, D. K. (1985). *The shopping mall high school: Winners and Losers in the Educational Marketplace.* Boston, MA: Houghton Mifflin.

Price, D., with Lee, M. (2005). *Learning communities and student success in postsecondary education.* New York: MDRC .

Quint, J. C., Polit, D. F., Bos, H., & Cave, G. (1994). *New chance: Interim findings on a comprehensive program for disadvantaged young mothers and their children.* San Francisco, CA: MDRC.

Raudenbusch, S., Fotiu, R. P., & Cheong, Y. F. (1998). Inequality of access to educational resources: A national report for eighth-grade math. *Educational Evaluation and Policy Analysis, 20*(4), 253–267.

Resnick, L. (Ed.). (1989). *Knowing, learning, and instruction: Essays in honor of Robert Glaser.* Hillsdale, NJ: Erlbaum.

Roueche, J. E., & Baker III, G. A. (1987). *Access and excellence: The open door college.* Washington, DC: Community College Press.

Rumberger, R., & Gándara, P. (2004). Seeking equity in the education of California's English learners. *Teachers College Record, 106*(10), 2032–2056.

Rutschow, E., Richburg-Hayes, L., Brock, T., Orr, G., Cerna, O., Cullinan, D., et al. (2011). *Turning the tide: Five years of achieving the dream in community colleges.* New York: MDRC.

Safran, S., & Visher, M. (2010). *Case studies of three community colleges: The policy and practice of assessing and placing students in developmental education courses.* New York: National Center for Postsecondary Research and MDRC.

Schoenbach, R., Greenleaf, C., Czicko, C., & Hurwitz, L. (1999). *Reading for understanding: A guide to improving reading in middle and high school classrooms.* San Francisco, CA: Jossey-Bass.

Scrivener, S., Bloom, D., LeBlanc, A., Paxson, C., Rouse, C. E., & Sommo, C., et al. (2008). *Opening doors: A good start: Two-year effects of a freshman learning community program at Kingsborough Community College.* New York: MDRC.

Seidman, E. (1985). *In the words of the faculty: Perspectives on improving teaching and educational quality in community colleges.* San Francisco, CA: Jossey-Bass.

Shaughnessy, M. (1977). *Errors and expectations: A guide for the teacher of basic writing.* New York: Oxford University Press.

Shulman, L. (1987). Knowledge and teaching: Foundations of the new reform. *Harvard Educational Review, 57,* 1–22.

Smith, B. (1991). Taking structure seriously: The learning community model. *Liberal Education, 77*(2), 42–48.

Snow, C., Burns, S. M., & Griffin, P. (1998). *Preventing reading difficulties in young children.* Washington, DC: National Academies Press.

Solorzano, D. (2001). Critical race theory, racial micro-aggressions, and the experience of Chicana and Chicano scholars. *Qualitative Inquiry, 8*(1), 23–44.

Solorzano, D., Ceja, M., & Yosso, T. (2000). Critical race theory, racial micro-aggressions, and campus racial climate: The experiences of African American college students. *Journal of Negro Education, 69*(1/2), 60–73.

Somers, M. A., Corrin, W., Sepanik, S., Salinger T., Levin, J., & Zmach, C. (2010). *The enhanced reading opportunities study final report.* Washington, DC: National Center for Education Evaluation and Regional Assistance, Institute of Education Sciences.

Spillane, J. (2006). *Distributed leadership.* San Francisco, CA: Jossey-Bass.

Staley, C. (2010). *Focus on college success.* Boston, MA: Wadsworth.

Steele, C. (2010). *Whistling Vivaldi, and other clues to how stereotype affects us.* New York: Norton.

Steele, D. et al. (n.d.). How identity safety influences student achievement. Unpublished paper. Stanford, CA: Stanford University.

Thomas, W. P., & Collier, V. P. (1995). *A longitudinal analysis of programs serving language minority students.* Washington, DC: National Clearinghouse on Bilingual Education.

Timar, T., & Maxwell-Jolly, J. (2011). *Narrowing the achievement gap: Perspectives and strategies for challenging times.* Cambridge, MA: Harvard Education Press.

Tinto, V., & Goodsell-Love, A. (1995). *A longitudinal study of learning communities at LaGuardia Community College* (ERIC Document ED 380 178). Washington DC: National Center on Postsecondary Teaching, Learning, and Assessment, Office of Educational Research and Improvement, U.S. Department of Education.

Tinto, V., Goodsell-Love, A., & Russo, P. (1994). *Building learning communities for new college students: A summary of research findings of the Collaborative Learning Project.* Syracuse, NY: National Center on Postsecondary Teaching, Learning, and Assessment.

Tinto, V., Russo, P., & Kadel, S. (1994, February/March). Constructing educational communities: Increasing retention in challenging circumstances. *AACC Journal, 64*(4), 26–29.

Venezia, A., Bracco, K. R., & Nodine, T. (2010). *One-shot deal? Students' perceptions of assessment and placement in California's community colleges.* San Francisco, CA: WestEd.

Visher, M., Teres, J., with Richman, P. (2011). *Breaking new ground: An impact study of career-focused learning communities at Kingsborough Community College.* New York: MDRC.

Weiss, M., Visher, M., Worthington, H., with Teres, J., & Schneider, E. (2011). *Learning communities for students in developmental reading: An impact study at Hillsborough Community College.* New York: MDRC.

Weissman, E., Kristin F. Butcher, K. F., Schneider, E., Teres, J., Collado, H., et al. (2011). *Learning communities for students in developmental math: Impact studies at Queensborough and Houston community colleges.* New York: MDRC.

Wiseley, C. K. (2011). *Effective basic skills instruction: The case for contextualized developmental math* (Policy Brief 11-1). Palo Alto, CA: Policy Analysis for California Education.

Woodlief, B., Thomas, C., & Orozco, G. (2003). *California's gold: Claiming the promise of diversity in our community colleges.* Oakland, CA: California Tomorrow.

Zachary, E., & Schneider, E. (2010). *Building a foundation for student readiness: A review of "rigorous" research and promising trends in developmental education.* Oakland, CA: MDRC.

Zeidenberg, M., Jenkins, D., & Calcagno, J. C. (2007). *Do student success courses actually help community college students succeed?* CCRC Brief No. 36. New York: Community College Research Center, Columbia University.

INDEX